BE GOOD, SWEET MAID

Other books in the *Women & Literature* series edited by Janet Todd:

Bibliography of Women and Literature, 1975–80
Women Writers Talking
Gender and Literary Voice (*Women & Literature*, new series, volume 1)
Men by Women (*Women & Literature*, volume 2)

BE GOOD, SWEET MAID

An Anthology of *Women & Literature*

EDITED BY JANET TODD

HOLMES & MEIER PUBLISHERS, INC.
New York . London

First published in the United States of America 1981 by
Holmes & Meier Publishers, Inc.
30 Irving Place
New York, N.Y. 10003

Great Britain:
Holmes & Meier Publishers, Ltd.
131 Trafalgar Road
Greenwich, London SE10 9TX

Copyright © 1981 by Holmes & Meier Publishers, Inc.

Library of Congress Cataloging in Publication Data
Main entry under title:

Be good, sweet maid.

    1. English literature—History and criticism—
Addresses, essays, lectures.   2. Women in literature
—Addresses, essays, lectures.   3. Literature,
Modern—History and criticism—Addresses, essays,
lectures.   I. Todd, Janet M., 1942–
II. Women & literature.
PR409.W65B4 1981   820′.9′9287   81-1461
ISBN 0-8419-0692-0   AACR2
ISBN 0-8419-0702-1 (pbk.)

Manufactured in the United States of America

Contents

BE GOOD, SWEET MAID

Introduction

JANET TODD

This anthology is drawn from two journals; the *Mary Wollstonecraft News-letter*, a mimeographed biannual, lived from 1972 to 1974, and its child—the sleeker, printed *Women & Literature*—from 1974 to 1979. Although Wollstonecraft's name disappeared from the title in the second incarnation, her compelling portrait continued on the cover and her influence remained within. It is appropriate that she should dominate, for she was one of the first and most effective feminist critics.

During the decade beginning in 1787, Wollstonecraft wrote short pieces for the *Analytical Review*, many on novels and advice manuals; in 1791 she probed Jean-Jacques Rousseau's *Emile* more lengthily in her most famous work, *A Vindication of the Rights of Woman*. In both short reviews and long analysis, she was concerned with the supposed severance of virtue and intellect in women. "Be good, sweet maid, and let who can be clever"—or worse, "Be pretty, sweet maid"— was the advice she found in Rousseau and a host of inferior writers; it was advice she never tired of combating.

Literature, Wollstonecraft insisted, should strengthen reason, not pander to sentimental visions of innate virtue. Goodness was for her a result of reason and effort, not ignorance or noble birth as in so much fiction for women. Given this view, she was most affronted by those works that rewarded female virtue with a coach and six. Such novels tended to "debauch the mind," "vitiate the heart," and inspire young women with "false notions and hopes."

Whether created by male or female authors, woman in literature is predominantly a sexual and not an intellectual being, Wollstonecraft noted. "Why do all female writers, even when they display their abilities, always give a sanction to the libertine reveries of men," she exclaimed. She criticized the sexual labeling of women as "sweet maid," old maid, wife, or whore, and pleaded for an understanding of those who had not succeeded in following society's preferred route from maid to wife, a route made harder for women by fiction's duplicities. She herself had suffered from the pejorative labels; her "sweet maid' stage had been short—she had no dowry to underpin her sweetness—and she became successively an old maid and a whore. The rigid categories of sweet maid and wife had failed to contain her and in her criticism, tentatively at first, she blamed literature for fooling her and other women into thinking they ever could.

The eighteenth century was the age of the woman author. A tiny minority in the seventeenth century, women writers had by the last quarter of the next century, become a formidable group. So Wollstonecraft could assess female literature in general, finding fiction, for example, derivative and "flimsy"—"*The Child of Woe* having no marked features to characterize it, we can only term it a truly feminine novel." In addition she could evaluate individual writers—especially major producers like Charlotte Smith and Elizabeth Inchbald, or innovators like Fanny Burney—and judge others by their standards.

When she was reviewing for the *Analytical Review*, Wollstonecraft came to associate the sentimental, emotional style that many women used (and which she herself employed in her letters and first autobiographical novel) with the "libertine" and "sweet maid" subject matter she had come to despise. So she yearned for a more "reasonable" prose, one not immediately marked as female, that she could use to escape the prejudices aroused by a "lady's" pen. Hers was then to be the enlightened style of the *Analytical Review* and of the radicals Fuseli and Godwin—who happened to be men— not the subjective gush of her Gothic and sentimental sisters. In this style she wrote *The Rights of Woman* and her journal criticism; though her subject matter and bubbling phrases distinguish her from the majority of *Analytical Review* writers, her prose is still predominantly the periodical's, and the writer and her public are presumed genderless. "I am then going to be the first of a new genus," she exulted as she set out on her career as critic, but her practice made the genus *female critic* a hybrid from the start.

The subjects of Wollstonecraft's criticism are in the main the subjects of the *Mary Wollstonecraft Newsletter* and *Women & Literature*: the creation of female images and the problems of female labeling, whether of wife and spinster or of author and critic. Again like Wollstonecraft in her reviews, the journals have evaluated women writers, considering how to deal with the acceptably great of the patriarchal tradition—with F. R. Leavis's honorary males, Jane Austen and George Eliot for example—how to judge anew the less securely appreciated such as Virginia Woolf, and how to promote and establish female authors like Violet Hunt, long-neglected or spurned. In style too the journals are successors—their articles have not attempted to forge a new critical language; instead, like Wollstonecraft's reviews, they have accepted the hybrid character of female criticism. Using the language and methods of the academy—our living, as the magazine was hers—we have aimed to influence all readers, irrespective of gender, and to change rather than to deny male critical discourse and judgment.

The anthology is arranged in chronological sections, and there has been no attempt to group articles according to approach or date of composition. The earliest from the *Mary Wollstonecraft Newsletter* is on Elizabeth Barrett

Browning and appears in the Victorian group; the latest, an interview with May Sarton, from volume seven of *Women & Literature*, is placed in the twentieth century. The two articles are separated by seven years and much has happened in feminist criticism between their writing. Yet they remain close in aim, for each allows a female author to speak out in a female context, to be a woman writer—not merely a writer who happens to be a woman.

Nina Auerbach opens the book with her article "Artists and Mothers," which finds the traditional parallel between artistic and biological production wanting. She notes that Austen and Eliot reject motherhood, which in their work entails confinement, pain, and death, and instead applaud work, which represents creativity and life. Ellen Serlen Uffen continues the discussion of Jane Austen, concentrating on the theatricals in *Mansfield Park*, which illustrate the dangerous loss of self-restraint and control that occurs when art simulates nature too closely. In this novel Austen uses her authorial control to uphold the eighteenth-century values of art, decorum, and stability in the face of the inevitable succession of a more boisterous, vital, and discordant new century. My own article, "Frankenstein's Daughter: Mary Shelley and Mary Wollstonecraft," links Mary Wollstonecraft with her daughter. It argues the relationship between the monster of *Frankenstein* and Jemima, the fallen woman of *The Wrongs of Woman*: both are excluded from family and society, both are superficially corrupted by social injustice, and both suffer from an ineradicable monstrosity or femaleness.

Beatrice Fink ends the Romantic section by treating the utopia of the Marquis de Sade. In "Ambivalence in the Gynogram," she argues that, although Sade espoused philosophical equality of the sexes, he maintained women's passivity and subordination to the patriarch. His ambivalence is revealed in the dichotomy of his formal elevation of the female—she controls the narrative voice—with his subordination of her in the plot. A similar apparent liberation but actual subversion is discovered by Leslie Rabine in the first article of the Victorian section. Analyzing George Sand's *Indiana*, the author demonstrates that, far from contesting the "myth of femininity," Sand subverts feminist principles into the traditional concept of womanhood, and so encourages obedience to convention.

In her article on Elizabeth Barrett Browning's *Sonnets from the Portugese*, Susan Zimmerman takes up the question of marriage, which, with creativity and madness, constitutes the most frequent theme of the critics. She distinguishes *Sonnets from the Portuguese* from the male tradition of the Petrarchan sonnet and places it within the tradition of epithalamium. While the male poet transcends sensual rapture to achieve spiritual love, Barrett Browning's speaker, soon to be married, must approach God through a man. So she sacrifices a direct relationship with the Divine for a changeable human love.

Not marriage but spinsterhood concerns Judith Weissman in her article on Trollope. She outlines Trollope's sympathetic treatment of the single woman, Lily Dale: in a society where there are ties of friendship and respect for the individual, Lily's worth need not be determined by her marital status. Constance Rooke notes a very different society in her article on the influence of Eliot's *Daniel Deronda* on Wharton's *House of Mirth*. She sees a correspondence between the two heroines caught in a rootless, unnurturing world of meretricious values. A means of self-expression both women employ, the *tableau vivant*, serves to dramatize the extent to which each is reduced in worth to an art object.

The Victorian period closes with Patricia Spacks's essay on the Brontës, "Rebellions of Good Women." She finds that in their novels, the female characters are not simply rebelling against conventional external restrictions, but are also laboring under an internal conflict between the need for independence and passion on the one hand and the desire for relation and service on the other. While male characters can create their own morality or combine selfless service with self-indulgence, the heroines are often destroyed by the conflict or at best resolve it in imagination. The section on the Modern period opens with a piece on Virginia Woolf's Miss La Trobe, who finds fulfillment rather than resolution in imagination. Miss La Trobe eschews the art object status of Gwendolyn and Lily Bart and becomes instead the artistic subject, wielding her art with power. Diane Filby Gillespie shows Woolf's heroine abandoning a masculine art which attempts to manipulate nature mechanically and instead accepting and expressing an intuitive internal reality.

Elaine Showalter's article on E. M. Forster returns to the theme of marriage, exalted by Barrett Browning's speaker and avoided by Trollope's Lily. Forster's negative feelings about the state are embodied in his critic Fielding in *A Passage to India* and are implicit in his political parallels between women's submission in marriage and the Indian people's subjection to British rule. Yet in the end Forster has Fielding marry, for, although it represents surrender, it also allows for continuity and new life.

Marie and Robert Secor investigate Woolf's contemporary, Violet Hunt, who in "Tales of the Uneasy" explores the third major theme of twentieth-century female literature—female madness and its sexual underpinnings. Marie and Robert Secor detect in the "Tales" the response of a sensitive, strong-willed woman to the weak and indecisive men who seemed to inhabit Edwardian England, and they speculate on the degree to which this fictional pattern represents Hunt's own unsatisfactory relationship with the dependent Ford Maddox Ford. Female madness is again the subject of the first article in the Contemporary period, a study of Joyce Carol Oates. Charlotte Goodman argues that Oates's characters are often destroyed by convention; seeking to escape the patterns of their mothers' lives through sexual relationships—as lovers, wives, and mothers—they ultimately fail and, unable to transcend the boundaries of these roles, sink into the safety of passivity and madness.

Marriage and creativity enter into the conversation between May Sarton and Dolores Shelley, in which Sarton candidly discusses the life of a woman artist, the sense of growth that comes from loving another person and the independence that comes from living alone. At one point she seems to be commenting on the first article of the anthology, Nina Auerbach's "Artists and Mothers," when she remarks, "I think it's very hard for a woman to be married and have children and be a first-rate artist." Asked by Dolores Shelley if the woman artist subverts "her desire for a family . . . through art," she conjectures, "not subverting exactly, but perhaps it uses the same kind of creative energy." This creative energy is clearly in evidence in the Quebec women writers Christiane Makward surveys. Much of their writing rejects the conventional literary homage to the mother, especially emphasized in a society dominated by Catholic theology and the pioneer stress on child-bearing; instead, eschewing the reverence and repression of the past, their work has become diverse, satirical, and celebratory—a far cry indeed from the "sweet song" of Charles Kingsley's maid.

Be Good, Sweet Maid, the anthology of the *Mary Wollstonecraft Newsletter* and *Women & Literature*, has been a communal effort of many people, and I am grateful to all who have made its publication possible by submitting articles and by subscribing to the journals. I would especially like to thank Florence Boos and Madeleine Marshall for their help in editing the journals and Mary Anne Lutz for her help in preparing this anthology.

The Romantic Period

Artists and Mothers: A False Alliance

Nina Auerbach

Do our wombs silently dictate when we write? Are woman's books poor replicas of unborn babies? In the popular image of the creative process, creativity and childbirth are often entangled, so that a childless woman writer seems wistfully to turn herself into a mother by some poignantly incomplete process of parthenogenesis. Virginia Woolf shyly touches on this assumption in "A Room of One's Own" as she forms an imaginary community of four great nineteenth-century woman novelists: "Save for the possibly relevant fact that not one of them had a child, four more incongruous characters could not have met together in a room."[1]

But Woolf evades defining the "possibly relevant" conjunction between childlessness and art. Did the Brontës, Jane Austen, and George Eliot write out of a thwarted need to give birth, sadly making substitute dream children out of their novels? Or did they produce art that allowed them a freer, finer, more expansive world than the suppressions of nineteenth-century motherhood allowed? Perhaps out of a defensive awareness of her own childlessness, Woolf allows us to hover between both suggestions, just as our picture of the childless woman writer has typically hovered on the borderline between deprivation and defiance.

Our perceptions about women are still so infused with biological mythology that even contemporary feminist critics may see the creation of a world in books as a token of a destiny missed rather than of one triumphantly forged. Thus Cynthia Griffin Woolff's feminist biography, *A Feast of Words: The Triumph of Edith Wharton*, uncritically echoes Wharton's sad self-doubt in her old age: "So rich in the offspring of her creative intelligence—'my children,' she used to call her fictions as she scolded them into compliance and dressed them and spanked them into shape (these were *her* terms in letters to her friends)—she was barren of biological progeny."[2] "Barren" and "biological" end the sentence with an alliterative, authoritative thud, negating the "feast of words" that made Wharton worthy of a biography in the first place. Even in feminist reevaluations of notable women, it is difficult to escape a retreat to the womb.

Well-known female psychiatrists have endorsed the idea that childbirth is the only significant reality in a woman's life, reducing every other need and impetus to the shadowy status of metaphor. Helene Deutsch's influential *The Psychology of Women: A Psychoanalytic Interpretation* (1945) defines its vision by the titles of its two volumes: *Girlhood* and *Motherhood.* The two stand as inescapable poles of the "normal," a monolithic destiny in which maturity means only maternity: all other goals are an evasion. Even in the early work of Karen Horney, whose feminism led her to break with Freud, the womb replaces God's word as the only true creator, of which civilization itself is but a poor proud replica. "The Flight from Womanhood" (1926) forces even men into complicity with the universal urge to define one's humanity in motherhood: "Is not the tremendous strength in men of the impulse to creative work in every field precisely due to their feeling of playing a relatively small part in the creation of living beings, which constantly impels them to an overcompensation in achievement?"[3] In all three of the above statements, motherhood is not one manifestation of our multifaceted creative gift, but a means of belittling the variety of human achievement. Horney reduces all men to the pathos of the aging Edith Wharton, trying in vain to spank a book that has no bottom.

This traditional view of motherhood as the "onlie begetter," by which all art is ultimately explicable and to which it is reducible, has cast a long pall over women's lives. Only recently have women begun to fight free of this shackling of their thoughts to their wombs, often with the help of sympathetic men such as the psychoanalyst Robert Seidenberg in his sensible "Is Anatomy Destiny?" (1970): "Without in the least knocking the value and delights of having babies, writing books would seem to be another thing again" (in Miller, p. 309). This sane understatement is long overdue. To me, at least, it is a relief to find a male analyst appreciating rather than diagnosing the clearheaded distinctions of such woman writers as Mary Ellmann—"this idealization of childbirth obscures the distinction between involuntary and voluntary achievement which we depend upon in describing any achievement as *creative*"—or Cynthia Ozick: "To call a child a poem may be a pretty metaphor, but it is a slur on the labor of art. Literature cannot be equated with physiology, and woman through her reproductive system alone is no more a creative artist than was Joyce by virtue of his kidneys alone, or James by virtue of his teeth. . . . A poem emerges from a mind, and mind is, so far as our present knowledge takes us, an unknowable abstraction."[4] In this decomposition of a sentimental equation, the artist's identity makes its own definition. It no longer needs to justify its existence by a pious metaphorical association with motherhood.

The very existence of this conflict between psychiatrists suggests their underlying difficulty in perceiving an adult woman without reference to children. As Helene Deutsch's categories suggest, a woman passes only from being a child to bearing one. Attempting to bring a new flexibility to these rigid imperatives, Jean Baker Miller deplores the absence of psychiatric paradigms for adult womanhood: "The attributes toward which women are still expected to aim are those that are linked with childish in infantile qualities, e.g., helplessness, dependency, and the like. Women are not expected to grow toward those attributes associated with men; to do so would be unfeminine. In fact, we seem to have no model for women's growth at all" (Hiller, p. 387) This vacuum where the adult female should be, the paradox whereby her existence is defined only in reference to children, explains much of our difficulty not only in creating our own lives, but in assessing the lives of women in the past. This difficulty is compounded when we look at the lives of childless women in the nineteenth century, struggling against universal approval of large families and paeans to the holiness of motherhood. For the nineteenth-century popular imagination, motherhood was not merely a bio-logical fact, but a spiritual essence inseparable from pure womanhood; thus, whatever their marital status, the large, anomalous band of "lady novelists" were most charitably regarded as a peculiar species of mother. Whether actual or metaphorical, maternity alone was the seal of respectable female maturity. The honorary motherhood bestowed on woman artists, in the nineteenth century as today, seems to have created a nagging confusion in the self-perception of two of the century's greatest and most determinedly childless novelists: Jane Austen and George Eliot.

Jane Austen's letters define a world where, after marriage, incessant confinements constitute the business of a woman's life, and often, as in the case of her sister-in-law Fanny who died bearing her fourth child, its premature termination as well. Children were inescapable and often welcome invaders of Austen's cottage at Chawton, though she never confused them with the manuscripts that could be slipped quietly under a blotter when nieces and nephews burst into the rooms; but confinement was more pernicious. The very word has undertones of enforced incarceration, even of burial alive, that echo in Austen's perceptions of motherhood. Her seemingly callous, un-apologetic distaste for childbearing has shocked generations of critics,[5] perhaps because their stereotypes become dislodged when a woman novelist lashes out against parturition. Her most widely-quoted description of mother-hood is a Gothic comedy of marriage's abortion and biology's grotesque invasion: "Mrs. Hall, of Sherbourne, was brought to bed yesterday of a dead child, some weeks before she expected, owing to a fright. I suppose she happened unawares to look at her husband."[6] Considering this ruthless vision of misadventure, it seems unlikely that Jane Austen's novels represent sighs over lost fulfillment.

Later in her life, she enthusiastically supported her niece Anna's attempt to write a novel, reading her manuscript with gusto and criticising it with professional scrupulousness; but she lost all interest in Anna when she married and had a child. In her passage from writer to mother, Anna sinks into a lower order of being, forfeiting her humanity, her youth, and perhaps life itself: "Poor Animal, she will be worn out before she is thirty.—I am very sorry for her" (23 March 1817, II, 488). Austen's dismissal suggests an unpassable abyss between writer and mother, human and animal, the dancing creativity of the mind and the monotonous attrition of the womb. In mother-hood, Anna has relinquished life rather than created it.

Jane Austen's anger at childbirth suggests less a squeamish shrinking from biology than a deep awareness of its potential to betray the aspiring con-sciousness. Yet when *Sense and Sensibility*, her first published novel, was in proof, she wrote exultantly to Cassandra: "No indeed, I am never too busy to think of S & S. I can no more forget it, than a mother can forget her sucking child" (25 April 1811, II, 272). This triumphant letter contains one of the very few conventionally maternal images in all of Jane Austen's writings, and it is also one of her sparse employments of formal figurative language. The unaccountable conventionality of this metaphor, compared to the indelible portrait of Mrs. Hall of Sherbourne, is underlined by its appropriation from *Isaiah* 49:15: "Can a woman forget her sucking child, That she should not have compassion on the son of her womb?" In casting about for a form for the unprecedented elation of success, Jane Austen seems to have turned to the Bible rather than life. Perhaps she might later have dismissed this sentence, along with its self-consciously Biblical simile, as "thorough novel slang." Though a Freudian might suggest that her unconscious broke through her defenses just this once, the second-hand language and metaphor make their emotional validity dubious: in Austen's letters as in her novels, true feeling cannot express itself in clichés. Though the tangible accomplishment of her first set of proofs made art and motherhood leap together in her language, the borrowed equation seems less a vehicle of spontaneous joy than an index of the paucity of language defining women's achievements. Jane Austen did not give us a new language, but in her later letters, she uses the old easy metaphors as a vehicle of cutting irony.

For as she gained confidence in her own achievement, she came to value art precisely for its separation from childhood, creating her books as pre-servatives of a precious space for the free, mercurial adult—a brief conscious-ness of mobile womanhood between the twin suppressions of girlhood and marriage. When Anna was still her colleague in fiction rather than an alien mother, Austen's suggestion that Anna delete her heroine's childhood con-tained her own mature credo: "One does not care for girls till they are grown up" (9 September 1814, II, 402). But "grown up' does not mean ground down into a "Poor Animal." Writing to her niece Fanny, to whom she turned tenderly after Anna's defection, Austen defined the incompatibility between the spiritual freedom her novels celebrate and the subsidence of motherhood: "Oh! what a loss it will be when you are married. You are too agreable in your single state, too agreable as a Niece. I shall hate you when your delicious play of Mind is all settled down into conjugal & maternal affections" (20 February 1817, II, 478–79). Was she thinking of Anna when she used the word "hate"?

The equation between childbearing and creativity arises again in a letter to Anna, in simple language this time and with a dangerous edge. Juxtaposing her own creation with that of her newly-delivered niece, Austen writes: "As I wish very much to see *your* Jemima, I am sure you will like to see *my* Emma, & have therefore great pleasure in sending it for your perusal. Keep it as long as you chuse, it has been read by all here" (? December, 1815, II, 449). In the earlier letter, the maternal image insisted on the identity of the writer's with the mother's ecstacy; here, no metaphor insists on unity, and the simple clauses are kept delicately and deliberately apart. Moreover, both writer and recipient must have been aware that in the past, it was Anna who had sent her novels to her aunt, and that Jemima was not dedicated to the Prince Regent at his own royal request. The simple parallelism of the syntax juxtaposing the two possessive pronouns makes the gulf between them, and between the clauses that contain them, glaringly clear. Separateness is now the essence of the metaphor. Jemima and Emma are a different order of child entirely, and in that difference lies both the wit and the irony of their conjunction.

Jane Austen's dream children, "my Elinor" and "my Elizabeth" of whom she is so proud, are precious precisely because they are not children: their adulthood is a brief reprieve from an infantilizing life. The sight of real children brough Austen no Wordsworthian sense of continuity and renewal; rather, she distrusted the confinement of the flashing adult self they represented. During her last illness, she wrote wearily, "I am quite tired of so many Children" (23 March 1817, II, 488), as if they were a symptom of the illness that was wearing down her life. The tone of this letter is echoed in her last and most romantic novel: in *Persuasion*, Captain Wentworth signals his continuing love for Anne Elliot by removing a burdensome child from her back; most nineteenth-century heroes would deposit the child in the heroine's arms. Adult love becomes the ally of art in redeeming the dutifully maternal woman by an alternative world.

Jane Austen's fiction subtly reinforces her allegiance to childless adulthood. Though the novels avoid autobiography and give us no portrait of the complete artist, Austen's strongest, if most undisciplined, heroine defines the life she is not equipped to live. The "imaginist" Emma Woodhouse aspires to shape art out of life, to turn her neighbors into characters for her plot, and among Austen's heroines, Emma is the most remote from motherhood. Not only is she motherless herself—which for Mr. Knightley explains her dangerous will to control—but she alone coolly rejects motherhood for herself in favor of an aunt's artistic distance. The future she wrongly predicts for herself is the life her creator actually lived: "There will be enough for every hope and every fear; and though my attachment to none can equal that of a parent, it suits my ideas of comfort better than what is warmer and blinder. My nephews and nieces!—I shall often have a niece with me.'"[7] Like Jane Austen, Emma preserves the fine distinction between the artist as aunt and the "Poor Animal" as parent. Though her own capacity for artistic distance is questionable, her sensitivity to hierarchical nuances could never blur two such radically unlike relationships.

Emma is unequipped to live her own prediction, but we never learn whether she will follow Anna's pattern, turning to maternity when she gives up her art under the glare of Mr. Knightley and the normal: as far as we see, the marriages that conclude June Austen's novels have no progeny. When the last chapter surveys the future, the heroines are never seen surrounded by a dimpled brood, as Victorian heroines infallibly are. In Austen's novels, the consummately adult art of life may fulfill itself in marriage, but motherhood seems antithetical to it. Like Charlotte Brontë's Jane Eyre, Austen too might have been troubled by a menacing nightmare of carrying a child as a portent of peril and loss. Far from endowing Austen with second-hand motherhood, her identity as an artist represented an escape from confinement into a child-free world with space for mind and spirit, time for change, and privacy for growth.

George Eliot was born as a literary sibyl in an age when it was less easy for mind to laugh away the "Poor Animal." Though individual mothers could still be paragons of idiocy, as are many of Eliot's own creations, Victorian motherhood came to incarnate humanity's holiest state, in which alone divinity returned to blend with flesh. Perhaps as a result, Eliot hymned maternity in theory as powerfully as she avoided it in practice. Her early essay, "Silly Novels by Lady Novelists," endorses the "precious specialty" women bring to fiction, "lying quite apart from masculine aptitudes and experiences."[8] In a later letter, Eliot develops this hint that maternity is the hidden generator of both womanliness and woman's art: "We can no more afford to part with that exquisite type of gentleness, tenderness, possible maternity suffusing a woman's being with affectionateness, which makes what we mean by the feminine character, than we can afford to part with the human love, the mutual subjection of soul between a man and a woman—which is also a growth and revelation beginning before all history."[9]

These genuflections to motherhood may account for the insufferably cute toddlers who tug at the reader in the early novels: Tottie, Eppie and their ilk may be Eliot's unconvincing attempt to demonstrate that she too is in possession of woman's "precious specialty." Though her one plausible child, Maggie Tulliver, is a "wild thing" whose estrangement repudiates all nurturing, Eliot's self-conscious protestations about the holiness of motherhood strike an uncomfortably false note in her work. They may also have inspired one of her most astute twentieth-century critics to this simplistic diagnosis of her genius: "What compelled this woman to create so compulsively, even after she had amassed a more than modest fortune by her writings? What was it that drove her to read scores of dry volumes on topography, art, history, prosody, mythology, law, religion, medicine, in order to sustain her occasionally flagging 'inspiration'? Was there a link between this obsession to give birth to fictional offspring and the sterility enforced by social convention on the loving 'Mutter' of Lewes' three legitimate sons?"[10]

If offered both dry volumes and wet diapers, I suspect Professor Knoepflmacher would choose the former under no "compulsion" beyond a sense of vocation, just as George Eliot did before him. Unfortunately, in accordance with the pieties of her age and with her own desire for inclusion and veneration, Eliot herself provides some fuel for vulgar misreadings of her career, for until the end of her life she repeatedly defined her own sense of moral mission in the imagery of motherhood. But if we look more closely at her own descriptions of the creative process, it seems that like her own characters in *Middlemarch* she allowed her thoughts to "entangle themselves in metaphors." For if her books evoked any aspect of motherhood to her, it was not the possession of tender fulfillment, but the unending frustration of parental estrangement: "My own books scourge me," she wrote of Sara Hennell (23 August 1863, *GEL* IV, 104), suggesting implicitly that a dream child like a real one is the future's revenge on the hopes that created it.

But books alleviate the pain of parenthood in that unlike children, their presence evaporates with time. Requesting that her publisher bring out *Silas Marner* before *Romola*, she wrote: "My chief reason for wishing to publish the story now, is, that I like my writings to appear in the order in which they are written, because they belong to successive mental phases, and when they are a year behind me, I can no longer feel that thorough identification with them which gives zest to the sense of authorship" (24 February 1861, *GEL* III, 382–83). Unlike the unalterable future a real child creates, one's future with one's book allows the renewal of forgetfulness. Ten years later, Eliot defines this healing departure more clearly to Sara Hennell: "But do not write to me about [*Middlemarch*], because until a book has quite gone away from me and become entirely of the non-ego—gone thoroughly from the wine-press into the casks—I would rather not hear or see anything that is said about it" (21 November 1871, *GEL* V, 214–15). Unlike motherhood, the essence of literary creation is the promise of inevitable detachment. As Jane Austen regained perspective on her works by shutting the manuscripts in a drawer for months at a time, so George Eliot exorcises the pain of her novels by forgetting them. The inconstancy of art bestows a completeness distinct from the perpetuity of motherhood. Eliot's awareness of the centrality of partings makes one suspect that it was character rather than "the sterility enforced by social convention" that made her one of a small band of Victorian women who we know practised birth control;[11] nor does it seem an accident that her first literary triumph was the lachrymose setpiece of the worn-down mother Milly Barton's death, as if the birth of the author into "the honours of print and pay"[12] was simultaneously the death of the mother and of motherhood itself.

For as her most recent biographer points out,[13] Mary Ann Evans' one authentic child was not a novel, but her own transfigured self: like Milton's Satan, she gave birth to a persona who would reign rather than serve. But ironically, in an age whose language of womanhood was inseparable from the language of family, her very imperiousness associated her with motherhood. Thus when Mary Ann Evans was eight, the gravity with which she shunned other children led them to dub her "little Mamma," not perceiving that a dislike of children might disqualify one for that title: habitual association links female authority only to motherhood. Later, when she had evolved into

George Eliot, her Victorian acolytes made of her a massively philosophic earth mother. Lewes gave the tone and the vocabulary to this collective adoration: he made her anomalous role in his household more conventionally palatable by bestowing on her the Germanic title of "Mutter," adding a lofty touch of Goethe to her relationship with his grown sons, who however were beyond the age of tending. As with "little Mamma," the title was more suggestive of role-playing than of reality. Eliot's testy response to a feminist who addressed her as "Miss Evans" shows her clinging to the name as an index of social acceptance: "when I tell you that we have a great boy of eighteen at home who calls me 'mother,' as well as two other boys, almost as tall, who write to me under the same name, you will understand that the point is not one of mere egoism or personal dignity, when I request that any one who has a regard for me will cease to speak of me by my maiden name" (1 April 1861, *GEL* III, 396).

Names here carry their own autonomous life; Eliot never examines the relationships they are intended to define. Later on, Lewes' "Mutter" became his "Madonna," under which affectionate title she presided over solemn Sundays at the Priory, but this Victorian Madonna is upstaged by no divine child: she gives birth only to her own regality. Indeed, George Eliot seems to have shied away from worshippers who presumed to call themselves the children of her cosmic motherhood. At the height of her eminence, a cult of adoring women adopted her as their "spiritual mother," begging to be called (as one of them put it) "by the sweet name of 'Daughter.' "[14] Eliot regarded this cult ambivalently perhaps not entirely because of its lesbian and separatist undercurrents. In confronting this swarm of clamorous, adoring progeny rather than in his distant fondness for Lewes' highly independent sons, Eliot seems to have found herself too close to the reality behind the matriarchal title; she was in danger of strangling in her Madonna's robes. The emotional demands of Edith Simcox, her most persistent and fervid "daughter," led her finally to repudiate both the name and the thing: "she did not like for me to call her 'Mother'. . . . she knew it was her fault, she had begun, she was apt to be rash and commit herself in one mood to what was irksome to her in another. Not with her own mother, but her associations otherwise with the name were as of a task, and it was a fact that her feeling for me was *not* at all a mother's—any other name she didn't mind."[15]

Only in the last year of her life, when her persona threatened to take on literal reality, was she able to work free of the charade that had at first dignified, then oppressed her. Paradoxically, her abandonment of this persona might explain her late, and brief, marriage to John Cross, for she evolved with him a new set of fantasy relationships that avoided the name, and the game, of motherhood. Though he was twenty years her junior, and turned to Eliot just after the death of his beloved mother, he never perceived himself as one of her progeny. Instead, they addressed each other teasingly during Lewes' lifetime as "Nephew" and "Aunt," in a manner recalling Jane Austen's allegiance to the aesthetic distance an aunt could claim. Moreover, she signed her first love letter to Cross by a private name remote from Lewes' "the Mutter": "The tender Beatrice" (16 October 1879, *GEL* VII, 211–12). Stimulated by their joint reading of Dante, her image of herself has progressed from cosmic, if childless, motherhood to that of an absolute spiritual essence purified of maternal qualities. Doubtless this role too left out essential elements in their relationship. Still, Eliot's late rejection of the posture of "Mother" may be one reason why she selected Johnny, who asked of her no noble maternal poses, rather than the dependent "daughter" Edith as her chief worshipping comforter after the death of Lewes.

For in rejecting the image of motherhood, Eliot was coming to terms with the reality of her past. Though Lewes bestowed the glorifying title on her, this indefatigably nurturing man was the sole mother in their relationship, restoring to her as best he could the comforting identities of "daughter" and "little sister" from which she was exiled.[16] For she had left her family, first emotionally and then in fact, when she was still in the position of dependent child to her imperious father and brother, and her life beyond them played out the cycle of familial roles only in wary, fitful charade. Her central self, and the apparent source of her art, was not the all-nourishing mother of her grandiose aspirations, but the more humble and dependent creature she had been in the family she left, whom she recalled in her autobiographical sonnet sequence, "Brother and Sister":

But were another childhood-world my share,
I would be born a little sister there.[17]

Lewes' mothering was sufficiently sensitive to enable its object to play at maternity, to gain the glory with which Victorian society endowed it without submitting to the sacrifice at its essence. The creator and persona George Eliot is the happiest offspring of Lewes' sense of play.

Though in her ambiguous role as "Mrs. Lewes," George Eliot took the name of "mother" solemnly, her novels do not. Infanticide is a persistent, and sometimes tempting, activity, and like Jane Austen's, Eliot's most artistically-inclined heroines are the least motherly. The powerfully-built Dorothea Brooke does not become the robust matriarch she might have, but surprises us by almost dying in childbirth; in the somber conclusion to *Middlemarch*, a description of Dorothea's maternity modulates into an image of a grim and solitary death. Maggie Tulliver, compact of passion an the need for love, violently mutilates her dolls in a manner that does not augur well for her nurturing future.[18] In George Eliot's novels, as in Jane Austen's letters, there is an implicit equation between motherhood and the ignominy of death, rather than creation and renewal.

But only in Eliot's last novel, *Daniel Deronda*, does a fully-fledged woman artist eloquently assert the distinction between motherhood and art: she is the Princess of Leonora Halm Eberstein, whose essence (like George Eliot's) has gone into her stage name, Alcharisi. Though the novel's action condemns her abandonment of her son, it condemns more radically the uniformity forced on women: the real crime is that, like Gwendolen Harleth,

Alcharisi can gain a modicum of adult freedom only by marrying. Alcharisi is the only female artist in Eliot's novels, and she stands strikingly aloof from woman's "precious specialty" as "Silly Novels by Lady Novelists" defined it: "Every woman is supposed to have the same set of motives, or else be a monster. I am not a monster, but I have not felt exactly what other women feel—or say they feel, for fear of being thought unlike others. When you reproach me in your heart for sending you away from me, you mean that I ought to say I felt about you as other women say they feel about their children. I did *not* feel that. I was glad to be freed from you."[19]

The artist does not embody the vague invocation in the Prelude to *Middlemarch* of "the common yearning of womanhood"; this artist, at least, is bravely exempt from it. Alcharisi's defiant apologia seems to spring from the same new self-acceptance that led George Eliot to deny herself as "spiritual mother" to Edith Simcox. She gives Alcharisi two ringing sentences that might stand as the definitive epitaph of her own identity as artist and "Mutter": "I was living a myriad lives in one. I did not want a child" (p. 689). This simple statement seems a truer record of her creative life than the mantle of the Madonna with which she decorated it. After a career of entanglement and role-playing, Eliot, like Austen, frees her art from the metaphor of maternity and allows it to stand alone, as its own justification and its own treasure.

George Eliot's liberation of art from the trappings of motherhood was a belated and difficult assertion, and it is for us as well. Even today, almost a hundred years after her death, it is a difficult insight for those who accept traditional psychiatric paradigms of women, which postulate, as George Eliot did in *Middlemarch*, a common yearning of womanhood" that denies the many possible goals and shapes female adulthood can choose. It is tempting but misleading to yoke artistic and biological creativity. In the lives of Jane Austen and George Eliot, two woman artists made inescapably aware of the social assumptions equating womanhood with motherhood, art is a liberation from that demand, not a metaphoric submission to it. It is the bounty of "a myriad lives in one," bringing release from limitation to a common destiny. Austen and Eliot both turned away from motherhood and embraced a creativity they defined as more spacious, more adult, more inclusive. Our study of woman artists, and of women, has still much to learn from their fine attunement to differences that are not monstrous, but part of our inherited wealth.[20]

Notes

1. Virginia Woolf, *A Room of One's Own* (1919; rpt. New York: Harcourt, Brace & World, 1957), p. 69.

2. Cynthia Griffin Wolff, *A Feast of Words: The Triumph of Edith Wharton* (New York: Oxford University Press, 1977), p. 342.

3. "The Flight from Womanhood: The Masculinity Complex in Women as Viewed by Men and by Women," reprinted in *Psychoanalysis and Women*, ed. Jean Baker Miller (Maryland: Penguin Books, 1973), p. 11.

4. Mary Ellmann, *Thinking About Women* (New York: Harcourt Brace Jovanovich, 1968), p. 63; Cynthia Ozick, "Women and Creativity: The Demise of the Dancing Dog" (1969), reprinted in *women in Sexist Society: Studies in Power and Powerlessness*, ed. Vivian Gornick and Barbara K. Moran (New York: New American Library, 1972), p. 439.

5. The most recent critic to disapprove is the iconoclastic Patricia Beer in *Reader, I Married Him: A Study of the Women Characters of Jane Austen, Charlotte Brontë, Elizabeth Gaskell, and George Eliot* (New York: Barnes & Noble, 1974), pp. 4–5.

6. 27 October 1798. In *Jane Austen's Letters to her Sister Cassandra and Others*, ed. R. W. Chapman, 2 vols. (Oxford: The Clarendon Press, 1932), I, 24. Hereafter cited in the text by date, volume, and page.

7. Jane Austen, *Emma*, ed. R. W. Chapman (London: Oxford University Press, 1952), p. 86.

8. *Westminster Review*, 66 (October, 1856), 461.

9. To Emily Davies, 8 August, 1868. In *The George Eliot Letters*, ed. Gordon S. Haight, 7 vols. (New Haven: Yale University Press, 1954–55), IV, 468. Hereafter cited in the text by date, volume, and page.

10. U. C. Knoepflmacher, "Mr. Haight's George Eliot: 'Warheit Und Dichtung,' " *Victorian Studies*, 12 (June, 1969), 430.

11. See Gordon S. Haight, *George Eliot: A Biography* (New York and Oxford: Oxford University Press, 1968), p. 205.

12. The ceremonial phrase belongs to her publisher, John Blackwood, as quoted in Haight, p. 214.

13. See Ruby V. Redinger, *George Eliot: The Emergent Self* (New York: Alfred A. Knopf, 1975).

14. Quoted in Haight, p. 452.

15. Simcox Autobiography, 26 December 1879. Quoted in Haight, p. 533.

16. Redinger makes this point, pp. 286–88.

17. George Eliot, *Poems* (London: The Hawarden Press, 1899), p. 170.

18. For further discussion of Maggie as an anti-maternal principle, see my "The Power of Hunger: Demonism and Maggie Tulliver," *Nineteenth-Century Fiction* 30 (September, 1975), 150–71.

19. George Eliot, *Daniel Deronda* (1876; rpt. Penguin English Library, Middlesex, 1967), p. 691. Future references to this edition will appear in the text.

20. This paper was originally presented, in somewhat altered form, at a Special Session at the 1977 MLA Convention, "Psychiatric Paradigms of Woman Artists," Chairperson Kathleen Fishbun.

The Art of *Mansfield Park*

ELLEN SERLEN UFFEN

Reginald Farrer, in an essay commemorating the one-hundredth anniversary of Jane Austen's death, wrote of *Mansfield Park* that it "is vitiated throughout by a radical dishonesty . . . [Austen's] purpose of edification, being not her own, is always at cross-purposes with her unprompted joy in creation."[1] This "dualism of motive," Farrer believes, is responsible for destroying the unity and sincerity of the novel. On the contrary, I suggest that the "dualism of motive," is intentional on Austen's part, is highly controlled, and is precisely the factor which creates the novel's unity. *Mansfield Park* is a book about change. It is a dramatized portrayal of the confrontation between the eighteenth and nineteenth centuries and their two opposing world views. Jane Austen presents the novel to us through a kind of Keatsian dichotomy of art and nature, but—here is the critic's bane—without the Keatsian half-doubts. Her art as a novelist as well as the values of an entire century, are at stake in *Mansfield Park* and their preservation is dependent upon her absolute and, at times, obvious authorial control.

The eighteenth century in the novel signifies the realm of art, the imposed order, refinement, decorum, stasis, and indeed, the civilization which are Mansfield Park. The house is emblematic of a century's ethos, and of the very style of the novel to which it gives its name. If the book is about "ordination" at all, as Austen's famous letter would indicate, it is primarily in the sense of initiation into the order of that world. The other pole of the novel is the nineteenth century, the realm of nature represented by the Crawfords and their encroaching city world—disorderly, vital, unstable because in constant progress toward the inevitable future. This dualism, which appears to be a curious reversal of the normal pastoral ideal, is connected with the cycle of change: what was once a part of the natural scheme of things is now a part of art, the ultimate perserver of the past. But this Keatsian cycle includes within it no Keatsian joy, no promise of renewal. What appears to be a happy ending is an illusion. The new world that is finally formed signifies only the death of the old world and no more. The novel, then, is profoundly ironic. If critics have sometimes missed the irony of *Mansfield Park* it is because the irony is of a type we do not normally expect in Jane Austen, one of sad resignation.

Mansfield Park is, thus, a very personal novel. Jane Austen, identifying herself not only as artist, but as eighteenth-century artist on the brink of a new, frightening, and potentially destructive nineteenth century world must, to save her identity, be even more the artist than she ever has been. Her fears are manifested in tone and in theme; the book is quite deliberately presented as a work of art. We are jolted, for instance, by the authorial "I," by Austen's unusually proprietary view of her heroine—"My Fanny"—but we are required here to remember what in most novels we forget in the course of the reading, that Fanny is a character in a novel. Jane Austen has created her, has given her life, and in a quite literal sense, "owns" her. Fanny Price is conceived as a literary heroine in the best eighteenth-century tradition.

Moreover, the novel is generally evocative of literature: "*Mansfield Park* continues," writes Henrietta Ten Hamsel, "and in some respects increases the use of popular eighteenth-century fictional conventions—the perfect heroine, the moralizing mentor, the seducing villain, the opposing relative, the cruel chaperone, the virtuous clergyman, the violent catastrophe, and the admiration of the Picturesque"; Everett Zimmerman sees Fanny as "standing midway between Pamela and Emma Bovary"; C. S. Lewis believes that she is "almost a Jane Austen heroine condemned to a Charlotte Brontë situation." The novel has been called a "cousin to the Morality plays," and the wilderness at Sotherton "a Spenserian forest where time and space are suspended."[2] Even the play-within-a-novel is a literary device, and the scene in which Mary and Henry plan the seduction of Fanny bears an uncomfortable resemblance to the devilish scene in *The Monk* where Ambrosio and Matilda plan the same for Antonia.

Edmund himself is to Fanny a literary hero—something out of medieval romance: "There is nobleness in the name of Edmund," she tells Mary Crawford, "It is a name of heroism and renown—of kings, princes, and knights, and seems to breathe the spirit of chivalry and warm affections" (p. 160).[3] And Fanny's effusions on nature are literary ones, controlled and predetermined responses in the language—"harmony," "repose," "rapture"—of the eighteenth-century Sublime. Contrasted to Fanny's Picturesque enthusiasm is Mary's view of nature: "I am something like the famous Doge at the Court of Louis XIV," she admits to Fanny, "and may declare that I see no wonder in this shrubbery equal to seeing myself in it" (p. 159). No literary heroine is she; Mary's brand of nature is the animate kind, the only one available in the city.

Fanny, then, is one of the keepers of eighteenth-century values in the novel, and they include the values embodied in the literature of the century. Literature itself, as Lionel Trilling has correctly noted in what is probably the most widely-read critical article on the novel, is at the very moral center of *Mansfield Park*.[4] Trilling, however, is referring specifically to the episode of the theatricals, but the question of literature as an art form is much bigger than this. The theme of art in opposition to nature reverberates throughout the novel and is illustrated most significantly in its three major episodes—in the excursion to Rushworth's estate, Sotherton, in the theatricals at Mansfield, and finally, in Fanny's visit to Portsmouth.

The scenes at Sotherton are carefully arranged in various gradations from art to nature indicated by the actual physical locations used, and also include some of the most loaded, symbolic language Jane Austen ever wrote. The group at Sotherton, composed of the visitors from Mansfield, and the Rushworths, mother and son, assembles, and the tour begins with the great house and its chapel, the traditional keeper of familial moral order. Mrs. Rushworth, concentrating on the various stages of its furnishings, explains the history of the chapel and concludes by saying that prayers are not longer read there by the domestic chaplain as was done before the present owners. Thereupon, Mary, not knowing that Edmund will soon be ordained, observes to him with a smile that "Every generation has its improvements" (p. 66). Fanny, however, regrets the loss of this custom, seeing it as "a valuable part of former times . . . so much in character with a great house . . ." (p. 66).

After the initial inspection the group gathers on the lawn to discuss the next stage of the tour:

> The lawn, bounded on each side by a high wall, contained beyond the first planted area, a bowling-green, and beyond the bowling-green a long terrace walk, backed by iron palissades, and commanding a view over them into the tops of the trees of the wilderness immediately adjoining. It was a good spot for fault-finding. (p. 69)

At this point, the assembly, "dispersed about in happy independence," form themselves into parties of three: Henry Crawford, Maria Bertram, and Mr. Rushworth; Mrs. Rushworth, Mrs. Norris, and Julia Bertram; Edmund, Fanny, and Mary Crawford. The last trio turn through a door and:

> A considerable flight of steps landed them in the wilderness, which was a planted wood of about two acres, and though chiefly of larch and laurel, and beech cut down, and though laid out with too much regularity, was darkness and shade, and natural beauty, compared with the bowling-green and the terrace. (p. 70)

The scene has progressed so far from the house and chapel to the planted lawn to the planted, but relatively "natural" beauty of the wilderness. The wilderness is landscaped nature, or art made to produce the illusion of nature and is therefore deceptive, not what it seems to be. Given their immediate circumstances, however, the illusion is enough to create in the visitors the feeling of freedom a truly natural state would offer. The wilderness soon begins to take on the aspect of a paradise to the participants and a false paradise to the reader, a place of temptation created, as were the earlier Renaissance paradises, by human desire.[5]

As it continues, the scene gets confused, with various groups weaving in and out of it and people losing themselves in its windings and "serpentine courses." But the confusions, the meetings, the people just missing each other become, at the same time, more and more organized. It seems almost as if the scenes were choreographed, perhaps as contrast to and as an artistic control over the actual events. Indeed, "The whole passage," says Robert Liddell, "now takes on something of the character of a ballet: formal, artificial, and amazingly beautiful."[6] As Fanny, characteristically fatigued by her walk, rests on a bench fronting the gate to the park, she is our witness to the drama with all of its entrances and exits. Mary and Edmund go off, "tempted" into the park by an unfastened side gate; Maria and Henry, foiled in their outing by a locked gate, maneuver their way around its edge under Fanny's gaze and "By taking a circuitous, and as it appeared to her, very unreasonable direction to the knoll, they were soon beyond her eye" (p. 77). A bit later Julia appears and goes after them, followed closely by Rushworth. Fanny convinces him to find his companions and eventually, even she is prompted by impatience to move. She comes upon Edmund and Mary and "it was evident that they had been spending their time pleasantly, and were not aware of the length of their absence" (p. 79).

One of the dangers implicit in the false freedom of the wilderness is loss of civilized self, which includes those moral obligations dependent on time. Edmund has kept Fanny waiting an entire hour when he meant to return within a few minutes. We recall the little exchange between Edmund and Mary earlier when he had looked at his watch to gauge how far they had walked in the woods. Mary had responded to his action by saying, "Oh! do not attack me with your watch. A watch is always too fast or too slow. I cannot be dictated to by a watch" (p. 73). At this point, then, she has scored her first triumph; she has succeeded in making Edmund lose all sense of time and place. Sotherton has served his purpose.

Initially the ostensible reason for the visit to Sotherton was an investigation into the possibility of its "improvement," a term which in *Mansfield Park* is always an indication of danger. It suggests a desire for radical change and it functions in the novel as a metaphor for the cultural disorientation heralding the destruction of tradition.[7] Significantly, it is Mary Crawford who terms the disuse of Sotherton's family chapel an "improvement," and Henry Crawford who instigates the present visit and who also several times suggests the need for landscape improvement at Thornton Lacey, Edmund's future residence. Jane Austen's strategy here, and later in the theatricals episode, according to Alistair M. Duckworth:

> Has clearly been to expose the dangers to the "estate" of excessive and unprincipled change. Her metonymy extends beyond metaphorical convenience, for by locating traditional systems in the fabric of the house, or in the landscape of the park, she has affirmed her faith in the substantial existence of certain preexisting structures of morality and religion, and . . . has suggested how essential to the continuity of an ethos is the actual physical disposition of its setting.[8]

Ironically, then, the day, "with all its imperfections," points precisely to the necessity for improvement, but in the ethical realm. The visit, which had begun more or less innocently, concludes by putting into relief the intrigues and deceptions whose working-out will constitute the action of the rest of *Mansfield Park* and, in the doing, sets the stage, as it were, for the theatricals, the next important variation on its themes.

The most controversial parts of *Mansfield Park* are undoubtedly those dealing with the theatricals and properly so since they are a microcosm of the underlying tensions of the whole book. The episode is also closely connected to the one at Sotherton in that here the characters are acting, or dramatically living the parts that they naturally fell into there. It differs in tone, however. The earlier scenes had a quality of literal, or physical furtiveness about them; here we have that same quality on the psychological level. At the very beginning, for instance, Henry Crawford suggests that Maria act Agatha, the part Julia had been secretly hoping for: Julia "saw a glance at Maria, which confirmed the injury to herself; it was a scheme—a trick; she was slighted, Maria was preferred; the smile of triumph which Maria was trying to suppress showed how well it was understood . . ." (p. 102). And so the scene continues; looks and gestures abound. Physical action is secondary.

The main critical question surrounding the theatricals is why all the fuss? What *not* act a play? We know that there were theatricals performed at the Austen home which Jane herself enjoyed enormously, so why is the same thing problematic here? It is, I suggest, because the major issue in this section is not so much the *fact* of the theatricals, as what they represent in the context of the novel. They are not "art"—that is a definition of the eighteenth-century universe of *Mansfield Park*—but are instead to be understood as another indication of the feared encroachment of the nineteenth-century world. More precisely, the realm of art associated with the ordered, decorous eighteenth century implies a great degree of constraint and self-discipline on the part of the artist. The theatricals, on the other hand, or the "acting" which they necessitate, to be done well, must be derived from the opposite ability, the ability to remove oneself from externally imposed definitions of self— from both psychological and social constraints. The fear of this happening in these scenes is compounded here in that what emerges when these constraints are loosened is not a "made-up" self, but one which too closely resembles a real self, now basking in its new freedom.

As the critical history of *Mansfield Park* now stands, there seem to be two fairly clear-cut camps which have formed themselves in relation to the problem of the theatricals—the followers of Edmund Bertram and those of Lionel Trilling. In an early discussion with his brother, Tom, Edmund clarifies his position:

> In a *general* light, private theatricals are open to some objections, but as *we* are circumstanced, I must think it would be highly injudicious, to attempt anything of the kind. It would show great want of feeling on my father's account, absent as he is, and in some degree of constant danger; and it would be imprudent, I think, with regard to Maria, whose situation is a very delicate one, considering every thing, extremely delicate. (p. 96)

In literal context it would be foolish to deny the feasibility of Edmund's argument, yet it speaks to only half the problem; it does not explain the tense undersurface of the scenes , the level of psychological drama enacted. It is this point that Lionel Trilling addresses. According to him, in these scenes, "What is decisive is a traditional, almost primitive feeling about dramatic impersonation . . . it is the fear that the impersonation of a bad or inferior character will have a harmful effect upon the impersonator, that, indeed, the impersonation of any other self will diminish the integrity of the real self." And this, in turn, is connected—most obviously in Edmund's case—with the choice of a profession; that is, the assumption of a role which makes another role impossible—"It is a commitment which fixes the nature of the self."[9]

Trilling's argument is convincing, but as applied to the actual situation depicted in the novel, it is ex post facto: the damage has already been done. The fear is not that the actor will become the mask—he already is that—but rather that the mask will no longer be necessary.[10] To put it another way, what the theatricals episode is really dramatizing is the release of energies which define the self. As Trilling has it, "That the self may destroy the self by the very energies which define its being, that the self may be preserved by the negation of its own energies—this, whether or not we agree, makes a paradox, makes an irony, that catches our imagination."[11] The energies have always existed, and acting a role just makes it easier to follow the natural inclinations under the guise of disinterested playing. This is what we are meant to understand by Fanny's observation that Maria was acting "well— too well," and that "Mr. Crawford was considerably the best actor of all" (p. 125). This observation, in fact, hardly needs the context of acting to support its justness. The context simply clarifies the reality. Each person, that is, can "be" his or her own real role without fear of detection. The episode illustrates the ultimate in typecasting: Maria can flirt with Henry, Mary with Edmund, Mrs. Norris can indulge her self-importance and Mr. Rushworth his vanity.

So the real danger in this episode is not that the natural selves of the players will become the artistic selves they are portraying, but rather the other way around: art is simulating nature so closely that those natural selves are coming loose of their civilized wraps. The wraps are primarily the effect of "education," a major part of which, as Trilling and others have noted, consists in learning to repress one's energies, to substitute decorum and order for instinct. In other words, education is the careful inculcation of a role that will become a lifestyle. Sir Thomas has not succeeded in properly educating his daughters because he has not taught them to believe strongly enough in the life's role. It is only later he realizes that "they had never been properly taught to govern their inclinations and tempers, by that sense of duty which can alone suffice" (p. 352). This realization, however, comes too late to influence the occurrences which are the natural consequences of this scene. At this present point, even Edmund yields to the temptation of instinct— albeit in the guise of "saving" Mary—by agreeing to act. It is Fanny here who is Sir Thomas' only success. When she says "I really cannot act . . . it would be absolutely impossible for me" (p. 111), her statement constitutes an admission of total repression of energy, the state of mind for which her physical debilitation is a metaphor.

Thus this episode is another version of the wilderness at Sotherton but a much more disturbing one in context because more blatantly subversive. By using art so openly, so indecorously, in the false service of nature, the performance constitutes a serious undermining of all the values of Mansfield Park. Moreover, by turning Mansfield itself into a theater and actually acting the play within its bounds, the action becomes a brazen desecration of the estate, a violation of civilization.

The values of Mansfield, however, are not completely clear to us—or to Fanny—until they are tested by contrast during her visit to her parents' home in Portsmouth. At this point in the novel Fanny, notwithstanding Sir Thomas' wishes, has been obstinately refusing to marry Henry Crawford. Her guardian means to teach her a lesson. He sends her off to Portsmouth, believing that "a little abstinence from the elegancies and luxuries of Mansfield Park, would bring her mind into a sober state, and incline her to a juster estimate of that home of greater permanence, and equal comfort of which she had the offer" (p. 280).

Sir Thomas could not have planned it better had he been the artist composing the scene. Fanny is greeted upon her arrival by a "trollopy-looking" maid who does not even notice her, so eager is she to convey to Fanny's brother, William, who had accompanied her, some news about his ship. Next, one of her younger brothers appears, pushes the maid aside and blurts out the same news. Her mother comes, Fanny is rushed into a tiny parlor, and from there the chaos begins in earnest. Fanny is disappointed at every turn: the house it too small, her mother is "a partial, ill-judging parent, a dawdle, a slattern," her father barely notices her presence, the servants do not attend to order, her brothers and sisters are totally undisciplined, continually "thumping and halooing" and squabbling over insignificant matters. Fanny, after the first day is "fatigued and fatigued again" and after the first week can think of nothing but Mansfield Park:

> Everything were she now was was full contrast to it. The elegance, propriety, regularity, harmony—and perhaps, above all, the peace and tranquillity of Mansfield, were brought to her remembrance every hour of the day, by the prevalence of every thing opposite to them *here* . . . At Mansfield, no sounds of contention, no raised voice, no abrupt bursts, no tread of violence was ever heard; all proceeded in a regular course of cheerful orderliness; every body had their due importance; everybody's feelings were consulted. If tenderness could be ever supposed wanting, good sense and good breeding supplied its place . . .
> (p. 298).

Interestingly, the whole tone of the novel changes when Fanny reaches her parents' home; the narrative picks up speed, everything bustles, bangs, runs, shouts in a manner reminiscent of Smollett and Dickens. The comedy of the episode catches the tone of the city; there is a physical vitality, a vitality of unrestrained impulse here, unlike the verbal or intellectual vitality evident elsewhere in *Mansfield Park*. In fact, what engages us immediately is precisely this exuberant quality which Fanny finds most obnoxious; but, still, what we feel at the end is a vague discomfort arising from paradox. We, with Fanny, are led to compare Sir Thomas' "absolute power" and its results at Mansfield with Mr. Price's lack of power and even lack of desire for power over his family. We compare, too, the good-natured ineptitude of Mrs. Price with the total torpitude of Lady Bertram, a luckier Mrs. Price. Our response to this episode is finally deeply ambivalent: the scene is a breath of fresh air after the restraints of Sir Thomas' regime at Mansfield, and even though we realize that a great deal of Fanny's present attitude is based on her own family's disregard of her, at the same time we know that her distaste is not entirely unfounded. We admit, however hesitantly and unwillingly, that the Prices could do with a little order.

Fanny returns to Mansfield Park as eagerly as two months earlier she had left it. Upon her arrival she is greeted by another sort of chaos arising from something unique to the house, scandal. Maria has left Rushworth and run off with Henry Crawford thus, as it happens, proving Fanny was right about him; and Julia, fearing new restraints at Mansfield because of her sister's actions, has eloped with Yates. Both of these events have occurred, not really surprisingly, far away from Mansfield, in London, which place Fanny was disposed to think "very much at war with all respectable attachments" (p. 329)[12]—in moral context, Portsmouth writ to the largest extreme—and which in eighteenth-century literature had traditionally been treated as a place of evil. It is there, for instance, that Clarissa is undone, that Joseph Andrews is tempted, that Moll Flanders has her base of operations. Moreover, we hear about what happened through letters, as if any direct contact with London would despoil Mansfield even further.[13]

But neither Fanny nor the reader is given much time to think about the events. A chapter after her return her creator enters to tie up the loose ends and thoroughly cleanse the scene:

> Let other pens dwell on guilt and misery. I quit such odious subjects as soon as I can, impatient to restore everybody, not greatly in fault themselves, to tolerable comfort, and to have done with all the rest. (p. 350)

One by one the dissenting and alien elements are neatly excluded from Mansfield Park: Mary Crawford remains in London living with the Grants, Dr. Grant having taken a stall in Westminster; Maria, now divorced from Rushworth, rejected by Crawford and unaccepted by her family, goes off with Mrs. Norris to "another country"; and Julia is far away with Yates. The people who remain at Mansfield are its owners and inheritors: Sir Thomas and Lady Bertram; Fanny and Edmund; Tom, newly purged of dissipation by his recent illness; and Susan, Fanny's sister and Mansfield's new Fanny. The novel concludes with the marriage of Edmund and Fanny and their removal to the parsonage previously occupied by the Grants, there to live out their days, presumably, in peace and harmony "within the view and patronage of Mansfield Park" (p. 360).

The ending, however, is more ambiguous than this simple plot summary would indicate.[14] Joseph M. Duffy, Jr. is close to the true problem when he says that Austen is really suggesting here a way to live with the social horrors that were to occupy later novelists in the nineteenth century: "Her prescription might almost be reduced to that of retirement from the world, yet it is retirement to an incredibly complicated existence. It is not retirement to natural simplicity but a strategically deliberate retreat to a stately life of art, ritual, and imposed forms."[15] The ending thus suggests an unnatural future existence at Mansfield Park and, fittingly, it is brought about equally unnaturally by the hand of the artist. Although Austen allows Fanny and Edmund to inherit their earthly paradise, their succession is a triumph only of her art. Here again, Duffy has seen the ambiguity: Mansfield Park, he tells us, or:

> The good society is man's eloquent artistic gesture in the face of menacing nature; but unless the social order is enriched from a life-giving force, its facade of elegance, propriety, and regularity can, and does, collapse. For these graces are fragile vestigial elements in a superficial society, as they are in the merely good-tempered, well-mannered individual, and they can be shattered by a force so simple and powerful as a natural inclination.[16]

Marriage in *Mansfield Park* does not look to the regeneration of society as does the traditional marriage at the end of comedy. The energy necessary for revitalization has been excluded here. Art, which resolved the world of the novel, is not enough to sustain it beyond the present generation. The real eighteenth-century world, that is, the world on which this fictional version is based, will soon be dead and Austen suggests, so will the novelistic art of the eighteenth century which is responsible for transposing this world into fiction. Hence people die in *Mansfield Park* but no one is born, and we cannot help feeling that no one is likely to be. The novel contains neither the promise of comedy nor the weight of tragedy, rather, simply and profoundly, the sadness of loss. Its denouement is a poignantly ironic comment on the lines of Jane Austen's favorite Cowper: "Oh sacred art, to which alone life owes/Its happiest seasons, and a peaceful close."

Notes

1. "Jane Austen, *ob.* July 18, 1817," *Quarterly Review* CCXXVIII (July 1917), p. 20. Cf. Lawrence Lerner, *The Truthteller: Jane Austen, George Eliot, D. H. Lawrence* (London: Chatto & Windus, 1967), p. 160: "Mary Crawford succeeds: she embodies the qualities that *Mansfield Park* was written to assail, but she also embodies more of the book's creative energy than anyone else—more than Fanny, and far, far more than the worthy and dreary Edmund, who comes to life only when he is material for comedy (as in Chap. XIV). *Mansfield Park* is a book divided against itself."

2. The quotations, respectively, are from: *Jane Austen: A Study in Fictional Conventions* (The Hague: Mouton, 1954), p. 101; "Jane Austen and *Mansfield Park*: A Discrimination of Ironies," *Studies in the Novel* 1 (Fall, 1969), p. 355; "A Note on Jane Austen," *Essays in Criticism IV (Oct. 1954), 359–71, rpt. in Jane Austen: A Collection of Critical Essays,,* ed. Ian Watt (Englewood Cliffs, N.J.: Prentice-Hall, 1963), p. 29; Denis Donoghue, "A View of Mansfield Park," in *Critical Essays on Janes Austen*, ed. B. C. Southam (London: Routledge & Kegan Paul, 1968), p. 41; Thomas R. Edwards, Jr., "The Difficult Beauty of *Mansfield Park*," *Nineteenth-Century Fiction* 20 (June 1965), p. 53.

3. All references to *Mansfield Park* are to the Riverside edition, ed. Reuben A. Brower (Boston: Houghton Mifflin, 1965).

4. *"Mansfield Park,"* in Watt, p. 132.

5. I borrow this idea from A Bartlett Giamatti's study of *The Earthly Paradise and the Renaissance Epic* (Princeton: Princeton Univ. Press, 1966), p. 85.

6. *The Novels of Jane Austen* (London: Longman, Green, 1963), p. 75.

7. Cf. Alistair M. Duckworth, *The Improvement of the Estate: A Study of Jane Austen's Novels* (Baltimore: Johns Hopkins Press, 1971), p. 45: "If Edmund Burke in his political prose following the French Revolution could use the imagery of excessive estate improvements to illustrate the horrors of the revolution, we need not be surprised that Jane Austen could suggest in the adoption of Reptonian methods dangerous consequences for the continuity of a culture."

8. Ibid., p. 57.

9. Trilling, pp. 132, 133.

10. That the actor is already the mask is suggested strongly enough simply in the casting list of Kotzebue's melodrama, *Lovers' Vows*, the play they have chosen to enact. I am indebted to Reuben A. Brower for supplying the following list in "A Note on Jane Austen and the Theatre" in his Riverside edition of *Mansfield Park*, pp. xxix-xxx: Frederick (the illegitimate son)—Henry Crawford; Agatha (Frederick's devoted mother)—Maria Bertram; Count Cassel (a brainless and amorous fop, with a fortune)—Mr. Rushworth; Baron Wildenhaim (the seducer, now a widower)—Mr. Yates; Amelia Wildenhaim (the coquettish daughter)—Mary Crawford; Anahalt (minister and tutor, in love with Amelia)—Edmund Bertram.

11. Trilling, p. 131.

12. Edmund agrees. Cf. *Mansfield Park*, p. 71: "We do not look in cities for our best morality. It is not there that respectable people of any denomination can do most good; and it certainly is not there, that the influence of the clergy can be most felt. A fine preacher is followed and admired; but it is not in fine preaching only that a good clergyman will be useful in his parish and his neighbourhood, where the parish and neighbourhood are of a size capable of knowing his private character and observing his general conduct, which in London can rarely be the case. The clergy are lost there in the crowds of their parishioners."

13. According to Q. D. Leavis, however, the reason the events are told in letters is that the novel, at an earlier date, was epistolary in form. This is no doubt true, but does not explain why Austen chose to retain that particular method of narration at this particular point. Cf. "A Critical Theory of Jane Austen's Writings (II): 'Lady Susan' into 'Mansfield Park,' " *Scrutiny* X (Oct. 1941). p. 123.

14. For some opinions of the significance of the ending see: Joseph W. Donahue, Jr., "Ordination and the Divided House at Mansfield Park," *ELH* 32 (June 1965), p. 178; Avrom Fleishman, *A Reading of Mansfield Park: An Essay in Critical Synthesis* (Minneapolis: Univ. of Minnesota Press, 1967), p. 56; Tanner, p. 159; Marvin Mudrick, *Jane Austen: Irony as Defense and Discovery* (Princeton: Princeton Univ. Press. 1952), p. 180.

15. "Moral Integrity and Moral Anarchy in *Mansfield Park*," *ELH* 23 (March 1956), p. 74.

16. Ibid., p. 86.

Frankenstein's Daughter: Mary Shelley and Mary Wollstonecraft

Janet Todd

In her introduction to *Frankenstein*, Mary Shelley wrote: "It is not singular that, as the daughter of two parents of distinguished literary celebrity, I should very early in life have thought of writing."[1] In the same introduction, she makes the point that creation does not come from a void, but from materials afforded a writer by circumstances. The two comments together suggest that Mary Shelley was aware of her literary debt to her parents and was acknowledging their inspiration. Some of the "materials afforded" were certainly the works of her mother, Mary Wollstonecraft.

The first reviewers of *Frankenstein* emphasized the novel's relation to William Godwin's *Caleb Williams*, published in 1794.[2] They noted resemblances in the plot, characters, structure and tone. The two heroes, the lower class "creature," Caleb Williams, and the upper class master, Falkland, are trapped in a pattern of pursuit, in which Caleb, in posession of his master's criminal secret, is hounded by Falkland until the pursuer becomes the pursued and Falkland is destroyed. In something of the same manner, although the pattern is reversed, the monster pursues Frankenstein until he in turn is pursued. Again, a great scene of Godwin's novel, where Caleb and Falkland confront each other not for mutual understanding but for the relief of their own tortured feelings, is paralleled by the climactic scene in *Frankenstein* on the sea of ice, where the monster and his creator meet to reinforce their ultimate incomprehension of each other.

In both *Caleb Williams* and *Frankenstein*, the protagonists, hunter and hunted, oppresser and oppressed, are male. However, in both, the absolute outcast situation of one of the protagonists—based in one case on an unchangeably low social position and in the other on a ghastly phyiscal appearance—is representative of the situation of women, especially fallen women. Like the monster, the woman is separated by her physical condition from the dominant male society and—in the case of the fallen woman—from the family as well. Since the family is the necessary bridge to the larger society, this exclusion is the most fundamental and searing.

In *Frankenstein*, the family, consisting of father, mother and child, or father, brother and sister, is constantly held up as the ideal state. To be deprived of this is truly to be deprived of society and, ultimately, of humanity. The fallen woman suffers just such an exclusion. This exclusion from society and the family is a major concern of Mary Wollstonecraft; it seems appropriate, therefore, to look in her work for an intermediary between Caleb Williams and the monster.

The importance of Wollstonecraft in Mary Shelley's life is revealed in many incidents and circumstances. The trips to her grave to find some solitude away from the chaotic Godwin household, Shelley's avowal of love over the grave, the Wollstonecraft picture hanging over the mantel mentioned by so many visitors to the house, and the references to Wollstonecraft made by Godwin and his literary friends when they commented on Mary's character or appearance must all have impressed on her the personality of her dead mother and have reminded her of the loss she had sustained and caused.

The literary influence of Wollstonecraft must also have been immense. Early in her life Mary Shelley read all of her mother's works, and her later journals reveal a constant rereading of them during her years with Shelley.[3] In *Frankenstein*, there are many hints of the influence of this reading, and several of the sentiments are those reiterated in the works of Wollstonecraft. For example, when Walton comments on the effect of ignorance and poverty on the mind, he echoes Wollstonecraft's views in *Letters from Sweden*, where the lack of curiosity and interest in the uncultured is noted.[4] Again, there are in *Frankenstein* comments about the blighting effect of trade, especially in the characterizations of Clerval's father. This was a constant theme of Wollstonecraft, emphasized in her later books after his disastrous relationship with the trading Imlay.[5] Many other echoes of Wollstonecraft's views are apparent throughout *Frankenstein*, but for a sustained similarity between the plot and characterization of *Frankenstein* and a work of Wollstonecraft, we must turn to her final, unfinished novel, *the Wrongs of Woman; or Maria*, which presents as one of its two heroines the fallen woman, Jemima.[6]

A central section of *The Wrong of Woman* is the first person narrative of Jemima, which has the same structural place in the novel as the monster's account of his life in *Frankenstein*. According to Wollstonecraft's intention, Jemima's life story is presented as typical of the lot of working class women, whose several ills she exemplifies. The illegitimate child of two servants, Jemima is abandoned by her father before she is born. Like Wollstonecraft herself, the mother dies a few days after giving birth to her daughter. Sent out to a baby minder, Jemima is from the outset of her life neglected and illtreated. However, instead of dying like most unwanted babies, she continues to grow, and soon she becomes a drudge for the younger children. This drudgery is exchanged for an even more hurtful one when her father decides to use her as a servant for his new wife. In their house, the stepmother reacts toward Jemima with the same repugnance and contempt as the father has already done, until she finds she can stand the obnoxious presence no longer, and Jemima is sent out as a servant. In the new establishment, she endures brutal treatment and is constantly taunted for her illegitimate birth. Her starvation diet forces her to steal, and she quickly adds the epithet of "thief" to that of "bastard."

Jemima is, in her own words, the "mark of cruelty" until her sixteenth year when "something like comeliness appeared on a Sunday." Automatically she is raped by the man of house, who then procures her frequent submission with threats. The result is inevitable. Thrown out of the house pregnant, she is forced to take refuge with beggars, and, although feeling some tenderness for her unborn child, she gives herself with much pain an abortion, so that she can eek out a subsistence as a beggar. Later she becomes a thief and a prostitute. She is despised by all, moved from street to street, and regarded as a monstrous blot on society.

The brightest period in this grim life occurs when Jemima finds refuge as the kept mistress of a licentious but cultivated "gentleman," in whose house she learns some book knowledge and refinement of manner and speech. Such acquirements, however, serve only to embitter her when, on his death, she is ejected as a moral outrage by his relatives, and is forced again to become a beggar and washer-woman.

By this stage in her life, Jemima has the awareness that it is primarily her sex rather than her lowly social condition that oppresses her and keeps her a permanent outcast from the society she wishes to enter. As she comments: "A man with half my industry, and, I may say, abilities, could have procured a decent livelihood and discharged some of the duties which knit mankind together; whilst I, who had acquired a taste for the rational, nay, in honest pride let me assert, the vituous enjoyments of life, was cast aside as the filth of society" (p. 65).

The rest of the narrative drags Jemima through the vicious institutions that oppress the poor; she goes to prison, the pauper hospital and the workhouse. In such surroundings, her character deteriorates, and she becomes indifferent and even at times malevolent; she "hated mankind." Finally she is taken on by the master of the workhouse as an attendant at his private asylum. She is chosen primarily because of her deadened emotions and her apparent moral insensitivity, now her most distinguishing characteristics.

In *The Wrongs of Woman*, Jemima represents the specific horror of being a woman deprived of family. Like Frankenstein's monster, she is conscious of no defining family and is therefore immediately an adult. Put to work when scarcely more than a baby, she already "looked like a little old woman, or a hag shrivelling into nothing," with "furrows of reflection and care" destroying the appearance of youth. So too the monster's ugliness removes him from the child, whom, at the outset of his life, he resembles in innocence. His yellow eyes and wrinkled skin are those of an old man, and people respond to the disparity between this appearance and his strength and vigor with the horror Jemima also excites.

Both Jemima and the monster realize their bereft condition, which they see as the cause of their horrific situation and their deteriorating characters. Jemima frequently and emphatically makes the point: "I was an egg dropped in the sand; a pauper by nature, hunted from family to family, who belonged to nobody—and nobody cared for me. I was despised from my birth" (p. 56). The monster expressed the same idea: "No father had watched my infant days, no mother had blessed me with smiles and caresses" (p. 106). At the end of her narrative, Jemima sums up her motherless state in a plaintive question. "Who ever risked anything for me?—who ever acknowledged me to be a fellow creature?" The monster echoes this: "But where were my friends and relations?"

The reactions of Jemima and the monster to their anomalous situations are similar: they seek surrogate parents, but in the fictive worlds of the novels, there are no surrogate families. Jemima tries to win the affection of her stepmother, at one point even making an impulsive gesture of affection toward her to kiss her; she is of course violently repulsed. So the monster, revealing himself to the father, De Lacey, begs for the affection of his family and is brutally cast off. Separated from the family which they can never enter, both Jemima and the monster become pariahs. The monster is called by his creator "a vile insect," "abhorred and miserable." Jemima sees herself "hunted from hole to hole, as if she had been a beast of prey, or infected with a moral plague." Full humanity is given only through the family; to be outside it is to be less than human, an animal or a monster."

If neither the monster nor Jemima can force an entry into a family, and so find a moral and social model, both yet find an intellectual one, Jemima in the gentleman she lives with for some years and the monster in the De Laceys, whom he sees through the chinks in the wall. Both the monster and Jemima are infinitely educable, although the monster's progress is intellectual self-improvement is certainly the more remarkable.

When mistress to the gentleman, Jemima improves herself intellectually through reading in his library and through conversation at his dinner table, "from which, in the common course of life, women are excluded." She is encouraged by her master in both reading and conversation until she reaches a point where her "sentiments and language" are superior to her station and sex. Returning to the life of the streets, she finds this superiority, far from being an advantage, a handicap. As a woman she can derive no benefit from it, and it serves only to remind her of the life from which she is excluded: "The book of knowledge is closely clasped, against those who must fulfill their daily task of severe manual labour or die" (p. 64).

The monster derives much of this learning from Felix as he seeks to educate his beloved Safie. Along with language, history, and geography, he learns the social facts which Jemina learnt through experience: "I heard of the division of property, of immense wealth and squalid poverty, of rank, descent, and noble blood." He learns too of the importance of the family: "how the father doted on the smile of the infant, and the lively sallies of the older children, how all the cares of the mother were wrapped up in the precious charge, how the mind of youth expanded and gained knowledge, of brother, sister, and all the various relationships which bind one human being to another in mutual bonds" (pp. 105-106). Such ideas, and with them the realization of his own abnormal extra-familial situation, are reinforced for the monster by his reading. *The Sorrows of Werter* serves primarily to emphasize that he is related to no one, while Plutarch causes him to feel even greater admiration than before for the forbidden domestic harmony presented by the De Laceys. Above all, *Paradise Lost* proves most relevant to his situation. The triune relationship of God, Adam and Eve presents the ideal familial pattern, from which he is forever excluded.

The monster's reading confirms his Godwinian observation, that virtue is essentially social, and for acceptance by society a family is necessary, since it is the primary social organization. Deprived of it, the monster follows his reading and experience and concludes: "If I have no ties and no affections, hatred and vice must be my portion." Prevented by his lack of family from exercising social virtue, his education, like Jemima's, serves only to embitter him. In Jemima's words, "To be cut off from human converse, now I had been taught to relish it, was to wander a ghost among the living."

It is in their presentation of Godwinian social theory that the monster and Jemima most coincide. Both are, initially at least, innately good, noble, and benevolent, and in both, vice is a wrenching of their human nature from its proper course. Both reiterate that it is misery and injustice which cause vice in them. Because she has been reduced to starvation, Jemima early learns to steal, although she does not thereby lose her consciousness of the evil nature of theft. Later, as a prostitute, preyed on by men, she preys on them by picking the pockets of the drunkards who abuse her with the names of slave, bastard, and whore. During her sorry career, Jemima has one chance of a domestic haven with a tradesman who offers to take her into his house. Before complying, Jemima advises him to eject the pregnant girl already under his roof. This is done and the girl in despair drowns herself. Considering this incident with remorse, Jemima can yet find justification for it: "I was famishing; wonder not that I became a wolf!" She does not completely exonerate herself, however, for she can still refer to herself in this incident as "a monster." Later in her life, smaller social sins cease to result in any self-condemnation: "I began to consider the rich and the poor as natural enemies, and became a thief from principle" (p. 68).

It is the monster's experience of cruelty and injustice that makes him morally monstrous. Constantly he asserts that he is evil because he is miserable. Driven out by the De Lacey family whom he had purposed to help, the monster declares "everlasting war against the species." He is filled with feelings of "revenge and hatred," inimical to his true character. Like Jemima, the monster feels that his vicious acts are inevitable given his social exclusion, and like Jemima he suffers in the execution of his evil: "Think you that the groans of Clerval were music to my ears? My heart was fashioned to be susceptible of love and sympathy, and when wrenched by misery to vice and hatred, it did not endure the violence of the change without torture such as you cannot even imagine" (p. 202).

The monster and Jemima are both diverted from benevolence by social injustice. In both cases their crimes are real and not glossed over. The monster murders Frankenstein's family and friend, and Jemima causes the death of her unborn child and of the pregnant girl. Both are portrayed as corrupted; yet both retain some essential goodness. Thus the monster and Jemima are allowed partial relationships. Jemima has been repulsed so often that she has lost all possibility of sexual or sensual feelings, and there is no suggestion that she can ever be a wife or mother. She can, however, relate to Maria, where there is no sexual and familial tie, and, through the relationship, Jemima is partly redeemed.

The monster well realizes that his exclusion implies first of all sexual and sensual exclusion. When he imagines an interchange of kindness with humanity, he exclaims, "But that cannot be; the human senses are insurmountable barriers to our union" (p. 130). At the end of the book, however, he excites some compassion in Walton when the latter's eyes are closed. In addition, he is given the last justifying word in the novel, so that the reader is left with an impression less of his crimes than of his sufferings.

A final direct similarity between the monster and Jemima is their association with reason or intellect. In the dualistic psychology of the time, reason opposes sensibility or emotion. While sensibility needs nurturing in a family, reason can exist without such support; in fact it may be strengthened at the expense of sensibility when a person is deprived of domestic life.

In *The Wrongs of Woman*, Jemima, the outcast, is associated with reason, while Maria, the middle class woman who comes from a defective but still functioning family, is associated with sensibility. Early in the novel, Jemima counters Maria's excessive emotion with her rather callous reasoning. For example, when Maria purposes to starve herself in romantic fashion, Jemima observes that few people carry this out and most start eating as they come to their senses. Always Jemima is aware of consequences, and sympathy is given, if it is given at all, only when it is judged advantageous to herself. Her sympathy for Maria occurs when she has proof that her master no longer trusts her and when she considers herself in need of a new patron.

The monster is associated with reason or intellect in two ways. First, he is the result of Frankenstein's intellect when it is divorced from the sensibility embodied in Elizabeth and his mother. The passion that sustains Frankenstein in his monstrous creation is intellectual, and there is in his laboratory no place for domestic and female sensibility. Secondly, the monster often shows an intellectual awareness not evident in Frankenstein, whose crises are marked by irrationality and impulsiveness. In their encounters it is Frankenstein who is moved by excessive emotion and who, on the sea of ice, has to be restrained by the monster.

The cause of this association with reason to the exclusion of sensibility is the same in Jemima and the monster, and can be traced, like their other ills, to their lack of a nurturing family, in which alone sensibility can be cultivated. Without a family, the rough blasts of society quickly check the development of a faculty which tends to self-indulgence rather than self-interest.

The similarities between the experiences and characters of Jemima and the monster are sufficiently striking to suggest that Mary Shelley had her mother's work somewhere in mind when she wrote her novel.[7] Two other circumstances reinforce this obliquely, since they associate the monster with the outcast woman: the fate of Justine in *Frankenstein* and the social situation of Mary Shelley when she was writing her book.

Justine resembles the monster through her rejection by her creator: "Through a strong perversity, her mother could not endure her, and ... treated her very ill" (p. 50). Since she does not have the monster's hideous appearance, however, she can be accepted for a time into the Frankenstein household. Yet, as in the case of the monster, the surrogate can never become the real: Justice is finally excluded from the family and killed for the crime of the monster, whose rightful position as child of the family she had in a way usurped. The main evidence against her is the picture of Frankenstein's mother, whom she had tried to accept as her own.

In her relationship to her own family, Justne is close to both Jemima and the monster. She resembles the monster rather than Jemima, however, in her effect on this family—an effect allowable in the poetic world of *Frankenstein*, but not in the "typical" world of *the Wrongs of Woman*:[8]

> One by one, her brothers and sisters died; and her mother, with the exception of her neglected daughter was left childless. The conscience of the woman was troubled; she began to think that the deaths of her favourites was a judgment from heaven to chastise her partiality (p. 51).

Here the excluding family is punished; in both books, however, the punishment falls directly and primarily on the excluded child.

More than most novels, *Frankenstein* seems to demand some biographical interpretation, owing to the extraordinary situation of Mary Shelley when she wrote it. The death of Mary Wollstonecraft in 1797 had left two motherless daughters. Shortly after Mary Shelley started *Frankenstein*, Fanny, the eldest, would kill herself, and her melancholy situation as supernumerary in the Godwin household must have been a contributing factor to her fate. Fanny's birth was the result of Wollstonecraft's departure from convention in her liaison with Gilbert Imlay, an account of which Mary Shelley could have read in her father's biography of her mother and in the letters published after her death.[9] Mary Shelley was aware of the misery of both Wollstonecraft and her illegitimate daughter, the seeming result of her mother's irregular conduct; yet she eloped with Shelley—whose wife was living at the time the first version of *Frankenstein* was written—and she stayed with him when there seemed no possibility of a marriage. Mary Shelley's first illegitimate child died, and her second, named William for her father, was not acknowledged by him. The child must have served as a reminder of the breach with a father whom she revered and whom it seemed she could never again approach. In her life, then, Mary Shelley had been unable to form the domestic circle she and her mother regarded as essential for virtue and for which the brief Godwin-Wollstonecraft marriage must have served as a model.[10]

By her birth, Mary Shelley had destroyed the one example near her of an ideal family, and an association of her with the destructive monster therefore becomes possible. Percy Bysshe Shelley's closeness to Frankenstein has long been noted; his family situation, including his love for his sister Elizabeth, his early enjoyment of alchemy and science, and his questing, passionate nature all suggest it. The two associations provide the book with a biographical interpretation which suits well the monster's kinship with Jemima. Mary Shelley has become a fallen woman, cast out from her family. Her situation is due partly to Shelley, who may repulse her as her monster was repulsed; it is also due partly to society and her father, to whom *Frankenstein* was dedicated—both had already turned from her.

Such a biographical interpretation is of course speculative. Its possibility, however, helps to confirm the idea suggested by the comparison of *The Wrongs of Woman* and *Frankenstein*, that the monster's predicament is the fallen or outcast woman's, and that the cause of this predicament is exclusion from society and, above all, the family.

Notes

1. Mary Shelley, *Frankenstein or The Modern Prometheus* (New York: Bantam Edition, 1973). The page numbers throughout the paper refer to this edition.

2. See, for example, *the Athenaeum*, no. 316, (Nov., 1833), 769–777. Other reviews noted the resemblances of *Frankenstein* to *St. Leon*, a later novel by Godwin, in which he gives an idealized portrait of Mary Wollstonecraft.

3. *Mary Shelley's Journal*, ed. Frederick L. Jones (Norman: U. of Oklahoma Press, 1947).

4. Mary Wollstonecraft, *Letters Written During a Short Residence in Sweden, Norway, and Denmark* (1796; Fontwell, Sussex: Centaur Press, 1970), p. 5.

5. For example, see Mary Wollstonecraft, *An Historical and Moral View of the Origin and Progress of the French Revolution and the Effect It Has Produced in Europe* (1794; New York: Scholars' Facsimiles and Reprints, 1975), pp. 518–520.

6. Mary Wollstonecraft, *Maria or The Wrongs of Woman* (1798; New York: Norton, 1975). The page numbers in the paper refer to this edition.

7. The main distinction between Jemima and the monster is of course in sex. Some possible reasons for the maleness of the monster are as follows: creator and creature should be of the same sex to avoid sexual implications and this sex should be male since it is bizarre to make a woman create life in other than a biological way; the creator requires a scientific education, usually denied to women; the monster, to wreak havoc on the world, must have great strength, even beyond ordinary men.

8. In her Preface, Wollstonecraft states that she aimed "to show the wrongs of different classes of women" and to portray "woman" rather than "an individual."

9. William Godwin, *Memoirs of the Author of 'A Vindication of the Rights of Woman'* (London: Joseph Johnson, 1798); *Posthumous Works of the Author of 'A Vindication of the Rights of Woman,'* ed. William Godwin (London: Joseph Johnson, 1798), Vols. III & IV.

10. Frankenstein's nostalgic picture of his childhood family is similar to Wollstonecraft's effeusions over domestic felicity. See, for example, *A Vindication of the Rights of Woman* (1792; New York: Norton, 1967), p. 91.

Ambivalence in the Gynogram: Sade's Utopian Woman

BÉATRICE C. FINK

Given the changing modes and moods of the Sadian text, the reader is forever sifting its components in order to gauge their relevancy or determine their validity. The signs at the reader's disposal are often ambiguous and sometimes misleading. They produce uncertainty regarding the function and priorities of specific structures. Are we dealing with a reality that is transposed or reversed? Do we face desire as projected through boundless imagination? Does deciding whether or not a passage is straightforward, satirical, or nonsensical yield arbitrary results? If the reader postulates a "true" Sade, how then is a false one formulated? Reading turns into decrypting.

To begin with, the decrypter not only must take into account all of several fictional languages—narration, discourse, simulation models or discrete systems—but also is obliged to explore and integrate the relationships existing among them. Narration and discourse, for instance, are actualized by simulation models or discrete systems in either of two manners. In the process of testing out alternatives to existing society, the model or system is turned into a laboratory. The many castles, religious retreats and other isolated strongholds that dot the itineraries of Justine and of Juliette in the novels bearing their respective names are in fact sealed enclosures in which experiments in group dynamics can take place without danger of outside interference. The intinerant female narrators are incorporated into these experiments for varying lengths of time. In the case of *Les 120 Journées de Sodome*, all the events take place in such an enclosure: the castle of Silling. Within these experiment stations, a process of ritual (re)enactment establishes another type of relationship between discourse/narration and model/system. In this case, the model or system takes on the trappings of a stage, complete with director, settings, principals and supernumeraries. Among the most impressive examples of staged ritual are *Juliette*'s dramatization of the Pope's philosophy, by means of orgy and murder on the high altar of Saint Peter's inside the Vatican enclave, and the seriatim tell-and-show routine of Silling's inhabitants, who have built a specially designed amphitheater for this purpose.[1]

Deciphering Sade is particularly challenging when the text is read as a female-encoded cryptogram, which we call a gynogram. The challenge lies in the very centricity of the female, and in the emergence of ambivalent patterns within the gynogram when female signs are plotted against a thought system founded on the dynamics of transgression. Gynocentrism in Sadian fiction is understandable in terms of adherence to novelistic tradition of the period on the part of a writer who was prone to using conventions and clichés in his literary formats. The basic explanation, however, lies in the manifest necessity of having inferiors in a never-ending process of domination.[2] Women, in other words, are indispensable targets of refutation and victimization within the confines of phallocratic politics.[3] They are a constant point of reference in much the same fashion as a divinity for a professed atheist. A casual survey of Sade's writings reveals that women, be they mothers, daughters, sisters, spouses, in-laws, outlaws, or other, are subordinated to men on a massive scale. The centricity derived of subordination is reinforced by the ubiquitous use of sex as a metaphor: of power, energy, transgression, etc. This makes women figuratively as well as logically integral to the text.

Gynocentrism is not, however, exclusively linked to subordination. In an interesting reversal, women control the progression of most Sadian prose fiction and are themselves subject to a certain amount of character develop-ment or growth (e.g., Juliette, Léonore, Eugénie de Mistival), while male characters remain unchanged. The growth feature results from the female's role of learner or initiate, which is almost exclusively her domain. Control of fictional progression occurs most frequently by means of female narrators. Except for liminary author intrusion, *Juliette* and the first two versions of *Justine*, consist of what is recounted or recited by their heroines. In *Aline et Valcour*, novelistic structure converges on Léonore, who has a dual role of reciter and motivator of the hero's quest, in addition to the polymorphism resulting from her pseudonyms. Although *Les 120 Journées de Sodome* is too fragmented to be described as a novel, it is basically a story about storytelling, that is to say metanarration. The metanarrational structure is supported by four "historiennes," or female reciters.[4] In addition, all of Sade's *bona fide* novels, save one (*Aline et Valcour*), have women's names as sole titles. The obvious—and correct—deduction to be drawn is that women are, in every sense, prime movers in terms of plot line.

An initial complicating factor, then, results from female centricity involving subordination on the level of applied theory and control on the level of literary form. This ambivalence is compounded when fictional centricity is plotted against the Sadian dynamics of transgression.

Transgression, or more properly transgressing, since we are speaking of an ongoing phenomenon, is itself ambivalent. On the one hand, it is a process of individuation, a perpetual overshooting of one's own mark. This is how, and why, the Sadian libertine maintains her/his momentum. Transgressing as individuation generates power drives which create the familiar strategy, or hierarchy, of dominance. The basic dichotomy in this case is strength/

weakness. Since this is not an exact equivalent of the male/female dichotomy, one does encounter dominant women in Sadian prose, such as Juliette, la Durand or Léonore. However, behind every powerful woman there tends to lurk an even more powerful man, as is the case with Juliette and Noirceuil.[5]

On the other hand, transgressing stands for a rejection of established social institutions and values, producing counter-systems; that is, those opposing or reversing "real world" systems. In this context, the transgressor is primarily an outlaw. While the liberated, libertine outlaw is free to exert power in ways condemned by the establishment (murder, rape, incest, blasphemy, etc.), the system within which he operates purportedly eradicates the inequities of the society from which he has withdrawn. The social protest dimension of Sadian transgressing thus introduces an equalitarian bias into outlaw doctrine. Given the obvious difficulty of reconciling equality with dominance, only imperfect or temporary resolutions exist. The one most commonly resorted to is binary: an equality of axiomatic character is set up among victims while co-existent intralibertine equality is conspiratorial or utilitarian in nature. Such is the basic class structure of nearly all Sadian retreats, and the basic statutory premise of *Juliette*'s "Société des amis du crime." On rare occasions, however, amidst a network of disquisitions downgrading women on biological grounds and by sophistic argument, we find the equalitarian bias exerted in favor of sexual equality; that is to say, as a mechanism for redressing the inequities of eighteenth-century society with regard to women. This is the point at which all of the ambivalences in the gynogram converge. It is also—and predictably—the point at which utopian paradigms emerge. Sade's utopian woman therefore deserves our special attention.

Sadian prose fiction offers two instances in which the doctrine of utopian sexual politics takes precedence over the politics of a phallocratic regime. The first is inserted in the *Philosophie dans le boudoir*'s fifth dialog, in the form of a treatise referred to as a "brochure" entitled "Français, encore un effort si vous voulez être républicains."[6] This is at once a proclamation of emancipation from the moral and political bonds of France's *Ancien régime* and argumentation for a republican France based on individual freedom, notably in the area of sexual practices. The second is *Aline et Valcour*'s island paradise of Tamoé (IV, 252–350). Contrary to the brochure, the society it proclaims as ideal is highly regulated and enforces conventional sexual behavior. Furthermore, it must be analyzed in novelistic context in order to be fully appreciated.

The brochure lacks a fully articulated utopian system. Its discourse is not space-encased, with the result that it has a *topos*, but no *topographia*. It is, however, utopian insofar as it projects a nonplace of wish-fulfillment, a conflictless society of great permissiveness where everyone is presumably happy. The basic premise of its eudaemonism being governmental non-intervention, emphasis is on behavior rather than on institutions. Following a preliminary disquisition on the dangers of religious belief in general and

Christian dogma in particular, discourse concentrates on mores, or those rules of social behavior which, we are told, alone constitute an authentic morality.

Since no form of hierarchy exists (with the exception of an abstract and unfelt governmental regulator), equality of men and women is implicitly inscribed into the text.[7] It is spelled out specifically in the section on sexual wherein traditional taboos—against prostitution, adultery, incest, rape, sodomy, and homosexuality—become meaningless once total sexual freedom is enshrined as a matter of principle. Everyone without exception, male or female, is thus free to indulge in these practices. Rather interestingly, the most concrete institutional recommendation in the entire brochure coincides with the area in which female equality is explicitly proclaimed: prostitution.

Given the overriding importance of sexual freedom, public brothels become key structures. "A number of clean, roomy, well-appointed and secure edifices shall be built in the cities; there, people of all sexes and ages will be subjected to the caprices of libertines" (III, 500). While the model is that of a brothel for male libertines, parallel structures are provided for females, whose "temperament is infinitely more ardent than ours" (III, 501). Women, states the speaker, "shall be entitled to the same sexual satisfactions as men; and, provided it is understood they are to submit to all those who covet them, their freedom to enjoy all objects of their desire must be guaranteed on equal terms" (III, 504–05).

Are we to conclude that the brochure contains a valid statement on equal rights for women? Several observations must be made before attempting an answer to this question. The brochure's discourse deals with anonymous units, not individualized characters. At no point are the theories and recommendations it contains tested out. Given the absence of case studies, it is difficult for us to determine if we are being confronted with the gamesmanship of protest, or a blueprint which is capable of being implemented. If we suppose, for the sake of argument, that the latter holds true, then we must ask if the workings of the system, which guarantees equal rights in theory, would do so in practice. A primary feature of Sade's utopian *laissez-faire* projection is that freedom for the agent postulates servitude for the subject or object. As Maurice Blanchot rightfully points out, nowhere does Sade fully work out the relationship of power to power; that is to say, the resultant of multiple and conceivably conflicting power drives. Once again, the text provides no definitive answer. Finally, there is the danger inherent in any "separate but equal" clause, such as we find in the brochure. When pointed textual references to female physiology and the precedence of male rights in the order of textual presentation are added to the list, the reader suspects that the balance of equality tips in favor of the physically stronger, as it does in the state of nature.

Contrary to the brochure, the island of Tamoé is a full-fledged utopia, both never-never land and norm. Utopias were fashionable in the eighteenth century, and Tamoé, like most of its contemporary counterparts, owes far more to tradition than to its inventor's inventiveness. What distinguishes this mythical island is its singularity within Sadian prose. Since it is essentially

Morean (*Utopia*-derived), it represents a social alternative to society based upon the notion of perfectibility rather than that of emancipation. While remaining iconoclastic, it is a metaculture, not a counterculture. As a result, its code of ethics retains a conventional flavor since virtue is, indeed, its own reward.[8] Its uniqueness is enhanced by inclusion in *Aline et Valcour*, which is itself one of a Sadian kind: epistolary novel and "roman philosophique." The novel also provides in Léonore, its heroine, an example of woman triumphant.

Specific paradigms characterize fictional utopias: a voyage (in space or time), an area having little or no contact with the world at large, an unexpected intruder, a guide who functions as narrator and dispenser of wisdom. Since utopian lifestyles revolve around unchanging rituals, linear time is supplanted by circularity. In Nowhere, there is nowhere to go; chronological time is spatialized.

While the above merely describes the basic givens of utopia in general, it does underline the appropriateness of such a structure for an author with a penchant for fantasy, ritual, and hermetism. In fact, why not consider the castles, convents, and other retreats scattered throughout Sadian prose as pornotopian or dystopian derivatives of an archetype whose integrity the author maintains only once? Viewed in this perspective, Tamoé's singularity remains on the level of myth, but disappears on the level of construct.

We are now in a position to enter the sanctum that houses Sade's utopian woman. *Aline et Valcour's* epistolary narrational framework—letters exchanged between the Blamont family and its entourage—includes two lengthy first-person narrations in which Sainville and Léonore respectively recount their globe-trotting adventures. It is Sainville, acting as intruder, who reveals the utopian isle to the reader. Ever hopeful of recovering his beloved wife Léonore, he comes upon a haven in storm-tossed waters unaccounted for by navigational charts. Both nature (rocky shores) and culture (habor fortifications) protect it from outside interference. Tamoé's natural insularity has been heightened by total isolationism, symbolized by the destruction of its fleet. Its inhabitants are friendly, and Sainville's rebuffed sailors soon discover that its women are dignified and proud. On his way to meet Zamé, the island's father figure leader, Sainville crosses the capital city, whose symmetry, greenery, and color-coordination constitute an urban planner's dream. Its cheerful uniformity and orderly appearance are the hallmarks of the island's lifestyle and of its founder's philosophy. Zamé heartily welcomes his wayfaring guest and wastes little time before going to a lengthy account of Tamoé's (and his own) past and an explanation of its institutions. Predictably, his narration is interspersed with a number of disquisitions setting forth standard Sadian positions on biological determinism and on the relativity and interdependency of law and crime. These tie in with suitably liberal penal legislation.

What is less standard is Tamoé's sexual politics. While sex remains a pleasurable pastime—for it is a natural one—it is linked, not with power and subjugation as in other Sadian retreats, but with harmony and order. Nor does it acquire, as elsewhere, the status of metaphor. D'Holbach and La Mettrie are outdistanced by Plato, as goals are defined in terms of virtue, justice, and a generalized state of equilibrium, rather than hedonism, self-expression, and change. Tamoé, in the hero's words, is a golden-age temple of virtue.

As Sainville becomes acquainted with Tamoan society through the dual means of a statement of aims and a well-planned tour of inspection, he is introduced to women and to the institutions that govern their lives. The twenty formative years Zamé has spent abroad have taught him that most of the so-called civilized world's problems are traceable to social and economic inequality, for inequality leads to instability, hence unhappiness. Women and men are equal before Tamoan law, not only for humanitarian reasons but also for the utilitarian purpose of eliminating all sources of disharmony. Economic equality automatically follows from the absence of private property: everything belongs to the state. There are no domestics or other traditional categories of subservient females. While educational facilities are segregated according to sex, women have the same learning tools at their disposal as men do. In fact, quite a number of them become bilingual. If there is a specialization of tasks, it is a purely functional one. Marriages are based on mutual consent, and spouses, as Zamé carefully points out, are companions to one another linked in friendship, not bondage. Divorce proceedings can be initiated by either party, for reasons of incompatibility or infidelity (a rare occurrence, given the nature of marriage policies).

The communal character of island life and the resulting downgrading of the family as a nuclear social unit further equalize woman's status: mothers do not rear their children and are therefore not housebound. Respect for sexual taboos as a means of enforcing social uniformity also works in favor of women. Zamé's policies in this area have eliminated two sexual practices that enhance male superiority in other Sadian contexts: incest and homosexuality.[9] Both of these practices, he claims, reinforce subgroups, hence factionalism, and are therefore counterproductive from the great society's point of view. Brothels and prostitution, traditional badges of female degradation, are non-existent. Insofar as corrective measures are concerned, there is no discrimination between the sexes.[10] Finally, there is nothing, in theory, to prevent a woman from becoming a freely chosen head of state once paternalistic monarchy gives way to republic upon Zamé's death. Utopian woman, it seems, has been legislated into equality with utopian man. In the process, she outdistances both her Sadian sisters and her real-life counterparts.

The institutions in her island residence acquire additional significance by being contrasted with those of another retreat on Sainville's route, the dystopian, pornotopian kingdom of Butua, which lies hidden in darkest Africa (IV, 188–248). Sade himself sharpens the opposition in an "editor's note," declaring that "he wishes to console his readers following the harsh verities he was obliged to depict in Butua by taking them to Tamoé" (IV, xxvii). The grimness of what is, in other words, must be exorcized by the wondrousness of what ought to be.

While related as constructs, Butua and Tamoé are antithetical as myths. Tamoé has attained a level of mature civilization; Butua is precultural, its inhabitants childlike illiterates. Where reason, nonviolence, and moderation govern Tamoé, passion, bloody violence, and excess reign supreme in Butua. Egalitarianism is replaced with rigid hierarchy, natural religion by priesthood and idolatry. Even eating habits are opposed: Tamoans are vegetarians, while Butuans fill their stomachs with human flesh.

The most striking contrast lies in the treatment of women. Butua is pure pornotopia: every aspect of life is libidinized in this dystopian garden where sex functions as both symbol and reality of unbridled pleasure and power . . . for the despot. Those hapless females living among "the cruelest and most dissolute people on earth" are the most wretched creatures in all of Sadedom. Sexual servitude is compounded by their being slaves to slaves; even males must submit to their master tyrant. Indoctrinated submission and torture have made Butuan women revert to an animal state. Like cattle, they constitute an exchange commodity in a barter economy as units of trade and taxation. The ultimate insult, in this cannibalistic kingdom, is that these third-rate sex objects are sacrificed but not deemed worthy of being eaten, for their flesh, like that of cows, is "fibrous and tasteless."

While Tamoé's message is unequivocal (Sade and his orator speak with one voice, while the dialogue between visitor and guide is catechismal, not dialectic), Butua's apologist, the prime minister Sarmiento, delivers orations whose inner dialectic renders them paradoxical. When justifying Butua's despotic regime and its misogyny on naturalistic and relativistic grounds, Sarmiento nevertheless prophesies that the cannibalistic kingdom "will crumble of its own accord" as a result of vice, corruption, and the collusion of priests. Author input in the form of notes and Sainville's refusal to be convinced or remain captive further confuse the issues. While Butua and the status of its women are characteristically Sadian insofar as they project limitless fantasizing through sexual metaphor, they are decidedly satirical in that they mirror, yet grossly distort, the realities of absolute monarchy and the state of nature.

Statistics lend support to Sarmiento's dire prophecy. Out of a total population that stands at 30,000 at the time of narration, 2,000 women are sacrificed monthly. If one adds the depopulation attributed to internal and external warfare, immolation, cannibalism, and abortion, Butua is programmed to self-destruct in the very near future. It thus contains no definite statement on women, being clearly marred by a number of flaws.

What is the reader to make of such a purposely flawed simulation model? By situating Butua immediately before Tamoé on the itinerant chart, Sade uses the former's chaos to enhance the latter's mythical cosmos. In other words, narrative/navigational directionality conditions the reader into accepting Tamoé's statement on women at face value, in the process heightening the ambivalence of the gynogram. Furthermore, by praising Zamé's virtue and legislation in the novel's concluding lines, the author lends discursive support to narrational intent. The reader is maneuvered—at least provisionally—into accepting the Tamoan model's truth value.

Virtue, in its Platonic (and Morean) sense of harmony, or highest form of pleasure, is Tamoé's *telos*; legislation, the means by which it is attained. But of what does legislation consist when statutory laws are minimized by design? Inner laws, the motivations and strivings of Zamé's subjects, are acquired characteristics, the result of painstaking conditioning by a European-educated master-mind. Legislation can thus be equated with manipulation based on theories of behaviorism and the ethico-psychological premise of *perfectibilité*. Zamé states explicitly on several occasions that his grand strategy is based on controlling the mechanics of the human psyche: "all aspects of man's heart must be considered by those desirous of directing him"; otherwise "one acts only absurdly or according to set rules, for set rules are the great war cry of imbeciles."[11] Civic virtue, the reign of "the just and the good,' exists in this utopia because, as in other utopias, all possible sources of conflict and temptation have been eliminated. Money, a prime source of greed, is unknown and the island's only gold mine has been carefully camouflaged so as to fall into oblivion. Institutionalized equality further discourages acquisitiveness. Isolation from aggressive nation-states and economic autarchy (except for minor dealings with neighboring islands) have cancelled the risk of war while precluding comparison with other lifestyles, thereby minimizing the unsettling weighing of alternatives. And if by chance any dissent should occur following this far-reaching cleanup campaign, it is in turn eliminated—by exile and social ostracism. That such a system, while providing for equal rights, is fragile at best is underscored by the fact that it rests on *stasis*, the delicate equilibrium of non-change. Like all sterile spaces, it is particularly vulnerable to germs. What will happen, one asks, when Zamé vanishes from the scene?

One may assume, for the sake of argument, that the indispensable sameness is maintained, that Tamoé is truly the myth of atemporality within a chronic universe, a spatialized interruption in the continuum of time. Let the godlike Zamé be immortal. We now ask: equal rights for whom, or rather for what? If thought, as Descartes would have us think, is the essence of man, then are we dealing with humans?

The islanders' uniformity and conformity are cultivated from infancy on by means of a centralized behavior-control mechanism. Education amounts to factual instruction. Artistic expression is downgraded to the level of craftmanship or folk entertainment, for fear it might stimulate creativity. Tamoans, that is, are trained to understand their institutions and perform technical tasks, not to judge or innovate.[12]

Equal rights, it appears, is actually one of several methods employed by Zamé to implement and support his policy of standardization. What Sade is telling us is that in some contexts there are alternatives to manipulation by fear and deprivation (and its inherent victimization of women). While such alternatives appear preferable in the light of Butua, they presuppose rigid behavioral constraints. And through whom? Quite naturally, the father figure.

In the last resort, it is the male who directs the passive but equal female. All Tamoans may be passive with respect to their beloved Zamé, but woman's lack of initiative extends to her relationship with her male coequals. She simply responds and enjoys being protected. Zamé's (personally selected) daughter-in-law delights in reciting her three French words to her cherished spouse: "Here is your property." The right to equal treatment, as any right, remains a dead letter if it is waived, if the will to self-effacement prevails. To the precarious balance of equality, to the dehumanization of equals, one adds the remark that equal rights seem to be made available only when women do not exercise them. It is somewhat like offering champagne to a teetotaler.

Let us now return to the plot lines of Léonore's and Sainville's accounts, both of which enhance the "philosophical" dimension of the novel. More fortunate in his quest than Candide, Sainville reunites with a woman as beauteous and untainted as ever. Léonore's adventures and mental evolution parallel those of Juliette in several important respects. Her liberated mentor Clémentine and a multiplicity of experiences have hardened her into calculated indifference and atheism, although she resists libertinism in the name of loyalty to Sainville. At the novel's end, it is she who comes out on top. She is loved and respected by her husband and controls the purse strings of a vast inherited fortune. She is also the only character who evolves in the course of the novel, and does so thanks to her wits.

The impression of lifelessness, of creatures whose contentment is contingent upon their being brainless, grows stronger when Tamoan women are set against Léonore, baffler of all the predatory males she encounters during her travels, including the kind of Butua. By overcoming all of the obstacles along her path in order to be true to her higher self, she acquires the attributes of the traditional questor. She thus functions not only as Sainville's goal, but also as a principal moving force behind the novel's momentum.

Sade's utopian woman and her shortcomings may be redefined in terms of a non-Léonore. She is a nameless, faceless unit, not a personality with several names and an overpowering sexual appeal. She has never had access to the only life-instilling forms of education, those of varied experiences which strengthen individuality, of energy-generating struggles. Nor does she, like the thinking Léonore, reach a higher level of existence through the verbalization of her beliefs. And she hasn't the slightest trace of imagination. This non-Léonore lacks the requisite Sadian ingredients of success and power.

Why is it that the island of virtue and equality is not woman's paradise, but merely her limbo? Tamoé teaches us that the master-victim relationship so common in Sadian retreats, is not the only language of dominance. Butua may in fact signify that it is not necessarily the best one. There exists another, that of unrelenting persuasion of the many by the one, a leader-led dichotomy. In the latter situation, woman may be satisfied with her lot but she operates on the basis of male-conditioned reflex.[13]

A close reading of the brochure and of Tamoé in terms of their female signs thus reveals that equality between the sexes is not attainable in any meaningful sense. In the last resort, such equality is either contingent upon some form of power or becomes a dead letter pursuant to psychological manipulation by a father-figure. The ambivalence introduced into Sade's gynogram by egalitarianism deriving from transgression-as-protest, or by utopian paradigms is more apparent than real. The prime function of both rhetoric and model in our examples is therefore one of deception. The case of Léonore, who is marginal to the utopian environment, merely underlines that Sade is on the side of the strong, that if a woman is favored enough by character, connections and money, she can become an independent agent— provided men are willing to cooperate.

Léonore, however, raises more questions than she answers. On the one hand, she is instrumental in resolving ambivalence by personifying what Tamoan women are not, thereby implicitly downgrading the significance of their equality. On the other, she is the nucleus of *Aline et Valcour*'s most significant narrational structure. She therefore illustrates a point of convergence in the gynogram of two levels of ambivalence: a semantic one, which we have qualified as apparent; a formal one, resting on a base of gynocentrism within a universe where females are either powerless or dependent on a male power vacuum in order to exert control. The latter ambivalence, which is particularly striking in *Justine*, lies beyond the scope of our analysis. Suffice it to say that it is inextricably tied to the dynamics of Sade's novels and that, as such, it is here to stay.

Notes

1. There are, of course, variations in this basic dyad, such as scenarios within *La Philosophie dans le boudoir*, which is itself constructed very much like a play. See Yvon Belaval's introduction to his edition of *La Philosophie dans le boudoir* (Paris: Gallimard/ Folio, 1976), pp. 7–34. On the theatricality of Sade's prose fiction, see Anne Lacombe, "Du théâtre au roman: Sade," *Studies on Voltaire and the Eighteenth Century,* 129 (1975), pp. 115–143.

2. Theoretically, the process of self-realization by means of dominance terminates when only one person remains alive. But this process may be thought of in Hegelian terms, that is to say as goal oriented rather than as ending at a specific point in time.

3. This does not imply that male subserviency is nonexistent, especially in the case of the physically or mentally weak. However, the basic differential set up by the author, whether in fictional or nonfictional context, is between members of opposite sexes. Naturalistic arguments and historical precedents are forever being resorted to in an effort at demonstrating that women are both biologically and culturally inferior to men. The most energetic mouthpieces of such discourse are the phallocratic elite, specifically high-ranking male homosexual libertines.

4. The role of reciter connotes power on a formal level but is not necessarily played out by a powerful character. While Juliette and Léonore have power, Justine does not. For an excellent

analysis of Justine's function as reciter, see Nancy K. Miller, *"Justine,* or, The Vicious Circle," *Studies in Eighteenth-Century Culture,* 5 (1976), pp. 215–228.

5. In this regard, see Nancy K. Miller, *"Juliette* and the Posterity of Prosperity," *L'Esprit Créateur,* 15, No. 4 (1975), 413–424. Two other interesting analyses of female status in the Sadian world are Jane Gallop's, "Sade, Mothers and Other Women" and Godelieve Mercken-Spaas' "Libertinage et Phallocratie." Both of these papers were read at the December 1975 annual meeting of the Modern Language Association as parts of a panel chaired by Nancy K. Miller on "Sade and Women." Portions of my article were discussed during the same panel.

6. D. A. F. Slade, *Oeuvres complètes* (Paris: Cercle du livre précieux, 1966–67), vol. III, pp. 478–524. This sixteen-volume edition will be used as reference throughout. In case of quotations, translations into English are mine.

7. In a recent lecture at the University of Maryland on "Modern American Feminist Utopias," given in the course of a symposium on "Female Systems and Cultural Change," Carol Pearson stressed lack of hierarchy as a predominant characteristic of the utopias in question.

8. Compare Tamoé's guiding ethical principle, "the idea that evil is ever able to produce good is one of the most frightening vertigos of stupid minds" (IV, 251), to frequent assertions elsewhere that virtue, therefore, vice, are meaningless terms.

9. Sadian libertines ignore sexual taboos for reasons of self-realization, but also turn them into specific tools of female exploitation.

10. There are two major offenses in Tamoé: murder, punishable by exile, and adultery, controlled by divorce and social ridicule. A moral play performed for the islanders' edification illustrates the equal impact of infidelity on male and female: the unfaithful wife displays all the signs of extreme penance in public, while the lover goes into voluntary exile (IV, 336–37).

11. IV, 328. *Cf.* "The art [of leadership] thus consists merely in knowing one's fellow citizens well, and in being able to take advantage of their weakness; they can then be led wherever one wants" (IV, 321), and "That is how this philosopher . . . working only with men's souls, succeeding in purging his fellow citizens" (IV, 348).

12. The fact that Tamoans are undifferentiated objects is further emphasized by the briefness of premarital socializing. Eight days seem to be long enough to get to know one's future partner.

13. Sade's belief in the contemporary doctrine of spermatism, according to which only males are active transmitters in the process of heredity, may well explain such a characteristic. See Jean Deprun, "Sade et la philosophie biologique de son temps," in *Le Marquis de Sade: Actes du colloque d'Aix-en-Provence* (Paris: Armand Colin, 1968), esp. pp. 193–95.

The Victorian Period

George Sand and
the Myth of Femininity

LESLIE RABINE

George Sand was one of the most popular novelists of nineteenth-century Europe, and her life itself became a legend. Recently, the legend of George Sand has been re-invigorated by a television series, sponsored in the U.S. by the Mobile Oil Corporation, which portrays her as the Liberated Woman before her time. She is also portrayed this way in many of her biographies, the most famous of which, by André Maurois of the Académie Française, claims: "She was the voice of woman at the time when woman was silent."[1] Yet, the writing of French historians like Edith Thomas and Marguerite Thibert shows that women were not silent in France between 1830 and 1850. There was at that time a strong, independent women's movement, which George Sand ridiculed, and whose efforts to win equality for women she called "childishness."[2] Many of Sand's critical biographers also say that her early novels, *Indiana* and *Lélia*, are pioneer works which express revolt against the position of women in marriage.[3]

But a textual study of *Indiana* contradicts this view of her novels in a parallel way that historical research contradicts the television story of her life. Such a textual study will show how the novel's rhetoric of rebellion conceals but is an integral part of a novelistic structure which encourages conformity to the feminine stereotypes then in force. While *Indiana* appears to contest the myth of Woman as Passive Object of Male Desire and Possession, in this novel the concepts of women's freedom and of the liberated woman are themselves mythified and incorporated into the traditional established conception of womanhood.

This parallel between Sand's own writing and the legend of her life makes it necessary to talk about the thorny problem of the author-work relationship before a discussion of the novel *Indiana.* My analysis of the novel will rely on the notion that through a representation of her heroine, Sand represents her own fantasies as well as their censorship. In addition, the expression of these fantasies, though socially imposed, is Sand's and no one else's because of her unique social situation as the only successful female romantic novelist in the situation of extreme female oppression that characterized France of the 1830s.

Critical approaches which divorce the work from a particular author either by a notion of the text as an authorless self-sufficient totality, or, on the other hand, of the author as a pure aesthetic self, or even of language or writing as the speaking subject of every text, do not allow for the specificity of what George Sand, woman and author, had to think, to say, and to write in order to be published in the male-dominated market economy of the early nineteenth century.[4] In his critique of the concept of the autonomous text, Pierre Kuentz says: "the modern myth of writing . . . pretends to forget, at the heart of this civilization, the social and economic conditions of 'publication.' "[5] One could also add that it makes us forget the way those conditions differ for men and women, and the different relation that men and women have to writing itself.

These notions which set limits around the text or which merge it into "the great work of fiction as a single entity, a totality,"[6] derive from the nineteenth-century myth of equality and are related to the myth of "sameness" which will be discussed later in relation to Sand. They assume a "universal" writer and/or order of language to which all writers belong with equal status. That assumption of universality conceals the reality of inequality and its consequences, especially if the author under consideration, a nineteenth-century woman like George Sand, is not equal. She is in a different and inferior position with respect to the social, psychological and symbolic structures that govern the author-work relation and the treatment of themes in romantic works: themes such as desire, sexuality, and self-identity. A short summary of *Indiana* will introduce us to the way these themes are treated by Sand and prepare for further discussion of her relation to her heroine.

Indiana, written in 1832, brought its young author overnight success. It is the story of a young heroine, Indiana, who has been raised on an isolated island in the West Indies by her cousin Ralph, a taciturn, stony-faced man, ten years her senior, and totally devoted to his cousin. Ignorant, frail of body, consumptive and timid, but possessed of strong moral force and courage, the beautiful Indiana is married off to an elderly industrialist, the brutal M. Delmare. As the story opens, Indiana, along with Ralph and her servant Noun, live at M. Delmare's isolated estate outside of Paris. Noun, Indiana's milk sister,[7] a Creole born almost the same day as her mistress, has fallen in love with Raymon de Ramière, the young nobleman from the next estate, who has seduced the sensual servant and made her pregnant.

Indiana, much admired in fashionable circles, although she scorns such society, is seen by Raymon at a ball, where they fall in love with each other. Soon after, Noun commits suicide. Indiana confesses her passion to Raymon, but it remains a purely spiritual passion. His many attempts to seduce her fail, because she is saved each time either by her own moral virtue, by Providence, or by her cousin Ralph. As Raymon tires of Indiana, financial

ruin forces M. Delmare to go to live in the West Indies. The heroine toler-
ates her husband's increasing tyranny, until finally, one day, he strikes her,
and she runs away back to France. When she finally finds Raymon, he has
married the sardonic and witty Laure de Langy, who forces Indiana out of her
house. Indiana, alone and abandoned in Paris, humiliated and poverty-
stricken, is on the verge of death when Ralph finds her. He informs her that
her husband is dead, and then nurses her back to health. Rejected by society,
the couple prepares a ritual suicide, but just before the plunge to their death,
they decide instead to live in intimate solitude in the wilderness.

It is evident from this summary that *Indiana* does fit into the more general
structure of the romantic novel. But Sand's novel is unique (as we will see)
precisely in the way that it imitates that structure and in the way her relation
to her heroine imitates the romantic author-hero relation. What is the relation between a romantic author and the fictional hero, and how is Sand's
imitation of it different? It resembles the self-relation of what Julia Kristeva
calls the "unitary subject" of Western capitalism who lives in the world as in
a hall of mirrors, "rejecting the other and putting himself in his place."[8]

In Alfred de Vigny's ultra-romantic play *Chatterton* (1835), the hero, a
poet named Chatterton, describes literary creation in terms of an abrupt
cleavage of the subject from all but itself, and ensuing self-identification
through doubling and self-reflection:

> Here I am, alone facing my work.—I am no longer concerned with smiling and
> being polite! with greeting and shaking hands! That comedy is played out: I'm
> beginning another one with myself.—I must, right now, make my will powerful
> enough to seize my soul and to carry it in turn into the resuscitated cadaver of
> the characters I evoke and into the ghost of those I invent! Or else I must make
> my will place with fanfare in front of the sick Chatterton, in front of the
> Chatterton who is cold and hungry, another Chatterton, graciously adorned for
> the amusement of the public, and I must have that one described by the other,
> the troubadour by the beggar. Those are two possible poetries, nothing goes
> further than that.[9]

In a similar (but not identical) way, Chatterton is "another" Vigny. The hero
of the romantic work is a doubly imaginary reflecton of the author. Himself a
fiction, he mirrors back to the author not his biographical image but his ideal
self-image, determined by a social ideal. And this is how the Vigny-Chatterton
relation differs from the author-hero relation in the play: *Chatterton* and
Indiana (as well as many other works written during this period, such as
René, Confessions d'un enfant du siècle, Le Rouge et le noir) represent the
same and highly contradictory social ideal. They all express the same dream
to be the superior and unique Individual, who is recognized as unique and
superior by an unjust capitalist society even as it rejects him or her.

Sand's novel *Indiana* differs from other works which revolve around this
romantic mirror structure, since women of the nineteenth century had neither
the status of self-reflecting subjects, nor the possibility of conceiving another
type of subject. *Indiana* is not part of "the great work of fiction as a single

entity, a totality," but an exterior imitation of it, or what Julia Kristéva calls a "mask" by which the woman "pretends" to play the role of the unitary subject.[10] Sand's contradictory imitation of the romantic mirror structure will be described as it occurs in the author-heroine relation and within the novel itself. Through it Sand reintegrates a liberating vision into the traditional vision of femininity.

In *Chatterton,* and in much of romantic fiction, the hero, the reflection of the author's ideal alter-ego, is at the center of the narration, the subject of the novel and its universe. The romantic heroine is his dream woman, the object of his fantasies, a mysterious projection of his imagination. But in *Indiana,* Sand creates the heroine, her own alter-ego, as this distant phantom of a man's dream, a being alien to herself. Simone de Beauvoir says that women do not have their own myths and their own poetry but that "it is still across the dreams of men that women dream."[11] For George Sand this statement is doubly true: not only is *Indiana* an imitation of the male nineteenth-century wish-fulfillment work, but also the wish or dream the heroine fulfills is to be the perfect dream-object of the male dreamer. As Raymon tells Indiana: "You are the woman I have dreamed, the purety I have adored, the chimera who has always eluded me . . ."[12]

Since the subject of Sand's novel is the object of someone else's imagination, the novel originates in a contradiction: it is centered around a character who can have no self-consciousness, who must always be seen, thought or dreamed by a male in order to exit. And in *Indiana* (as in Sand's other "feminist" novels such as *Lélia* and *Isidora*), we almost always see the heroine through the eyes of a male character or of several male characters. It is not the heroine's consciousness which interprets the world for us, but the consciousness of the male characters which interprets and mediates our vision of the heroine.

In *Indiana, Lélia* and *Isidora*, there is a proliferation of male characters who multiply this mediation by observing other men observe the heroine. In one of the principle scenes of *Indiana*, Raymon has entered Indiana's bedchamber where he sees a portrait of Cousin Ralph:

> Yet it aroused in Raymon a violent feeling of anger.
> "What!" he thought, "This Englishman, young and bold, has the privilege of being admitted into the most secret apartment of Madame Delmare! His insipid image is always there, looking coldly at the most intimate acts of her life! He keeps watch over her, guards her, follows all her movements, possesses her all the time! (p. 92)

We see Indiana through the eyes of a portrait seen through the eyes of a man, and our admiration for the heroine is doubled by this double male vision, as well as by her ability to excite such violent emotion in Raymon, for whom the picture of a man has more consciousness than does a real woman.

George Sand can envision her own ideal alter-ego only by seeing it at a distance through a series of male observers, or by imagining it as a phantom contained within a series of male imaginations; this is strikingly brought out by the opening paragraph of *Lélia,* Sand's most famous early novel. Instead of introducing us directly to her heroine, Sand introduces Lélia through the words of a male character Sténio, who observes the heroine (she is unconscious of being observed) and perceives her as distant, inaccessible and unknowable: "There must be in you some horrible mystery unknown to men ... You are an angel or a demon, but you are not a human creature. Why do you hide from us your nature and your origin?"[13]

This conception of woman as having an unknowable nature and origin is discussed by Luce Irigaray in her critique of Freud, where she relates it to the conception of the "unitary" subject, living as in a hall of mirrors. Her analysis in *Speculum de l'autre femme* helps explain why Sand perceives a woman as seen and thought by a series of men and why the Sandian heroine can have no self-consciousness.

The unitary subject is determined by what Irigaray calls the "désir du même" ("desire for the same," or "desire for the self"). The subject seeks to protect himself from the "Other," from death, from his absence to himself, reproducing his original self as the same and identical, so as to exclude from the unity and homogeneity of his self-reflecting world anything truly different from it and from himself. Western philosophy, religion, and art (especially romantic art) reinforce this closed system of self-reflection. Irigaray comments:

> ... the desire of the same, of the self-identical, of the self (as) same, and moreover of the similar, of the alter-ego, and in a word of the auto ..., and of the homo ... of man dominates the economy of representation.[14]

This "economy of representation" is, like any economy, a system of production and reproduction: a system of images, signs and symbols produces and reproduces the relation of sameness, of oneness, of self-identity and self-presence. The above quotation refers to Freud's representation of sexual "difference" in his essay "Femininity" where woman and female sexuality become nothing more than the inverted reflection of man and male sexuality, "the negativity which supports, and confirms, the homogeneity of masculine desire."[15]

Freud's "economy of representation" in "Femininity" (as analyzed by Irigaray) parallels Sand's in *Indiana* (or rather Sand's, as we will see, is the mirror image of it). Both claim to reject the traditional view of women, but reproduce it by the way they each deny a female representation of origin and thus a female self-representation, which might challenge the male structure of origin and self.

Irigaray's point of departure is this statement from the beginning of Freud's "Femininity":

> A boy's mother is the first object of his love, and she remains so too during the formation of his Oedipus complex and, in essence, all through his life. For the girl too her first object must be her mother ... But in the Oedipus situation the girl's father has become her love-object ... In the course of time, therefore, a girl has to change her erotogenic zone and her object—both of which a boy retains."[16]

According to Irigaray, Freud's theory necessitates the "erasure for/by the woman of her relation to the origin—and thus her original relation to her mother and to her sex, which would finally be 'superficial' and 'secondary' enough, although 'Manifest'—for the eminence of the Phallus to impose itself."[17]

Freud's attempts in "Femininity" to qualify his first statement, to take account of the many empirical cases which contradict it, only lead him, according to Irigaray, into deeper contradictions, all of which stem from the central contradiction in his theory: his pretention to represent sexual difference is really a representation of sexual sameness. In spite of his insights, he cannot actually represent the nature of female sexuality and its own history of patriarchy and its successive ideologies, "in order to rediscover an archè even more archaic behind this beginning which Greece represents, and the concept of origin that Greece set up."[18]

Because she has had to efface her relation to her origin, and its experiences of identification with the parent of the same sex and of auto-eroticism, woman is prevented from forming any system of auto-representation of self-regard, any system that would symbolize her own desires and sexual reality. Like the heroine of Sand's novel, the heroine of Freud's theory is deprived of self-consciousness, because an independent configuration of desire and of self would violate man's assurance of self-identity and even the concept of identity (crucial to the ideologies not only informing Freud's theory, but also romanticism and formalist criticism). The woman must be looked at by the man, who sees her not as what she might be, but as lack and absence of what he is and has. But even as "lack" and "absence", or "outside" of man's closed system of images, woman still threatens the plenitude of male self-presence and self-identity:

> As gap, fault, default, lack, absence, outside of the system of representations, of self-representations. Of man. A nothing which might divert, disjoin, disintegrate infinitely the coherence of their systematic of "presence," of "re-presentation," and "representation." A nothing threatening to the process of production, reproduction, mastery, capitalization of meaning, dominated by the phallus.[19]

But Indiana never does threaten to upset the coherence of this system, and Sand never really violates the prohibition to symbolize feminine desire. In the novel, the heroine is the space within which Ralph and Raymon look at each other and see reflected in each other the *same desire*. Sand does more than not threaten the "economy of male self-representation"' as we will see, she reestablished it in its totality and re-affirms it all the more solidly in that she writes as an "independent" female author, acting autonomously.

If the heroine Indiana is to function within this structure described by Luce Irigaray, she can have no self-consciousness for yet another reason. Although she is the image of the author's ideal alter-ego, Indiana cannot think or say the *original desires* that gave birth to her as the wish-fulfillment heroine. She is the ideal woman who fulfills the desire to be sexually attractive, to be free from social laws, and to be happy, but Indiana *has* no sexual desires, and no active desires for freedom and happiness. An impossibly contradictory character, she is on the one hand described as the romantic rebel with a "will of iron" for whom "mental resistance to every kind of moral constraint had become . . . a second nature" (p. 69). But on the other hand, she willfully chooses the "dignity" of "submission" and "resignation" in order to be different from "a woman of the common type" who could have "dominated this man (M. Delmare) of a vulgar stamp" (p. 198).

This rebel chooses to obey M. Delmare, to resign herself to her fate, and above all to maintain the purity of her passion for Raymon, because she is not only "virtuous and chaste" (p. 189) but naturally and effortlessly so. She naturally and effortlessly conforms to all the moral laws dictated to the French woman of 1830, as opposed to the other feminine characters in *Indiana*, who only hypocritically pretend to conform to them. Or, as Raymon sees it: "What a difference between this chaste being who seemed to ignore the possibility of a conclusion to her love, and all those women concerned only with hastening it while feigning to flee from it" (p. 163). Indiana's lack of desire makes her all the more an object of male desire.

She can effortlessly and naively maintain her moral virtue, because her author inverts nature and culture. Indiana is sexually virtuous *because* she has not been corrupted by civilization, *because* she has been raised on an isolated island, and *because* she has had no education. "As ignorant as a real Creole," she is guided only by the "righteous ideas and the simple laws of good sense and humanity" (p. 164). Through the rhetoric of "will" and "resistence," Sand reaffirms the myth of an eternal feminine Nature which is socially and sexually passive by instinct, and which is only spoiled by worldly knowledge and education. In the nineteenth century, women were severely constrained to conform to that myth, and Indiana fulfills the fantasy of conforming without the pain and anguish of suppressing desire, or of having no desire to suppress.

Indiana is indeed a strange ideal alter-ego. Prohibited from expressing feminine needs and desires and from creating self-representations, Sand attempts to separate Indiana from the original desire that she fulfills. The heroine *fulfills* the desire to epitomize the social ideal of nineteenth-century womanhood, and *arouses* desire in men without *feeling* the desire to do either.

Although Sand tries to isolate some elements from the total structure of desire and its repression, the novel (as we will see) reestablishes that total structure. Louis Althusser's method of "symptomatic reading" seeks to relate all the elements of a text, including the "absent" elements to the *"typical systematic structure* unifying all the elements of the thought to be brought to light." This method has loosely guided me here and will help in examining a key passage of the novel, in order to describe how the scattered and fragmented elements of Sand's thought combine to reveal the myth of femininity and its perpetuation.

In Sand's "feminist" novels, *Indiana* and *Lélia*, the heroine's absent desire is displaced and reexpressed through a doubling of the heroine. In both novels, a secondary female character is the sister or milk sister of Lélia or Indiana, but is not presented as an imaginary alter-ego of the author. She is the sensual opposite of the heroine, a character with which the author in no way identifies. It is this character, Pulchérie in *Lélia* and Noun in *Indiana*, who expresses the complex internal conflicts, and who attempts to think and express feminine desire, revolt, and guilt.

In addition to this doubling of the heroine, there is also a conflict within the narrator herself (or himself, since Sand presents the narrator of *Indiana* as a young man). He relates events in such a way that the secondary female character appears more sympathetic, more socially victimized, more generous and more perceptive than the heroine. Unable to control the story that constantly escapes him, he continually intervenes to reinterpret the action, to censure and punish the secondary character, and to remind us that it is the heroine with whom we must sympathize in a rivalry between the two women.

The contrast between the two female characters and the conflict within the narrator appears in the scene where Raymon enters Indiana's bedchamber. An analysis of this scene shows the attempt to represent feminine desire, its repression and its reinsertion in the enclosure of male desire. Noun, having discovered her pregnancy, tries to win back the love of Raymon. In the absence of Indiana, she dresses up in Indiana's clothes and appropriates the use of Indiana's bed-chamber, hoping that this finery and luxury will touch Raymon. He, meanwhile, is desperately trying to find a way to rid himself of the servant girl so that he can concentrate on his love for her mistress. In the bed-chamber, the objects awake in him an increasingly intense obsession for the absent Indiana. (The implications of the striking class difference between the two women, a difference which Irigaray's theory does not explain, will be discussed later.)

Both at the beginning and the end of the scene in the bed-chamber, Raymon sees Noun reflected in a mirror and takes the image for "the phantom of a woman," (p. 83) whom he believes to be Indiana. At the beginning of the scene, he sees only a simple reflection, but by the end of the scene, this image has become a complex system of fragmented and repeated images:

Gradually, the vague and floating memory of

> Indiana blended into Raymon's intoxication. The two mirrors, which reflected in each other to infinity the images of Noun, seemed to be peopled with a thousand phantoms. He espied in the depth of this double reverberation a more slender form, and it seemed to him that he could discern, in the last blurred and hazy shadow that Noun reflected, the fine and supple shape of Madame Delmare (p. 86).

This passage speaks eloquently about the non-representation of feminine desire (erotic desire, "desire for origin," and "desire for the same"). It is evident in the symbolism of the passage, and in the words that are scattered throughout, that at an "infinite" distance from consciousness in the "last" "depth" of "memory," Noun and Indiana are one and the *same* being. They are two fragments which could possibly unite to form a total feminine subject but not within the structure of mirror imagery portrayed here. Neither Indiana (the subject of the novel) nor Noun (who tries to impose her desires in this scene) is the subject of the mirror system in the above passage. Only the man, Raymon, can be the subject of that system, which is inscribed within *his* gaze and *his* imagination as part of *his* desiring economy. Noun does not look at herself in the mirror, it is the mirrors which reflect her double image to each other, while Raymon looks at their infinite reverberation. Furthermore, the two fragments of the split feminine being are represented in such a way that they cannot be aware of each other. Only Ramon is aware of their resemblance and relation.

This passage suggests what Julia Kristeva and Luce Irigaray have indicated: that the model of the subject based on continued self-reflection is really a male model. Since the passage uses a mirror system of images, feminine desire for self-identify is inevitably expressed as the masculine desire that the woman be someone *other than herself,* and that she correspond to his preconceived stereotype of femininity. This text also begins as an attempt to express feminine erotic desire (through Noun) and ends as an imitation of male erotic desire, just as the novel is an imitation of a male romantic novel:

> Raymon, having examined her in the mirror without turning his head, brought his gaze to bear on everything that could give him a purer reflection of Indiana, on her musical instruments, her paintings, her narrow, virginal bed. He became intoxicated with the vague perfume that her presence had left in this sanctuary; he trembled with desire in thinking of the day when Indiana herself would uncover its delights to him; and Noun, her arms crossed, standing behind him, contemplated him with ecstasy, imagining that he was enraptured by the sight of all the cares she had taken to please him (p. 86).

As the expression of erotic desire breaks through in this passage, the feminine potential subject splits not into two but into three fragments (Indiana, Noun, Raymon). And it is the strange recombination of those fragments which most strongly perpetuates the feminine myth. During most of the novel, Indiana is the conscious Woman as Object while Noun represents unconscious feminine desire; but in this scene their functions are exchanged: Noun is conscious presence while Indiana appears as absence and illusion. Indiana, the subject of the novel, is more distantly absent, and more morally pure, the more ardently the novel expresses sexual desire. She is the subject of the novel, but she is not the subject of discourse or desire. Noun is here the subject who loves, who desires, who 'contemplates," and who "imagines." But as such, she is unloved, undesirable, and unworthy of contemplation by a man. Described here in an almost burlesque manner, Noun is punished by the narrator for trying to impose herself as subject. The writer's desire to express desire finally explodes through Raymon. Only the male can dominate this triangle as the subject who is both desirable and desiring, and who determines what type of femininity has value.

At the basis of a specular system of images is a quest for the answer to the question "who am I?" In this passage the feminine subject, fragmented into three partial subjects, answers the question three ways: "I" am nobody (Indiana); "I" am undesired and undesirable (Noun); "I" am the man who loves the woman who exists only as "I" imagine her (Raymon). The circle of male self-reflection closes, and the woman is "outside." If the several fragments of this feminine subject were combined, it would say: "I can be loved only if I hate myself and hate other women in me, but my reward will be to be admired in the imagination of a man whom I imagine according to what a pre-existing value system has taught me to imagine."

The scene of Indiana's bed-chamber reestablishes the total male "economy of representation" analyzed by Irigaray. It is a closed system which uses mirror images of women to provide the male character with self-presence by making Raymon the only character doubly present in the scene: he is actually present, and his presence is reflected in the sight of another character, Noun. Indiana must be absent from the scene in order to be "present" in Raymon's imagination and to represent *his* desire to him. Noun, who is actually present (but unnoticed by Raymon), is the feminine "nothing" which threatens to destroy the coherence of Raymon's desire system. It is she who must be destroyed, and shortly after this, she commits suicide. George Sand in this novel, reproduces the myth of Woman as Lack and Absence.

While Luce Irigaray's theory explains the role of Indiana, it does not totally explain the role of Noun, and the relation between the two female characters. Noun is used in this scene on a manifest level as an example of the immorality to be condemned in contrast to Indiana's virtue, and at the same time, on an implicit (and unconscious) level, she is used as the unattractive contrast to Indiana's irresistible sexual attraction. It is not a coincidence that Sand makes the pure and desirable woman a white bourgeoise while the sensual and unattractive woman is a lower class Creole.

In fact, the contrast between Indiana and Noun in this novel reflects the way in which class differences of women were used in the elaboration of an ideology that could maintain the established social order of nineteenth-century capitalism. In the final analysis, the novel reflects the entire ideological structure in which the nineteenth-century myth of femininity functions. Here again, I am guided by Louis Althusser's method:

> . . . we must go further than the unmentioned presence of the thoughts of a living author to the presence of his *potential thoughts,* to his *problematic,* that is to the constitutive unity of the effective thoughts that make up the domain of the existing *ideological field* with which a particular author must settle accounts in his own thought.[21]

At this point in her career, George Sand did not settle accounts with the existing ideology, for she was largely unconscious of what the figure Noun represents: the use of Noun in the novel demonstrates how the prostitution of lower class women was necessary to preserve the chastity of bourgeoise women for the sake of bourgeois men, and their system of property inheritance. The use of Noun shows how *both* chastity *and* sexual attraction are the privilege of bourgeoisie women, while the lower class woman is condemned for being deprived of these privileges, just as proletarian women of the 1830s were held responsible for their "immoral" lives and their poverty. The novel, and especially the passages quoted above, even reveals that that chastity and virginity are simply the ornaments of voluptuousness for a man like Raymon, while it participates in the hypocrisy of the moral code that Raymon's class creates and maintains. Finally, in the novel, the lower class woman must be sacrificed to maintain the innocence of the bourgeoise woman and the stability of the social order.

But the novel does more than illustrate the function of feminine stereotypes and feminine morality within a larger structure of class ideology. George Sand reproduces a more sophisticated and ambiguous version of the ideology in a novel that encourages obedience to the feminine stereotype. *Indiana* encourages women to resign themselves to the established order and to live in a fantasy world instead of acting to alter their situation, and, although the novel does to a certain extent show the punishments of rebellion and the rewards of resignation, this is not its principal method of propagating the ideology.

The message of the novel is perhaps stronger in that it is contradictory. It does not simply reproduce the stereotypes but merges feminine aspirations for freedom into them. Indiana does revolt: she runs away from her husband after he beats her. But she runs away to Raymon only when she does it as a "sacrifice," and when "she does not in any way go to him in search of happiness" (p. 285). Thus Indiana's revolt is contained in her resignation. She does attempt to survive alone in the world, but she is finally saved from a humiliating death by Ralph's coincidental intervention instead of by her own actions. Thus her independence is contained in her dependence on a man, and the novel itself must rely on a fantasy ending to save Indiana from the habitual fate of women.

Indiana cannot act to secure her own happiness, because it is in this refusal to so act that Sand implies the heroine's superiority to "all those women" who lower themselves to prevent being dominated by their husbands and to fulfill in secret their sexual desires (see pp. 10 and 11). In a novel which could certainly not be accused of promoting feminine solidarity, the heroine is superior because she epitomizes all the conventional values of the society that Sand appears to condemn. In like manner, the huge success of *Indiana* resulted perhaps from Sand's ability to make an upper class reading public feel superior to the upper class characters in the novel while at the same time flattering its prejudices.

In the novel, a host of faceless characters, the "false friends" (p. 246) who represent "Opinion," condemn Indiana and make her the object of scandal, because they believe she has revolted for her own pleasure and that she has been seduced by Raymon. The only difference between the society *in* the novel and the society who *reads* the novel is that the reading society knows the heroine has not violated these prohibitions. There is no basic difference of values and opinions, but the reading society can feel superior and enlightened.

Indiana's superiority depends on the continued (or permanent) inferiority of "all those women"; the readers' superiority depends on the continued prejudice of the "false friends"; and perhaps Sand's superiority depended on the continued inferiority of women in society. This may be why she denounced the feminist movement of her time. Here again the parallel between Sand's writing and her life emerges. Both as a writer and as a celebrity, she made the freedom of one woman separate from the freedom of other women, and perhaps this is why she has been selected to "represent" the ideal Liberated Woman by the mass media and the Mobil Oil Corporation. Although this analysis has focused on only one text, a similar analysis could be applied to Sand's televised biography and similar cultural products to see if they too treat the subject of women in a way that incorporates into the dominant ideology—which seeks ever to reproduce itself and society as the same—aspirations which are potentially different from it.

Notes

1.   André Maurois, *Lélia, on la vie de George Sand* (Paris: Hachette, 1952), p. 8. (Unless otherwise indicated, all the translations in the paper are mine.)

2.   George Sand, quoted in Edith Thomas, *Les Femmes en 1848* (Paris: Presses universitaires de France, 1948) p. 67. See also Marguerite Thibert, *Le Féminisme dans le socialisme français de 1830 à 1850* (Paris: Marcel Giard, 1926), pp. 374–378. The women's movement, led by women from the Saint-Simonian sect, began in 1833. When the Second Republic was declared in the Revolution of 1848, the feminists, led by Jeanne Deroin, Désirée Gay, Pauline Roland, and Suzanne Voilguin, formed *La Voix Des Femmes*. Their program demanded workshops for unemployed women; labor unions, public clinics, and better medical education for women; the right of women to divorce, to enter universities and liberal professions, and to vote and hold office. Theoretically, they were very advanced. It was after *La Voix des Femmes* nominated George Sand as their candidate to the National Assembly that she attacked the feminist movement in an attempt to dissociate herself from the feminists in the eyes of the middle-class public. In 1849, the feminist newspaper was banned and laws were passed forbidding women to attend political meetings. In 1850, Jeanne Deroin and Pauline Roland were arrested, tried, and condemned for attempting to form a trade union. Jeanne Deroin was exiled and Pauline Roland deported to a penal colony. Edith Thomas and Marguerite Thibert give detailed accounts of the debate between George Sand and the feminists of 1848. Many of the important documents and articles concerning their polemic are printed in the feminist journal *La Voix des Femmes,* in the issue of April, 1848.

3.   John Charpentier, *George Sand* (Paris: Jules Tallandier, 1936), p. 173; Emile Moselly, *George Sand* (Paris: *Les Femmes illustres,* Editions d'art et de littérature, 1911), p. 109; Wadimir Karénine, *George Sand: sa vie et ses oeuvres* (4 vols.; 2e ed.; Paris: Plon-Nourrit et Cie., 1899), I. 360. Karénine says: ". . . one of the first, she struggled against the humiliated and oppressed position of women in marriage. And *Indiana* is worthy of attracting our attention as a first attempt at revolt."

4. These notions can be found in many, many critical works, but many of them are illustrated in the critical anthology *Les Chemins actuels de la critique* (Paris: 10/18, 1968). A critique of structuralist criticism by Serge Doubrowsky, "Critique et existence" (pp. 215–229), sums up many of these positions: "Signs upon signs, writing upon writing, according to certain regulated relations certainly, but without a *person* to signify or to write: discourse forms a totality which refers only to itself . . . If the notion of 'author' or 'creator' is a myth it's for the good reason that it is not the writer that thinks his language, but language which thinks in him" (p. 217). The idea of the pure aesthetic self in general is stated by Paul de Man," Ludwig Binswanger et le problème du moi poétique" (pp. 63–78): "Such a development would necessarily bring about the intervention of objective factors from the physical, biological, social and intersubjective orders, which have nothing to do with the autonomous domain of aesthetic activity . . . To the empirical self which is open to the whole of reality is opposed the aesthetic self which aims for a different totality" (p. 70). The idea of a pure aesthetic experience and of the text as speaking subject are stated by Boris de Schloezer, "L'Oeuvre, l'auteur et l'homme" (pp. 128–140) "In the aesthetic experience, this object to which I relate is no longer an object, but a subject . . . it is the voice of the work itself, which tells me nothing but what it is: it is a speaking presence speaking about itself" (p. 135).

5. Pierre Kuentz, "Le Tête à Texte," *Esprit,* No. 12, décembre, 1974, pp. 946–962, p. 951.

6. René Girard, "From the 'Divine Comedy' to the Sociology of the Novel," *Sociology of Literature and Drama,* Elizabeth and Tom Burns, eds. (Baltimore: Penguin Books, Inc., 1973) pp. 101–108, p. 104.

7. Her "milk sister" or "soeur de lait" means the daughter of her wet-nurse.

8. Julia Kristeva, "Le sujet en procès," *Artaud* (Paris: 10/18, 1973), pp. 43–108.

"If this originary repression (refoulement originaire) institutes the subject at the same time that it institutes the symbolic function, it also institutes the distinction signifier/ signified, in which Lacan sees the determination of "every censure of a social order." The unitary subject (sujet unaire) is the subject which is instituted by this censure of a social order (p. 44).

"If such is, according to Marx, the status of the individual in the bourgeois system, then one could say, reading this statement in the light of recent notions, that in and by the State and religion, capitalism requires and consolidates the paranoid moment of the subject: unity rejecting (foreluant) the other and putting himself in his place (p. 51).

See also Julia Kristeva, "Pratique significante et mode de production," *Tel quel,* No. 60, Hiver, 1971, pp. 21–33. The subject constitutes itself as the unified, unchanging, stable, coherent of a unified, unchanging, stable, coherent state, by the acquisition of language, and especially syntax, which completes a rupture between conscious life governed by the symbolic function and the repressed "process" and "impulses" which violate the law of One.

9. Alfred de Vigny, *Chatterton* (Paris: Classiques Larousse, n.d.), p. 63.

10. Kristeva, pp. 71 and 74.

"In the paranoid group she is effaced, object of exchange among the brothers of the community or precious matron. It remains for her, as Hegel saw, to be the eternal irony of the brotherhood, to take the mask of a brother, and thus disguised as a man, eternal Clorinda, to join the game of negations; the only way to have a voice in the social and cultural chapter (p. 71).

Because this is the law of the community, up to and including capitalism: this law which has nothing to do with her, which does not signify her, she pretends to follow it.

11. Simone de Beauvoir, *Le Deuxième Sexe* (2 vols.; 57e éd.; Paris, Gallimard, 1949), II, 235.

12.   George Sand, *Indiana* (Paris: Garnier, 1962), p. 76 (All other references to this book are in parentheses after the quote. The translations are mine.)

13.   George Sand, *Lélia* (2 vols.; Paris: Calmann-Lévy, 1854) I, II. Translation mine.

14.   Luce Irigaray, *Speculum de l'autre femme* (Paris: Les Editions de minuit, 1974), p. 26.

15.   Ibid., p. 74.

16.   Sigmund Freud, "Femininity," *New Introductory Lectures on Psychoanalysis,* translated and edited by James Strachey (New York: W. W. Norton and Company, Inc., 1965), 112–135, pp. 118–119.

17.   Irigaray, p. 129.

18.   Ibid., pp. 75–76.

19.   Ibid., p. 57.

20.   Louis Althusser, *For Marx,* translated by Ben Brewster (New York: Random House, Vintage Books, 1969), p. 67.

21.   Ibid., p. 66. (Italics in text.)

Sonnets from the Portuguese:
A Negative and a Positive Context

SUSAN ZIMMERMAN

Elizabeth Barrett was already thirty-nine when Robert Browning came into her life. Long ago she had turned the corner from youth and set her face towards death. She had grieved and wept enough for a whole lifetime; she had endured the deaths of her mother and her brother Edward and her own ill health. Now she had won a victory: she had managed to renounce the world. Life could no longer disappoint her, because she expected nothing from it. Moreover, her literary reputation was at its height:[1] here, too, she had won a decisive victory. For both these reasons, and also because she had never married, Elizabeth Barrett had a peculiar sovereignty denied to most women of her generation. Like two other spinster-poets, Christina Rossetti and Emily Dickinson, she felt a direct relationship with God.

Suddenly this successful poetess, strong-willed enough to have conquered the fear of death, a mature and settled woman, was asked to become a wife and lover. She, who had finally learned to love heaven, must now turn back to earth, must surrender her chastity of thirty-nine years, must marry and devote herself once again to life. Moreover, she must relinquish her direct relationship with God, standing henceforward in relation to her husband as he does to God and as the church does to Christ. Her sovereignty must give way, for a wife is bound by the commandment of God to the fallen Eve: "... thy desire shall be to thy husband husband, and he shall rule over thee" (*Genesis* 3:16).[2]

No wonder Elizabeth Barrett was in conflict: surely love is sweeter than death, and yet such a great change was certain to be difficult. A poet, she naturally turned to pen and paper. What better form for an examination of her own reactions to love than the sonnet sequence? Within such a framework, male poets over the centuries had explored tenderness and passion; they had dealt openly with emotional conflict and had sometimes found solutions. So Elizabeth Barrett shaped her doubts and desires into forty-four graceful fourteen-line poems; inside the orderly structure of the Italian sonnet, she was free to express her own chaotic feelings.

Like the love poetry of Sidney, Shakespeare, Dickinson, and Meredith, the *Sonnets from the Portuguese* seem to invite biographical criticism. Unfortunately, such criticism tends to detract from rather than add to our understanding of the work. Certainly this is true in the case of Mrs. Browning. The early critics and biographers, knowing the barrenness of her life before meeting Browning and the happiness that resulted from her marriage, tended to see only the positive aspects of the coming of love. The conflict that is worked out through the sonnets has generally been underestimated.[3] My rather unorthodox reading of the famous Browning love story is given above to point out the reality of the poet's struggle. For Elizabeth Barrett (at least, as her story is told in the sonnets), love was both a giving and a taking away. The sequence works towards a resolution of the two: a joyful acceptance of what love has to offer and a generous giving of what love must take. We shall see that the final resolution depends more on the imagery and associations than it does on the thoughts expressed.

From the first, we are led to believe that the poet is writing a Petrarchan sequence. Perhaps she herself expected that she would. The plan is traditional: a series of sonnets, incorporating a slight plot, which examines closely an emotional conflict and describes in detail the changes that take place in the mind of a poet in love. Petrarch had done it, Sidney and Spenser had done it; Shakespeare, in his more mysterious way, had done it as well. Yet how could a woman in her position interpret the tradition? There were four distinct possibilities. She could ignore it; but in that case why write a sonnet sequence at all? She could accept it, thus casting herself in the role of the cruel mistress; but, as Christina Rossetti pointed out, such an identification is not particularly attractive.[4] She could invert it, thus assuming the role of the lover; but it would have been unmaidenly for a female poet to address a man in the terms used by the male poets who came before her. Moreover, the poet-lover is generally trying to seduce the beloved, and seduction is an activity Miss Barrett would hardly have wanted to associate with herself. Finally, she could use the tradition wherever it seemed fitting, accepting, ignoring, or inverting it according to context. This approach had interesting possibilities, but in Mrs. Browning's sonnets it threatened to produce a muddle. If she had been more conventional, the ending might have been less happy, for within the context of the great sonnet cycles of the past, her romance seems doomed to failure. We would, I think, have expected an ending either melancholy or philosophic or perhaps both.

Most sonnet sequences deal with a young man who has fallen violently and unfortunately in love. He has become a slave to his passions. Sidney's Astrophil says:

> Now even that footstep of lost liberty
>   Is gone, and now, like slave-born Muscovite,
>   I call it praise to suffer tyranny. . . .[5]

He does not in the least appreciate the services of the love-god:

> See there that boy, that murth'ring boy, I say,
> Who, like a thief, hid in dark bush doth lie
> Till bloody bullet get him wrongful prey.[6]

For the persona of Shakespeare's sonnets, too, love is an enthrallment and a humiliation:

> Being your slave what should I do but tend
> Upon the hours, and times of your desire?[7]

And:

> So true a fool is love, that in your will,
> (Though you do any thing) he thinks no ill.[8]

Like Astrophil, he is abused by the god of Love:

> Thou blind fool Love, what dost thou to mine eyes,
> That they behold and see not what they see?[9]

So we would not expect either of these sequences to end in marriage to the lover or gratitude to Cupid. Yet, in comparison to these, the woman in the *Sonnets from the Portuguese* is treated by Love with astonishing violence:

> . . . a mystic Shape did move
> Behind me, and drew me backward by the hair;
> And a voice said in mastery, while I strove,—
> "Guess now who holds thee?" (I)[10]

For her, the coming of Lover is terror. Other poets had been embarrassed; their sleep had been disturbed and their appetites had dwindled. But when Elizabeth Barret first realizes the change in her life, her reaction is extreme:[11]

> . . . I sank and quailed
> As if God's future thundered on my past (XXVIII).

She is conquered; she surrenders her sovereignty forever, because, she says "thou overcomest so":

> And as a vanquished soldier yields his sword
> To one who lifts him from the bloody earth,—
> Even so, Beloved, I at last record,
> Here ends my strife. If *thou* invite me forth,
> I rise above abasement at the word (XVI).

Such abasement before another human being far outweighs the self-abasement of previous lovers. Sidney and Shakespeare struggled with their own passions, not the beloved but Love itself was the real enemy. But Elizabeth Barret can only "rise above abasement" at the invitation of the victorious lover.

Another emotion that has tormented many lover-poets is a feeling of unworthiness. Shakespeare says:

> To leave poor me, thou hast the strength of laws,
> Since why to love, I can allege no cause.[12]

And:

> I may not evermore acknowledge thee,
> Lest my bewailed guilt should do thee shame.[13]

Perhaps among the most bitter is sonnet 87, full of reproach and shame:

> Farewell! thou art to dear for my possessing,
> And like enough thou know'st they estimate,
> The charter of thy worth gives thee releasing:
> My bonds in thee are all determinate.
> For how do I hold thee but by they granting,
> And for that riches where is my deserving?
> And cause of this fair gift in me is wanting,
> And so my patent back again is swerving.[14]

A proud lover like Astrophil still considers himself a wretch in comparison with Stella, the queen of virtue. But Astrophil's self-doubts are not serious; and even Shakespeare's confessions have their positive side. For the bitter mockery of some of the sonnets bolsters the poet's pride. Rather than believing he is truly unworthy, he may be suggesting that only the excessive pride of the youth makes it appear so.

In Elizabeth Barrett's sonnets, however, there seems to be no such self-assertion to counterbalance her feelings of inadequacy:

> The chrism is on thine head,—on mine, the dew,—
> And Death must dig the level where these agree (III).

> And dost thou lift this house's latch too poor
> For hand of thine (IV)?

>   For frequent tears have run
> The colours from my life, and left so dead
> And pale a stuff, it were not fitly done
> To give the same as pillow to they head.
> Go farther! let it serve to trample on (VIII).

> I will not soil thy purple with my dust,
> Nor breathe my poison on thy Venice-glass,
> Nor give thee any love—which were unjust (IX).

Her voice is insistent, she says without a trace of the mockery we sometimes find in Shakespeare, "We are not peers/ So to be lovers" (IX).

When her fear of unworthiness is conquered, it is only through the power of the lover; he alone makes her worthy of him. And even "love, mere love" (X) that makes her "not all unworthy" (XI) she owes to him: "I cannot speak/ Of love even, as a good thing of my own" (XII).

Were a Petrarchan lover to feel such serious doubts and fears, we would expect him to throw off the yoke of love and regain his sovereignty. We would certainly *not* expect a marriage to be based on such a relationship.

There is another way in which Mrs. Browning's progress is surprising. Petrarch had passed through the earthly love of Laura to a spiritual love; so Beatrice had captured Dante's soul for God. Sidney had written:

> Leave me, O love which reachest but to dust;
> And thou, my mind, aspire to higher things;
> Grow rich in that which never taketh rust,
> Whatever fades but fading pleasure brings.[15]

Wyatt, too, had turned from sexual love to philosophy:

> Farewell, love, and all thy laws forever,
>   Thy baited hooks shall tangle me no more;
> Senec and Plato call me from thy lore
> To perfect wealth my wit for to endeavor.[16]

In his own colorful way, Wyatt expressed the disgust of many former lovers when he said, "Me lusteth no longer rotten bough to climb."[17]

Mrs. Browning, on the other hand, has already prepared herself for heaven before the sonnets begin. Rather than trying to raise her soul, she must now lower it; she must return to life:

> Then my soul, instead
> Of dreams of death, resumes life's lower range.
> Then, love me, Love! look on me—breathe on me!
> As brighter ladies do not count it strange,
> For love, to give up acres and degree,
> I yield the grave for thy sake, and exchange
> My near sweet view of Heaven, for earth with thee!
> (XXIII)

There is in this sonnet a real sense of sacrifice. Sidney wanted to escape "rust" and "fading pleasure"; but Mrs. Browning is giving up something of value. She "yields" the grave as other ladies have yielded wealth and station, and her early prospect of heaven had been "sweet." If we had read only Petrarch, Dante, Herbert, and Sidney, we would find it difficult to believe that anyone would choose such a debasement of the soul. To turn from God to another human being, from the certainty of heaven to the changeableness of human love seems preposterous.

Knowing, then, that the poet's goal is different from those of earlier writers of sonnets, that her attitude towards her lover and the god of Love is different from theirs toward their mistresses and Cupid, and that her self-image is different, we may begin to wonder what, if anything, she shares with them. The answer, I think, is very little. She has used the hallowed form, the one framework in which personal self-examination was approved; but within it she has not created a Petrarchan (or a systematically anti-Petrarchan) lover. Neither of the two lovers in the sequence suffers hot and cold spells, or tears and sighs; for Elizabeth Barrett, the opening of the sequence marks the end of her tears and sighs. Neither of the two makes a complaint about the cruelty and coldness of the other. If anyone could have done so, it would be the male figure; but she anticipates and turns aside such a rebuke:

> . . . am I cold,
> Ungrateful, that for these most manifold
> High gifts, I render nothing back at all?

> Not so, not cold,—but very poor instead
> Ask God who knows (VIII).

So she refuses to accept the role of the courtly lady; nor does she want the kind of love offered to Stella. Nothing would distress her more than extravagant praise of her beauty, which was a standard technique employed by courtier poets:

> If thou must love me, let it be for nought
> Except for love's sake only. Do not say
> "I love her for her smile—her look—her way
> Of speaking gently,—for a trick of thought
> That falls in well with mine, and certes brought
> A sense of pleasant ease on such a day—" (XIV).

Neither will she accept the role of the courtly lover, who sued his lady for "pity": Neither love me for/ Thine own dear pity's wiping my cheeks dry" (XIV). The courtly lover pleaded for love, but Mrs. Browning has already won her love: now she asks only what she can give in return. The courtly lover was desperately anxious for consummation. Mrs. Browning is resisting it. The courtly lover would have been delighted to win the lady's favour without suffering the torments of love; Mrs. Browning wants to keep the lover in her heart, her dreams, and her eyes (VI), but says: "Go from me" (VI), and "Stand further off then! go" (V).[20] In her resistance, she seems to resemble the lady who is being courted, yet in sonnet III, she becomes the wandering minstrel-lover, normally a male figure who is courting: "A poor, tired, wandering singer, singing through/ The dark, and leaning up a cypress tree" (III).

We expect the writer of love poetry to identify himself as a poet, musician, or singer. Shakespeare and Sidney both discuss their professions; Wyatt's love-poems also refer to his pen and his lute. But in *Sonnets from the Portuguese*, the references are confused. As in earlier love poetry, the male figure is a poet and singer:

> Most gracious singer of high poems (IV)!

> My poet, thou canst touch on all the notes
> God set between His After and Before (XVII).

Accordingly, the woman is the instrument:

> ... like an out-of-tune
> Worn viol, a good singer would be wroth
> To spoil his song with.... (XXXII).[21]

Or she is a helpmeet to the great musician:

> God's will devotes
> Thine to such ends, and mine to wait on thine.
> How, Dearest, wilt thou have me for most use?
> A hope, to sing by gladly? or a fine
> Sad memory, with thy songs to interfuse?

A shade, in which to sing—of palm or pine?
A grave, on which to rest from singing? Choose (XVII).

This identification is difficult to maintain, however, since it is the woman who is writing the sonnets. She admits that she, too, is a poet; but contrasts her poor skill with his "golden fulness" (IV):[22]

My cricket chirps against thy mandolin.
Hush, call no echo up in further proof
Of desolation! there's a voice within
That weeps . . . as thou must sing . . . alone, aloof (IV).

Thou, bethink thee, art
A guest for queens to social pageantries,
With gages from a hundred brighter eyes
Than tears even can make mine, to play thy part
Of chief musician. What hast *thou* to do
With looking from the lattice-lights at me,
A poor, tired, wandering singer. . . . (III).

Yet before he came to her she sang, and some listened:

Deep thanks to all
Who paused a little near the prison-wall
To hear my music in its louder parts. . . . (XLI).

She writes, like the poets before her, of the difficulty of expressing love: "And wilt thou have me fashion into speech/ The love I bear thee . . . (XIII)? So Sidney shaped a sonnet out of the struggle for expression:

But words came halting forth, wanting invention's stay:
Invention, nature's child, fled step-dame Study's blows,
And other's feet still seemed but strangers in my way.
Thus, great with child to speak, and helpless in my throes. . . .[23]

And Shakespeare asked: "Why is my verse so barren of new pride?"[24] But Shakespeare particularly had the confidence of his poetry: "Not marble, nor the gilded monuments/ Of princes shall outlive this powerful rhyme,"[25] Triumphantly he challenged Time:

. . . I forbid thee one most heinous crime,
O carve not with thy hours my love's fair brow,
Nor draw no lines there with thine antique pen,
Him in thy course untainted do allow,
For beauty's pattern to succeeding men.
Yet do thy worst old Time: despite thy wrong,
My love shall in my verse ever live young.[26]

John Donne too had confidently immortalized his love in verse:

We'll build in sonnets pretty roomes;
As well a well wrought urne becomes
The greatest ashes, as halfe-acre tombes. . . .[27]

Even this source of pride traditionally granted the poet-lover is denied Mrs. Browning. She would like to immortalize her thankfulness and love, yet she cannot have the power of the consummate poet, for that role is taken by her lover. He alone could teach her how:

> Instruct me how to thank thee!—Oh, to shoot
> My soul's full meaning into future years,
> That *they* should lend it utterance, and salute
> Love that endures, from Life that disappears (XLI)!

So Mrs. Browning is not clearly the lover or the lady, the immortalizing poet or the immortalized beloved. What is she? A woman, a wife. Only a wife could reconcile herself to mastery; only a woman could love in the role of lesser poet, and could love a man without rejecting God (for, as I pointed out earlier, her love of a man is the channel to God: her husband is intermediary). It is all right—even desirable—for a wife's station in life to be lower than her husband's. For her it is not blasphemous to say:

> My ministering life-angel justified
> The word by his appealing look upcast
> To the white throne of God, I turned at last,
> And there, instead, saw thee. . . . (XLII).

The arrival of human love to her soul becomes analogous to mankind's salvation through the love of Jesus. The redemptive power of love, the unexpected quality of Grace, the unworthiness of the soul all sanctify the love in these sonnets by linking it to the love of God.

It seems to me that if we view the *Sonnets from the Portuguese* as a marriage poem, its shape is much clearer than if we view it as a traditional sonnet sequence. To establish this new context, let us examine an ancient and sanctified poem of love and marriage, the *Song of Solomon.*

In both poems, the male figure is associated with royalty. In the *Song of Songs*, he is a king, the woman says, "The king hath brought me into his chambers" (1:4). In *Sonnets from the Portuguese*, he is a "princely Heart" (III). Both men are master singers, Solomon presumably being the writer of the greatest of all songs. They are men of power and beauty, and their love is sure. Both wear crowns (Browning's is a "bay-crown" XIX); both are consecrated—the king at his coronation, Browning because of the "chrism" on his head (III). They are dark-haired: the king's "locks are bushy, and black as a raven" (5:11); Browning's cut lock is "so black!" (XIX). The king's "eyes are as the eyes of doves" (5:12); Browning gives "dovelike help" (XXXI). The men look for the women, calling to them from behind a barrier:

> . . . he looketh forth at the windows, shewing
> himself through the lattice (*S. of S.,* 2:9).

> What has *thou* to do
> With looking from the lattice-lights at me . . .
> (*S. from the P.,* III)?

The two women, on the other hand, are blemished but attractive. The bride of Solomon says, "I am black but comely. . . . Look not upon me, because I am black . . ." (1:5–6). Elizabeth has lived in darkness and shadow, and yet "love, mere love, is beautiful" (X). She knows that her love makes her as comely as the black bride:

> . . . what I *feel*, across the inferior features
> Of what I *am*, doth flash itself, and show
> How that great work of Love enhances Nature's (X).

Both the Shulamite and the poetess are chaste: "My dove, my undefiled is but one" (6:9). And both are reluctant to put off their purity. The Shulamite has cleansed her body when her lover comes to her door, so she replies:

> I have put off my coat; how shall I put
> it on? I have washed my feet; how shall
> I defile them (5:3)?

Elizabeth Barrett has cleansed her soul for heaven; like the bride of Solomon, she is at first reluctant to "defile" it, but finally surrenders for the sake of love:

> I thought the funeral-shears
> Would take this first, but Love is justified,—
> Take it thou,—finding pure, from all those years,
> The kiss my mother left here when she died (XVIII).

She, too, is a dove:

> Open thine heart wide,
> And fold within the wet wings of thy dove (XXXV).

Within the context of the *Song of Songs*, the coming of love to Mrs. Browning is like the coming of spring to the land. It is a "baptism" into new life (VII); words of love are to her dead hopes like the call of the cuckoo in spring is to the dead earth:

> Remember, never to the hill or plain,
> Valley and wood, without her cuckoo-strain
> Comes the fresh Spring in all her green completed (XXI).

The staff of dead wood that was to be a "pilgrim's staff" blossoms in his presence and produces "green leaves with morning dews impearled" (XLII). The unexpected return of spring to Mrs. Browning's life becomes more poignant if we have read the *Song of Songs*:

> My beloved spake, and said unto me, Rise
> up, my love, my fair one, and come away.
>   For, lo, the winter is past, the rain is
> over and gone;
>   The flowers appear on the earth; the
> time of the singing of birds is come, and the
> voice of the turtle is heard in our land. (2:10–12).

Here at last is a positive context in which to view Elizabeth Barrett's romance: her beloved spoke to her and said, "Rise up, my love, and come away." The winter had passed; the time for tears was over and gone: over the earth appeared the flowers and birds, especially the turtle-dove.

The bride of the *Song of Songs* is "as a lily among thorns" (2:2) and her lover "feedeth among the lilies" (2:16) so Mrs. Browning can assert joyfully:

> Very whitely still
> The lilies of our lives may reassure
> Their blossoms from their roots. . . .
> God only, who made us rich, can make up poor (XXIV).

The Shulamite is an example of a woman who was blemished yet worthy of love; who turned her lover away from her door, yet found him again; she cries out with love to the king:

> Make haste, my beloved, and be thou
> like to a roe or to a young hart upon the
> mountains of spices (8:14).

So we know that eventually Elizabeth Barrett too will be able to open her heart to her lover, that she will accept everything he has to give and surrender everything he must take. The last sonnet before the envoy celebrates the boundlessness of her new love:

> How do I love thee? Let me count the ways.
> I love thee to the depth and breadth and height
> My soul can reach, when feeling out of sight
> For the ends of Being and ideal Grace
> I love thee to the level of every day's
> Most quiet need, by sun and candlelight.
> I love thee freely, as men strive for Right;
> I love thee purely, as they turn from Praise.
> I love thee with the passion put to use
> In my old griefs, and with my childhood's faith.
> I love thee with a love I seemed to lose
> With my lost saints,—I love thee with the breath,
> Smiles, tears, of all my life!—and, if God choose,
> I shall but love thee better after death (XLIII).

Finally, in the envoy, the poet sees that she herself, like the Shulamite, is "a garden enclosed" (4:12). She is no longer ashamed of her heart's flowers, her poems, for she knows that love has produced from a bed of "bitter weeds and rue" something of beauty and worth:

> . . . here's eglantine,
> Here's ivy (XLIV)!

"Love is strong as death," says Solomon (8:6). "Many waters cannot quench love" (8:7). And Mrs. Browning becomes a witness to the truth of this statement:

> . . . I, with bosom-swell,
> Make witness, here, between the good and bad,
> That Love, as strong as Death, retrieves as well (XXVII).

That Love retrieves is the final lesson of *Sonnets from the Portuguese*. It is a lesson we would not expect from a traditional sonnet sequence, where philosophy is always superior to earthly love and sovereignty to subordination. We must keep in mind that this writer is a woman preparing herself for marriage, not a lover suing his mistress for "pity." Only if we read Elizabeth Barrett Browning's poems as we do other epithalamia (notably the *Song of Solomon*) can we see that earthly love is a proper subject for celebration.

Notes

1. Only five years later she was considered for the position of Poet Laureate.

2. I emphasized the positive aspects of spinsterhood here because they are seldom considered. We must recognize that no married lady of the last century could have devoted her life to poetry as Emily Dickinson did; and I doubt that Elizabeth Barrett would have become such a well-known poet if she had married at eighteen or twenty.

3. Goldstein discusses it intelligently. He sees the struggle as quite a conventional one, between reason and the emotions. He points out how difficult it is for the poet to adjust to the change in her life. He does not, however, discuss the sacrifices the poet is asked to make for love, or the violence of the love imagery. (Melvin Goldstein, "Elizabeth Barrett Browning's Sonnets from the Portuguese in the Light of the Petrarchan Tradition," unpublished doctoral dissertation, the University of Wisconsin, June 1958).

4. In her Preface to "Monna Innominata," Christina Rossetti says of Beatrice and Laura that they "have come down to us resplendent with charms, but (at least to my apprehension) scant of attractiveness" (*The Poetical Works of Christina Georgina Rossetti*, London, Macmillan, 1904, p. 58). Her own sonnet sequence is an attempt to interpret the role of the courtly lady in a more positive light.

5. Robert M. Bender, ed., *Five Courtier Poets*, New York, Washington Square, 1969, pp. 333–334.

6. Bender, p. 342.

7. William Shakespeare, *The Sonnets*, London, Cambridge University Press, 1966, p. 31. (sonnet 57).

8. Shakespeare, *loc. cit.*

9. Shakespeare, p. 71 (sonnet 137).

10. *Sonnets from the Portuguese*, New York, Avon, 1966. Sonnet numbers will be internally documented.

11. I use the names of the poet and her lover as shorthand. I mean, of course, the personae presented by the poet.

12. Shakespeare, p. 27 (sonnet 49).

13. Shakespeare, p. 20 (sonnet 36).

14. Shakespeare, p. 46 (sonnet 87).

15. Bender, p. 332.

16. Bender, p. 18.

17. Bender, p. 19.

18. Goldstein (See note 4) devotes his whole thesis to a study of the *Sonnets from the Portuguese* in relation to the Petrarchan tradition. His commentary on the sonnets themselves is good; however, his exploration of Mrs. Browning's use of the Petrarchan tradition is disappointing. He points out that she uses the Italian sonnet form rather than the Shakespearean, and that both Petrarch's *Rime* and the *Sonnets* are confessional and Christian. The only other insight he offers is that her pilgrimage is in the opposite direction frrom Petrarch's (p.262). He does not discuss any of the other differences between Mrs. Browning's sonnet sequence and the more traditional ones of the Petrarchan convention. He sums up:

> . . . like the poets before her, Mrs. Browning selected of a now hallowed English tradition what was important to her and added to the tradition her own distinctive marks (p. 259).

He does not feel, as I do, that her Petrarchanism becomes confused—even unrecognizable—and that her sonnet sequence takes on a completely different shape (which I find analogous to that of the *Song of Songs*).

19. See especially the "kiss poems" in *Astrophil and Stella*.

20. In this she is somewhat reminiscent of Stella (though, as I have said, she cannot really be identified with her): "Trust me while I thee deny, / In myself the smart I try. . . ." (Bender, p. 385). Stella resists for the sake of her own honour, however; Mrs. Browning primarily for the sake of her lover.

21. This sonnet has much in common with Emily Dickinson's "My Life had stood—a Loaded Gun". In both cases, it is the male figure that determines the activity of the female.

Emily Dickinson admired Mrs. Browning very highly, and I suspect the influence was strong. Consider for example this poem of Emily Dickinson's:

> My Worthiness is all my Doubt—
> His Merit—all my fear—
> Contrasting which, my quality
> Do lowlier—appear—
>
> Lest I should insufficient prove
> For His beloved Need—
> The Chiefest Apprehension
> Upon my thronging Mind—

(*Complete Poems*, ed. T. H. Johnson, Boston, Little, Brown, 1960, p. 368).

Some of Dickinson's most unorthodox ideas might have found their germ in the poetry of Mrs. Browning. Mrs. Browning sees her lover on the throne of God; Dickinson puts God and the lover into open conflict for her soul. Mrs. Browning and Emily Dickinson both see human love as sanctifying their lives and raising their station in life. Both link Love, Death, the lover, and God. Some of the similarities between these two women are striking. A convincing sample comparison would be between sonnet XXXVIII ("First time he kissed me. . . .") and Dickinson's poem number 506 ("He touched me, so I live to know"). Both the women are transfigured by the touch of the lover. Emily Dickinson feels she has "brushed a Royal Gown"; Mrs. Browning that she has had "the chrism of love." Compare also their subtle ambivalence towards marriage (see Dickinson's "She rose to His Requirement—dropt," and "He put the Belt around my life").

22. The contrast is interesting, because at the time Elizabeth had a much greater literary reputation than had Robert. That she really believed her work inferior (as most of us do now) is, to my mind, unlikely. But it was necessary for her to see their poetic talents as commensurate with their personal worth. She felt that Browning had more to offer; therefore it was natural, in the context of the sonnets, to characterize him as the greater poet.

23. Bender, p. 333.
24. Shakespeare, p. 40 (sonnet 76).
25. Shakespeare, p. 30 (sonnet 55).
26. Shakespeare, p. 12 (sonnet 19).
27. John Donne, "The Canonization," *Donne*, New York, Dell, 1962, p. 33.

"Old Maids Have Friends": The Unmarried Heroine of Trollope's Barsetshire Novels

JUDITH WEISSMAN

For my friend Jane Alpert

Anthony Trollope deserves more praise than he has received for standing up to his readers and refusing to marry Lily Dale, the heroine of the last two Barsetshire novels, to her long-time suitor. Lily Dale is a unique character in the eighteenth-and nineteenth-century English novel—a woman who is jilted and then, with pride and dignity, declares herself an old maid. Old maids in literature are virtually all objects of humor or pity, but Trollope's unusual sympathy and tenderness towards his characters, the source of the greatness of all the Barsetshire novels, enables him to treat her with respect.[1] In the course of the six novels, Trollope gradually becomes more and more concerned with writing about women, until in *The Last Chronicle of Barset* he portrays a whole country community, bound together primarily by friendships between women, which can embrace an old maid like Lily Dale.[2]

In the first four Barsetshire novels—*The Warden, Barchester Towers, Doctor Thorne,* and *Framley Parsonage*—Trollope attempts to build his stories around a fairly conventional comic marriage plot, but has little success.[3] The plots are contrived, and the young lovers are relatively uninteresting. Trollope is so uncomfortable with romantic comedy, in fact, that he forces his readers to recognize his uneasiness with narrative comments like, "The end of a novel, like the end of a children's dinner party, must be made up of sweet-meats and sugar plums."[4] Trollope's heart is not with his young lovers, but with his old people, especially those who are unmarried or widowed, and with their tender and lasting friendships. Most novelists concentrate on bringing heroes and heroines together in marriage, which provides an elegant and ceremonious ending for the novel; and most novelists neglect friendship, though it is as important as romantic love in the lives of many people. Friendship is not centered in a ceremony that can contribute to artistic form, and Trollope's interest in friendship cannot be separated from the structure of his Barsetshire novels: they are loose, rambling chronicle novels—different from all previous English novels—which build up a sense of the ongoing life of a community instead of focusing primarily on the beginning of a new nuclear family.

Trollope fully develops his country community only in the last two Barsetshire novels, *The Small House at Allington* and *The Last Chronicle of Barset*. Unmarried people predominate in these novels not because Trollope wants to suggest the sterility of the dying life of the country, as some critics have claimed, but because Trollope writes best about people like the Earl and Lady Julia de Guest, Christopher Dale, Hopkins the gardener.[5] These characters are, in general, less superficially attractive than the unmarried eccentrics of the earlier novels, like Septimus Harding and Monica Thorne, but they are also more seriously moral, and demonstrate love and loyalty that the earlier characters are never called upon to show.

After Bell Dale is married, the three Dales who remain together as the central family of Allington are all unmarried, and Trollope's presentation of all of them, especially the two women, Lily and her mother, is unusually sympathetic for the period. For example, his narrator respects Mary Dale's devotion of herself to her daughters, but nevertheless says, "I think that Mrs. Dale was wrong. She would have joined that party on the croquet ground, instead of remaining among the pea-sticks in her sun bonnet, had she done as I would have counselled her."[6] Comments like this are so matter-of-fact that their moral greatness has been slighted.[7] Although Trollope admits the faults of earlier characters, at no point before this does he say that he wishes that one of his favorite characters could have been different—and thus make us aware that he is refusing to change that character in order to fulfill his own idea of proper development. Trollope's refusal to change Mary Dale is evidence of a moral consciousness equal to that of writers usually considered much greater than he. It has the same meaning as Blake's proverb of Hell, that the most sublime act is to set another before you; it embodies the kind of sympathy that George Eliot keeps praising in *Middlemarch*, and is free from the self-congratulatory quality that mars many of her declarations of sympathy with characters like Mr. Casaubon.

Mary Dale's daughter Lily, the heroine of this essay, is the first young woman in the Barsetshire novels whom Trollope treats as tenderly as he does his older characters. Through her, Trollope goes beyond his earlier skepticism about comic endings of novels and openly defies the convention which declares that heroes and heroines shall be married and become a symbol or order in the world and continuity in society. Lily Dale is the first important heroine in the English novel who falls in love with someone who clearly does not deserve her, suffers, and neither learns some kind of lesson that enables her later to fall in love with the right person—like Dorothea Brooke or Amelia Sedley—nor comes to a tragic end—like Scott's Rebecca.[8]

Not endowed with the extraordinary wisdom of the nineteen-year-old heroines of other novels who manage to choose the right man, she is won by the good looks, superficial charm, and spurious affection of Adolphus Crosbie, a man whom she calls a "swell" as soon as she meets him. We wince at his inquiries about her dowry and cringe at the hollowness of his talk about what a little angel she is; we know that her mother, Johnny Eames, her cousin Bernard, and Hopkins (who says he would like to punch Crosbie's head even before he jilts Lily) are right to distrust him. The narrator leaves no doubt in our minds about Crosbie, saying, while Crosbie is still in Allington, "No; he was not a generous man,—a very ungenerous man" (p. 134).

Trollope lets us know immediately that we must distrust Crosbie because he is not particularly interested in sharpening our power to see through lies and hyprocrisy, as Jane Austen is in her subtle presentation of Wickham, a rather similar villain. Our disillusionment about Wickham follows the moral and intellectual development of Elizabeth Bennet, who is in many ways like Lily Dale. Witty and rather aggressive in comparison with their quiet older sisters, both win us with their openness, honesty, and freshness; and both are fooled by and infatuated with handsome seductive liars. Jane Austen, however, would never tell us that Wickham is a scoundrel before Elizabeth knows it, because she would then destroy our identification with Elizabeth's sharp intelligence and rationality, the faculties through which she finally learns to see and judge truly. In a novel of Jane Austen's, any woman who remained deceived by foppery and dishonesty would be unworthy of our regard.

Trollope asks us to be gentler with Lily Dale than Jane Austen would. Knowing that she is being deceived, we also must see that high intelligence is not enough to free an extremely passionate young woman (Trollope is surprisingly explicit about Lily's physical pleasure in touching and kissing Crosbie) from her attachment to an unworthy man. Without presenting her as self-destructive or masochistic, he lets us see that her love for Crosbie is influenced by some unfortunate cultural commonplaces. For example, when she tells Crosbie that she wants to show him off because he is her bird, whom she bagged with her own gun, she reveals that she looks at love as a game and a contest in a way that her sister Bell, who loves more quietly and happily, does not. She seems to believe in the eighteenth-century maxim that a reformed rake makes the best husband, and glories in her conquest of the "swell." Because she is nineteen, inexperienced, and passionate, her love for Crosbie is foolish; but it is not surprising, and Trollope asks that we not condemn her. The reader wants to join her friends and family in defending and comforting her; we want to punish Crosbie for jilting her and want to make her know that he is worthless. But Trollope's purpose is to make us learn to sympathize with her, because he believes, sadly, that "love does not follow worth, and is not given to excellence;—nor is it destroyed by ill-usage, nor killed by blows and mutilation" (p. 291). He is not praising Lily's great devotion to Crosbie, but is simply trying to make us remember that we cannot always believe in the orderly patterns of novels like Jane Austen's, in which love does follow worth.

The desperation of Lily's love for Crosbie is partly the result of a cultural change that is beyond her control, and probably even beyond her consciousness—the movement of economic power from the country to the city. Crosbie can come into the country from London and exploit Lily, almost as Alec D'Urberville can exploit Tess, both because she is too innocent to see through him and because Barchester is now lacking in young men with whom she might have fallen in love, or against whom she might have judged Crosbie. Johnny Eames is the one eligible young man whom she knows, and although her family and friends all want him to marry her and cure her misery, she and the reader both know that he really is not good enough for her. He is decent, pleasant, and devoted to Lily; but he has left the country for a job in the economic bureaucracy of London and has also left behind an ideal of manliness that Trollope associates with the old-fashioned country community. In both *The Small House at Allington* and *The Last Chronicle of Barset* he carries on a flirtation in London with a woman whom he despises, the first time in relative innocence, the next time in total cynicism; but unlike Tom Jones, he does not grow as a result of his contact with the corruption of the city. Trollope does not judge Johnny very harshly, but we cannot help seeing that his careless proposal to Amelia Roper is not absolutely different from Crosbie's to Lily. Crosbie and Johnny are both city men, and though Crosbie is infinitely worse than Johnny, they both lack the character of the older generation of Barsetshire men.[9]

In *the Last Chronicle of Barset* Trollope continues the story of Lily and Johnny and increases our sympathy with her refusal to marry him in two ways: he makes her grow more than Johnny does, and he develops the contrast of the country and the city in order to emphasize the superiority of Lily's community to Johnny's. London, in Trollope's view, contains some admirable people, like Mr. Toogood, but it is predominantly a world of dull civil servants and dishonest speculators and money lenders, people who embody the quiet disintegration of humanity. It is significant, in connection with Lily Dale's refusal to marry, that most of the marriages in *The Last Chronicle of Barset* take place in London and are between dull or unpleasant people. The ostensibly comic ending created by the large number of marriages in the book turns on comic tradition much more harshly than the quiet ironies at the ends of *Barchester Towers* and *Framley Parsonage* do; marriage is almost as unpleasant here as it is at the end of *Measure for Measure.*

Only the marriage of Grace Crawley and Henry Grantly, which takes place in the country, is moving. The romance is a repetition of the plot of *Doctor Thorne* and *Framley Parsonage*, but now is more than a perfunctory feature of the plot around which the interesting characters exist. Because Henry Grantly, his father, the Archdeacon, Grace Crawley, and her family all ask for and are given love and support from their friends in Barsetshire, the marriage plot is primarily a vehicle through which Trollope can affirm the vitality of the community. In the course of the six Barsetshire chronicles,

Trollope has made the community greater and greater, more and more loving. Although he can make no promises that this community, made up largely of people who have grown better with age, will endure in the face of the threat from London, nevertheless he has asserted its value. Such communities are rare in the English novel; Jane Austen's Highbury is comparable, but it is not tested by crime and death as Trollope's Barsetshire is. Here, in the last Barsetshire novel, Trollope has turned his earlier skepticism about the validity of a comic pattern that ends in marriage and the beginning of a new nuclear family into a vision of a positive alternative, a larger community of people bound together by extended families and friendships.[10]

Lily Dale must be understood as part of this Barsetshire community. Four years after being jilted by Adolphus Crosbie, she is still living with her mother, still being courted by Johnny Eames, and still being encouraged by her friends and family to marry him. But she has both learned to value her community in a new way and also gained the strength to resist it with an eloquence and seriousness that she lacked in *The Small House at Allington*. Always aware of the value of her friends—her one quarrel with Crosbie was over his request that she give up her friendship with Johnny Eames—she now has a real place in the community, treasuring the friendships of people as different as Mrs. Hearn and Grace Crawley, Johnny Eames and Hopkins.

The most striking change in Lily at the beginning of the book is that she speaks critically, rather than flippantly, about men. What she tells Grace Crawley about her Uncle Christopher clearly shows that she has thought seriously about love:

> His heart, and mind, and general disposition, as they come out in experience and days of trial, are so much better than the samples of them which he puts out on the counter for men and women to judge by. He wears well, and he washes well. . . . The Apollos of the world,—I don't mean in outward looks . . .—but the Apollos in heart, the men—and the women, too,—who are so full of feeling, so soft-natured, so kind, who never say a cross word, who never get out of bed on the wrong side in the morning,—it so often turns out that they won't wash.[11]

She is referring, obviously, to Adolphus Crosbie, but is neither sentimental nor bitter. In recognizing that he is one of a very seductive type about which she had been ignorant, she has come to appreciate the kind of people who have been the heart of the Barsetshire novels—odd, staunch, loyal, and devoted to their friends.

She also speaks more openly of the unfairness of sexual roles as they are socially defined than any of Trollope's genial narrators ever do:

> Now, with women, it is supposed that they can amuse themselves or live without amusement. Once or twice in a year, perhaps something is done for them. There is an arrow shooting party, or a ball, or a picnic. But the catering for men's sport is never ending, and is always paramount to everything else. And yet the pet game of the day never goes off properly . . . So they go back to their clubs and their cards, and their billiards and abuse their cooks and blackball their friends (p. 77).

Nothing in George Eliot or John Stuart Mill, both known for their concern for the oppression of women as Trollope is not, surpasses this as a condemnation of the shallow exploitive life that is allowed to men. The intellectual recognition implicit in Lily's words, that she was to Crosbie the object of a socially acceptable male sport, has contributed to the emotional distance from her suffering that is now part of her strength.

She also tells Grace explicitly that women are victims in the game of courting (apparently without considering that things might change):

> A man may assure himself that he will find for himself a wife who shall be learned, or beautiful, or six feet high, if he wishes it, or who has red hair, or red eyes, or red checks,—just what he pleases; and he may go about till he finds it, as you can go about and match your worsteds. You are a fool if you buy a colour you don't want, but we can never match our worsted for that other piece of work, but are obliged to take any colour that comes, and therefore it is that we make such a jumble of it (p. 238).

Her new wisdom is shared by her mother, who reflects, after meeting Henry Grantly:

> And Grace had chanced to come across this man, and to please his eye, and satisfy his taste, and be loved by him. And the result of that chance would be that Grace would have everything given to her that the world has to give worth acceptance. . . . But her daughter, her Lily, had come across a man who was a scoundrel, and, as the consequence of that meeting, all her life was marred! Could any credit be given to Grace for her success, or any blame attached to Lily for the failure? Surely not the latter! (p. 224)

Trollope does not suggest a complete reformation of sexual customs, but the women of the Dale family radically criticize one of the cruelest presuppositions of our culture, one reinforced by almost all English novels—that a woman's marital status reflects her worth. Both of these women have gained wisdom without losing warmth; Lily does not condemn herself for having loved extravagantly, but encourages Grace to abandon herself to love and to worship Henry Grantly for remaining loyal to her when her family is disgraced. She wants to believe in Henry because she wants to believe, in spite of her own experience, that "there is something of the poetry and nobleness of love left" (p. 222).

She wants romantic love to exist, but in the course of *The Last Chronicle of Barset* learns not to want it for herself. Though early in the book she tells Grace rather sadly that she knows that she is considered an old maid, she does not really accept this definition of herself until the end of the book. She must first reconsider both her love for Crosbie and her lack of romantic love for Johnny Eames before she can be at peace with herself. When Crosbie sends her mother a letter claiming that he has always loved Lily and would to see her again now that he is a widower, Lily must decide whether or not to see him. She tells her mother, finally, that she still loves him, but nevertheless will not see him, for "he would condemn me because I had borne what he had done to me, and had still loved him—loved him through it all. He would feel and know the weakness;—and there is weakness. I have been weak in not being able to rid myself of him altogether" (p. 185). Even here she has come a long way from her extravagantly romantic and self-glorifying declarations of widowhood in *The Small House at Allington.* And she finally gives up this emotional attachment which she condemns in herself when she goes to London. Staying with her new friend Emily Dunstable, who is enjoying her engagement to Bernard Dale, Lily feels her own bitterness at being single and expresses it more openly than she ever does at Allington: "things have gone wrong with me" (p. 425). This unhappiness, though temporary, is very deep and saves her from the charge of priggishness in her refusal to marry, made by Trollope himself in his autobiography and also by many critics. She is shocked into a new understanding of herself and a newly coherent resolution to be single by two accidental meetings with Crosbie in London:

> To tell the truth, the vision of the man had disenchanted her. When last she had seen him he had been as it were a god to her; and though, since that day, his conduct to her had been as ungodlike as it well might be, still the memory of the outward signs of his divinity had remained with her. It is difficult to explain how it had come to pass that the glimpse which she had had of him should have altered so much within her mind;—why she should so suddenly have come to regard him in an altered light. It was not simply that he looked to be older, and because his face was careworn. It was not only that he had lost that look of an Apollo which Lily had once in her mirth attributed to him. I think it was chiefly that she herself was older, and could no longer see a god in such a man. She had never regarded Johnny Eames as being gifted with divinity, and had therefore always been making comparisons to his discredit. Any such comparison now would tend quite the other way. Nevertheless she would adhere to the two letters in her book. Since she had seen Mr. Crosbie she was altogether out of love with the prospect of matrimony (pp. 436–7).

Trollope's narrator is rather reticent, perhaps because he does not want to imply superiority to Lily by articulating her feelings more clearly than she could. Nevertheless, we understand: the realization that she has loved a phantom for years makes Lily see the weakness, as she calls it, in her personality, a weakness that she believes makes marriage impossible for her. And the narrator simply respects her judgment, as he respects her mother's choice of self-denial. To analyze and comment too closely would be to intrude, and the heart of Trollope's greatness is his belief in the sanctity—and privacy—of the individual self. More than Fielding or Dickens or Austen, or even, I think, Eliot or James, Trollope gives us a sense that the personality is a mystery with which he must not meddle.

Whatever Lily learns from seeing Crosbie again brings her to the most haunting and sorrowful statement that she ever makes about herself. The second time that she refuses to marry Johnny she says that she no longer loves Crosbie but still cannot love him, and explains herself only with a metaphor. "If you take a young tree and split it, it still lives, perhaps. But it isn't a tree. It is only a fragment" (p. 627). She uses the common Romantic analogy between the mysteriously growing personality and the tree, but uses it negatively: the personality that develops as a tree grows can also be as irreversibly hurt as a tree and as powerless to correct itself. Lily, like her Uncle Christopher, her mother, and the Earl de Guest, lacks the resilience to love again and will not pretend to be different from her true self and claim to love Johnny Eames for the sake of pleasing everyone who cares about her.

Very different, however, from this sorrowful self-knowledge is the jaunty dignity with which she publicly defies her family and friends, both old and new, who try to persuade her to marry Johnny. Mrs. Arabin especially pushes her to new wisdom by asking that she marry Johnny to reward him for his goodness on behalf of the Crawleys. Virtue is rewarded by marriage in most English novels since *Pamela*, and Mrs. Arabin, good and kind as she is, does not yet understand why Lily will not turn herself into a character in a novel that other people would like to see written. Lily understands herself fully only after she answers Mrs. Arabin foolishly, saying that she has to stay with her mother. "As soon as these words were out of her mouth, she hated herself for having spoken them. There was a maudlin, missish, namby-pamby sentimentality about them which disgusted her" (p. 622). It is not love for Crosbie or loyalty to her mother that prevents her from marrying Johnny Eames; it is her refusal to violate herself. She has developed the great personal integrity that characterizes Trollope's older characters and has become a true individual—the kind of person valued by the many Victorian writers who feared that the growing pressure of conformity would destroy all personal strength and dignity. Lily demonstrates her defiant pride when she says, soon after her conversation with Mrs. Arabin, "I know in what college I'll take my degree, and I wish they'd let me write the letters after my name as the men do. . . . O.M., for Old Maid. I don't see why it shouldn't be as good as B.A. for Bachelor of Arts. It would mean a great deal more" (p. 623). It is daring simply for Lily to suggest, in the mid-nineteenth century, that she might get a college degree; it is defiant for her to claim that the words old maid might have the same connotations of independence as the word bachelor, and that a single woman might deserve the same respect as a single man. Her declaration that she intends to remain single is as clear a symbol of her education as a college diploma.

The subjects of her education have been her self and her relation to the community. Without wavering in her love for her friends and family, she demands that they learn to understand her. When Emily Dunstable reminds her that she has gone against the wishes of all her friends in refusing Johnny Eames, she answers, "That is true, and yet I have settled it rightly, and I would not for worlds have it unsettled again. There are matters on which friends should not have wishes, or at any rate should not express them" (p. 628). Marriage is a community concern when people like Grace Crawley and Henry Grantly wish to be married and must overcome the objections of their families, but the community has no right to interfere, or even comment, when someone has chosen not to be married. Lily will, we understand, have her way in Barsetshire; "in these days she could assume a manner, and express herself with her eyes as well as with her voice, after a fashion, which was apt to silence unwelcome questioners, even though they were as intimate with her as was her cousin Bernard" (p. 628). Barsetshire can learn from and yield to the individual in a way that Middlemarch, George Eliot's country community, cannot. It is, after all, a community of eccentric individuals, and Trollope is satisfied to see Lily become a woman like her mother or Lady Lufton or Monica Thorne or Lady Julia de Guest. These women and the men like them are not outcasts or misfits, for they bind the community together through friendship. As Lily tells Johnny Eames, "Old maids have friends" (p. 28); unmarried people often have more love to give to friends than married people have. She understands the goodness of the Barsetshire community better than the people who want her to marry. She knows, as we do, that its special blessing is to embrace the people who have been neglected in the English novel—people who are old, or lonely, or silent, or even unmarried.

Notes

1. Trollope's tenderness towards his characters has been discussed by several critics; among the best are Hugh Walpole, in *Anthony Trollope* (New York: MacMillan, 1928), p. 55; and Bradford Booth, in *Anthony Trollope: Aspects of His Life and Art* (Bloomington: Indiana University Press, 1958), p. 190.

2. The women of Barsetshire are barely considered in the essays on Trollope's women—"The Servility of Dependence: The Dark Lady in Trollope," by Charles Blenderman, in *Images of Women in Fiction: Feminist Perspectives* (Bowling Green: 1972); and "Trollope's Young Women," by P. Hansford Johnson, in *On the Novel: A Present for Walter Allen on his Sixtieth Birthday from his Friends and Colleagues* (London: Dent, 1971).

3. The superficiality and conventionality of Trollope's romantic plots have been discussed by Bradford Booth (*op. cit.,* p. 190) and A. O. J. Cockshut, in *Anthony Trollope: A Critical Study* (London: Collins, 1955), p. 111.

4. *Barchester Towers* (New York: Random House, 1950), p. 742.

5. In "The Unfortunate Moth: Unifying Theme in *The Small House at Allington*," *Nineteenth Century Fiction* 26: 127–144, Juliet McMaster argues that most of the characters are self-destructive. She concludes: "in that each has to some extent resolved 'evil, be thou my good,' all his characters belong in some self-tormenting pandemonium, and its inner sanctum is the Small House at Allington" (p. 144). As I will argue, her judgmental psychology is antithetical to Trollope's profound respect for the individual. Robert Polhemus, in *The Changing World of Anthony Trollope* (Berkeley and Los Angeles: University of California Press, 1968) says that by writing about a large number of unmarried people in *The Small House in Allington* Trollope "purposely creates a pattern of infertility in a stagnant and impotent society" (p. 91). He also has applied a false standard of psychological health to these characters without noticing the extraordinary amount of love that exists among them.

6. *The Small House at Allington* (New York: Dutton), p. 20. Subsequent quotations are from this edition and are in the text.

7. Passages like this, together with Trollope's moral stand concerning Lily, necessitate a reconsideration of the critical tradition that praises Trollope for doing such a very fine job of simply describing things as they are: This tradition is epitomized by Michael Sadlier's remark in *Trollope–A Commentary* (New York: Farrar, Straus, 1947) that "in the tale of English literature he is—to put the matter in a phrase—the supreme novelist of acquiescence" (p. 367).

8. Lily Dale has been the subject of more critical commentary than any other character in the Barsetshire novels. I suspect that part of the reason is that Trollope himself virtually disowns her in his autobiography by calling her a female prig and claiming not to understand why his readers love her so—even though the words he has given her, especially in *The Last Chronicle of Barset*, contradict everything that he says about her in his autobiography. Most critics have agreed with his later comments rather than with his fictional creation. Juliet McMaster sees her as the most self-destructive person in a whole group of self-destructive people. Bradford Booth claims that she has become so warped that in *The Last Chronicle of Barset* Johnny Eames is too good for her (*op. cit.*, p. 52). Robert Polhemus calls her perverse, selfish, and sentimental (*op. cit.* p. 94). James Pope Hennessy quotes and agrees with a comment by Sir Edward March, that a group of young women in Trollope have the strange conviction that once they have loved one person they can never love again, and that this conviction not only renders the women unhappy, but makes them "almost unendurable nuisances to their families and friends," in *Anthony Trollope* (London: Jonathan Cape, 1971), p. 252. He ignores, at least in the case of Lily Dale, the facts that some of the men in the community, like her Uncle Christopher and the Earl de Guest, share her love ethic, and that she is a joy to her family and friends.

9. G. M. Harvey, in "Heroes in Barsetshire," *Dalhousie Review* 52: 458–468, discusses the connection between Trollope and Carlyle in their ideas about the growing dominance of gray bureaucracies and the gradual disintegration of human beings. He sees that Johnny is not a hero, but calls his flaw egoism rather than weakness.

10. I disagree with Robert Polhemus' reading of *The Last Chronicle of Barset*. He claims that "the title itself announces that the old individualistic Barset way of life is finished and has no future" (*op. cit.*. p. 133). I believe that the life of the community is much stronger here than in any of the other Barsetshire novels.

11. *The Last Chronicle of Barset* (Boston: Houghton Mifflin, 1964), p. 133. All subsequent quotations are noted in the text and are to this edition.

Beauty in Distress: *Daniel Deronda* and *The House of Mirth*

Constance Rooke

In an essay on Edith Wharton's *The House of Mirth*, Richard Poirier compares that novel to *Middlemarch* and asserts that "Mrs. Wharton's critical admiration for George Eliot seems to have become a determining factor in *The House of Mirth*."[1] He believes that Wharton has adopted George Eliot's vocabulary, but that it has "the ring of platitude because it is given no nourishing connections to the dramatic substance of the novel."[2] Wharton's difficulty, he claims, is that "sharing George Eliot's attitudes, she is deprived of George Eliot's resources—a society in which there really were 'grave and endearing traditions' still in visible and even audible evidence."[3] Poirier is thinking particularly of the importanc of "roots" in the formation of character and quotes the following account of the heroine's deprivation in *The House of Mirth*:

> And as she looked back she saw that there had never been a time when she had any real relation to life. Her parents too had been rootless, blown hither and thither on every wind of fashion, without any personal existence to shelter them from its shifting gusts. She herself had grown up without any one spot of earth being dearer to her than another: there was no center of early pieties, of grave endearing traditions, to which her heart could revert and from which it could draw strength for itself and tenderness for others. In whatever form a slowly-accumulated past lives in the blood—whether in the concrete image of the old house stored with visual memories, or in the conception of the house not built with hands, but made up of inherited passions and loyalties—it has the same power of broadening and deepening the individual existence, of attaching it by mysterious links of kinship to all the mighty sum of human striving.[4]

Poirier contrasts Lily Bart's poverty in this respect with the moral wealth of the Garths who are so deeply rooted in the world of *Middlemarch*. There is, however, a more appropriate and far more striking comparison to be made with the last of George Eliot's novels, *Daniel Deronda*. In the following passage the verbal echoes (of roots, the spot of earth, kinship, memories, blood, tenderness, and endearment) are as inescapable as the sameness of the idea:

> Pity that Offendene was not the home of Miss Harleth's childhood, or endeared to her by family memories! A human life, I think, should be well rooted in some spot of native land, where it may get the love of tender kinship for the face of earth, for the labours men go forth to, for the sounds and accents that haunt it, for whatever will give that early home a familiar unmistakable difference amidst the future widening of knowledge: a spot where the definiteness of early memories may be inwrought with affection, and kindly acquaintance with all neighbors, even to the dogs and donkeys, may spread not by sentimental effort and reflection, but as a sweet habit of the blood. At five years old, mortals are not prepared to be citizens of the world, to be stimulated by abstract nouns, to soar above preference into inpartiality; and that prejudice in favour of milk with which we blindly begin, is a type of the way body and soul must get nourished at least for a time. The best introduction to astronomy is to think of the nightly heavens as a little lot of stars belonging to one's own homestead.[5]

In each case it is the absence of this ideal beginning for moral growth which occasions the reflections of the author. Admittedly, the Gwendolen Harleth whom we are to pity for her lack of roots must be measured against the exemplary Daniel Deronda who has been morally enriched by both houses referred to in the parallel quotation from *The House of Mirth*—the literal homestead and "the conception of the house not built with hands" which Deronda acquires when he becomes aware of himself as a Jew. But it is worth noting that Deronda leaves England to pursue a Zionist ideal, and we may conclude that his exit is not so much a natural consequence of the direction he has discovered for himself as his Zionism is an authorial invention whose purpose is to get him out of an unhealthy England. The society in which Deronda and Gwendolen have lived is very nearly as morally defunct as Lily's New York in *The House of Mirth*. Both George Eliot and Edith Wharton are obliged to go outside the dramatic substance of the societies they portray, as well as to fringe characters of a humble sort, in order to shadow forth a sanctified community.

The early lack of rootedness shared by Gwendolen and Lily extends to their larger deprivation, the absence of an ethically viable society. Hypocrisy and materialism are among the most conspicuous qualities of the world in which Gwendolen and Lily move, but the related issue of woman's place in that world is of particular interest to the novelists and to us. One intention of this paper is to establish *Daniel Deronda* as a significant influence upon *The House of Mirth*. That Wharton had read *Daniel Deronda* is proven by her references to that novel in a review of Leslie Stephen's *George Eliot*; that she was influenced by it in writing *The House of Mirth* will be shown by a comparison of the texts.[6] Indeed, the parallels are so extensive that *The House of Mirth* might be thought simply derivative were it not for the important circumstance that Wharton was contending with a social as well as a literary model. The second intention of this paper, therefore, is to suggest that the parallels between the two novels reveal their common and essential concern with the perverse socialization of woman. In particular, the *tableaux vivants* appearing in both novels will be examined as symbolic of woman's plight.

Lily Bart and Gwendolen Harleth are beautiful young women whose characters have been warped by the corrupt societies in which they live, and whose appetites for luxury, power and pre-eminence run counter to their better aspirations. As willing creatures of a corrupt society, both women are subjected to satirical attack by their authors; but as helpless creatures, victims of a society that has not provided them with either salutary values or an honorable means of growth, Lily and Gwendolen are—both in intention and in effect—intensely sympathetic. In fact, their pursuit of exalted financial and social status may be excusable to us and even admirable as an expression of energy. When another expression of energy becomes possible, when an extremely difficult but ethically viable route is shown to them, both women attempt it, Their careers are parallel in the sense that both grow toward moral responsibility and away from the commitment to luxury and dominion. In both novels, ascending and descending curves are described simultaneously. Gwendolen experiences moral qualms prior to her marriage, and these accelerate as her satisfaction in the status she has achieved decreases. Lily's social status and so her opportunities for making a brilliant match decline in a regular progression throughout the novel, each loss being occasioned by an impulse which reveals her increasing moral probity.

Gwendolen and Lily have experienced in early youth the pleasures of wealth and the less happy consciousness of that wealth being markedly less than each feels she deserves by virtue of her general superiority. Both then lose their limited means and go on to experience painfully straitened circumstances. They rebel at the vicissitudes of fortune, at the injustice to their own deserts, and determine not simply to regain but to surpass their original positions in society. In times of relative poverty both go to obscure European watering places, where they bemoan the loss of a proper setting in which to be viewed by those who are of any real social account. Both gamble—at roulette or bridge—in order to recoup their losses. It is borne home to both women that when one player wins, another necessarily loses—and that there may therefore be culpability in success. Both lose at their gambling, but as a symbolic consequence win ethically in the end. Lily undergoes two major financial setbacks: one occurs when her parents go bankrupt in their attempt to maintain a foothold in New York society, and the other Lily occasions herself when she loses her aunt's favor. Similarly, Gwendolen's first loss occurs when her mother goes bankrupt, and the second she yields to in order not to profit from an immoral marriage.

The general superiority that each woman feels can be judged in two ways. We may decide that such vanity is very simply excessive, absurd, and reprehensible; or we may feel that it is at least in part a debased version of that crucial sense of self-worth which is denied to most women. Each takes herself originally at the valuation of others, and each is superbly conscious of herself as a beautiful, high-spirited, accomplished, and charming woman. The values which they assign to these qualities may be out of all proportion to their worth, but the values have been assigned first of all by society and not by the women themselves. Gwendolen and Lily have had the good fortune to satisfy these requirements and in consequence have developed a sense of themselves as superior individuals. It is interesting in this connection that neither woman prizes herself simply for the qualities which have led to self-confidence. Each supposes that she will effectively deserve her exalted position by the exercise of a fine aesthetic sense and a diffused benevolence.

Both women are duped by the limited demands that are placed upon their intelligence. While Lily is justified in the belief that her mind works quickly, her intellectual pursuits are in fact restricted to the astute discovery of what little she needs to know about Americana in order to ensnare a wealthy and moronic collector, and to the conveyance (wherever she goes) of an attractive copy of the *Rubiyat*. Neither has she been trained in any purely marketable skill:

> Having been accustomed to take herself at the popular valuation, as a person of energy and resource, naturally fitted to dominate any situation in which she found herself, she vaguely imagined that such gifts would be of value to seekers after social guidance; but there was unfortunately no specific head under which the art of saying and doing the right thing could be offered in the market, and even Mrs. Fisher's resourcefulness failed before the difficulty of discovering a workable vein in the vague wealth of Lily's graces. (*HM*, 310)

When her money runs out altogether, Lily supposes that she will be able to earn a living by the artful trimming of hats. And even this proves a delusion. Similarly, Gwendolen proposes to escape the ignominy of becoming a governess by offering herself instead as an accomplished actress or musician—until she also is confronted by the truth that the drawing room has been a too polite testing ground for her abilities. Despite their gifts, both women are insufficiently trained to be anything but ladies. And the business of a lady is to be married.

When Gwendolen shows a strange reluctance to accept Grandcourt, her uncle (although a clergyman) remarks that a fortune so great " 'almost takes the question out of the range of mere personal feeling, and makes your acceptance of it a duty' " (*DD*, 179). It is a mark of their integrity that both Gwendolen and Lily experience distaste at the thought of being encumbered by a husband who has been married for his money. They try to pass off the looming male presence as a bore or an inconvenience, but both women are covertly afraid of the sexual rights which their husbands will possess. They encourage themselves in the faith that society's double standard of admissable behavior for single and married women will finally be operating in their favor; they hope that by sacrificing one sort of liberty they will have won another.

But Gwendolen, in marrying Grandcourt, and Lily, in pursuing a rich husband, do what they *know* is wrong. In each case, the essential fault—

marrying for money—is aggravated by a complication of the plot. Gwendolen discovers that Grandcourt has been supporting as his mistress one Lydia Glasher and their four illegitimate children. This knowledge prevents Gwendolen from marrying him until the choice narrows down to that or misery as a governess. The Lydia Glasher affair is roughly parallel to an obstacle that arises in the path of Lily's determination to marry Sim Rosedale. Lily is in possession of some damaging letters that have passed between Mrs. Bertha Dorset and Lawrence Selden, and has been urged by Rosedale to use them to restore her reputation (which is in the hands of Bertha) and so make it possible for Rosedale to marry her. Lily resists this inducement to commit blackmail, capitulates, and resists at last—largely because the letters are addressed to a man she loves. Similarly, Gwendolen's reluctance to injure Lydia Glasher is increased by the analogy she perceives between Lydia's illegitimate son (who ought to be Grandcourt's heir) and the apparently illegitimate Daniel Deronda—whom Gwendolen loves. A further parallel consists in the loyalty that both women exhibit here toward their sex. Throughout the novel, Lily has been like a sister to Bertha Dorset, and even now that Bertha's treachery has been revealed she is unwilling to injure her for gain. Likewise, Gwendolen scorns profit from another woman's loss, and extends her analogy to see in the embittered Lydia an image of Deronda's mother whom she assumes to have been wronged.

Lawrence Selden and Daniel Deronda are obviously parallel figures. Both are gentlemen of moderate means who are acceptable socially, but who have "points of contact outside the gilded cage" (*HM*, 64). Both have friends in humble stations to whom they behave gallantly, and Selden has a "republic of the spirit" (*HM*, 79) to match Deronda's dream of Israel. Both have exquisite taste, and both are acted upon by positive early influences. But the most conspicuous indication that Deronda has served as a model for Selden is that both men occupy the curious position of half-lover, half-mentor for the heroine. In both novels, the love of the heroine for the mentor is understated, and in both it is assigned a redemptive value. Neither woman is allowed to marry the mentor who holds himself superior to her. Each woman is morally saved by his influence, and similarly each is failed by his inability to love her enough or at the right time. Each woman believes that the male mentor has her better self in his keeping, and each cares extremely what he thinks of her. Each needs the mentor to show her what life has to offer outside the gilded cage, and each attempts to console *him* when he leaves her trapped within it. Our intense sympathy for Gwendolen and Lily makes it difficult to like the superiority of which Deronda and Seldon are so conscious. We are too apt to prefer the original pride of the heroine to her redemptive but humiliating education at the hands of her mentor. In the case of *The House of Mirth*, we are clearly supposed to be somewhat critical of the male mentor; but in *Daniel Deronda*, the author (at least consciously) intends us wholly to approve of his behavior.

A particularly remarkable parallel between the two novels is that in both the heroine has occasion to go yachting in the Mediterranean. The circumstances vary, but there are tonal similarities: the yacht is in both cases an image of poisoned luxury, and the qualities of drifting and of danger are pronounced in both. Furthermore, Deronda and Selden make appearances in port as accidentally arrived and half-willing rescuers who work to avert catastrophe for the heroine.

Other parallels involve the operations of conscience within the heroine and the related issue of her dealings with other women. Both Gwendolen and Lily exhibit a nervous susceptibility, a restlessness, and a tendency to run away which peculiarly express the stirrings of a desire to be good. Both engage in minor, compensatory acts of charity to other and less fortunate women, yet both are prone to holding themselves aloof from such women. Gerty Farish, who is Selden's cousin in *The House of Mirth*, has a heart of her own and aspirations of her own which Lily is prevented from seeing by her distaste for what she takes to be Gerty's "acquiescence in dinginess" (*HM*, 103). Similarly, the world of *Daniel Deronda* is populated by an army of modest and almost invisible sisters (including Gwendolen's own) whose needs deserve to be remembered along with those of an insistent Gwendolen. At the end of each novel the heroine makes a gesture toward solidarity with her own sex and with the human community at large. In neither case, however, is there much occasion to celebrate. Gwendolen is left clutching the vague and feminine ambition which has been assigned to her by Deronda, that she should "live to be one of the best of women, who make others glad that they were born" (*DD*, 882). She has little sense of what one does next to achieve such a goal, and she has neither lover nor fortune as consolation. Lily's moral redemption ends in suicide: as she dies, Lily imagines that she is embracing the infant daughter of a poor woman to whom she had behaved charitably. Thus, Gwendolen and Lily have at last escaped their vanity and found solace in virtue. They have moved from one stereotype to another, and so expired.

The original entrapment of the heroine is understood and dramatized far more powerfully than her release. In each novel, this trap is imaged by the *tableau vivant* which allows the heroine to display her beauty as if framed for the viewing of male society. *Tableaux vivants*—living pictures—were immensely popular in the last century as a kind of mutedly theatrical parlour game. The *tableaux* were elaborate representations, by a silent and motionless person or group, of a frozen scene from a work of art or literature. Requiring much preparation for a relatively short-lived and dubious effect, they may well strike us as absurd. Equally absurd is that women like Lily Bart have been "brought up to be ornamental" (*HM*, 345). Just as the *tableau vivant* is a mockery of art, so the education of Lily is a mockery of life: "She was like some rare flower grown for exhibition, a flower from which every bud had been nipped except the crowning blossom of her beauty" (*HM*, 369). The "aesthetic amusement" (*HM*, 80) to be derived from the *tableaux vivants* is not quickly to be divorced from sexual appreciation, and is fed by the spectacle (a word often applied to Gwendolen Harleth and Lily

Bart) of lovely women calculatingly revealing themselves as such.

Prior to the scenes in which the *tableaux vivants* are enacted, both women reveal an expertise in self-display. When Gwendolen first enters the music room at Offendene—an aristocratic sort of residence which will provide her beauty with a proper setting—she seizes upon an opportunity to become what her mother calls a charming picture: " 'Here is an organ. I will be Saint Cecelia: someone shall paint me as Saint Cecelia. . . .' She had thrown off her hat and gloves, and seated herself before the organ in a most admirable pose" (*DD*, 55). Gwendolen is perpetually concerned with "the effect of her beauty on a first presentation" (*DD*, 84). She is, however, not content with a merely passive showing of her charms, but wishes to act in a manner appropriate to the type she represents. Thus, when dressed in clothing suggestive of a serpent, she almost unconsciously assumes the movements of a serpent, and when called upon to take part in the Archery Meeting, she dresses herself to represent the goddess Diana. In all of this there is a pathetic nuance, a suggestion that the art object yearns to become an artist.

Lily's energies are also largely occupied in producing a picturesque effect: "The spot was charming, and Lily was not insensible to the charm, or to the fact that her presence enhanced it . . . the combination of a handsome girl and a romantic scene struck her as too good to be wasted. No one, however, appeared to profit by the opportunity" (*HM*, 71). That Lily assumes a posture even in solitude is a tribute to the thoroughness of her education, and that she regrets the absence of a viewer reveals that she has understood its purpose. Lawrence Selden takes a keen interest in her perfectly managed displays and tells Lily that she is indeed an artist: " 'It's part of your cleverness to be able to produce premeditated effects extemporaneously' " (*HM*, 77). The male, at any rate, is surely a connoisseur: "Selden stood where she had left him. He knew too well the transiency of exquisite moments to attempt to follow her" (*HM*, 160). Likewise, in *Daniel Deronda*, Grandcourt congratulates himself upon the recognition that "a cruder lover would have lost the view of her pretty ways and attitudes, and spoiled all by stupid attempts at caresses, utterly destructive of drama" (*DD*, 361). The special poignancy of Gwendolen's display is that, as Grandcourt knows, there will come a time when caresses in fact destroy the drama by turning it to nightmare. She will discover then that an object does not own itself.

Gwendolen is herself the instigator of the *tableaux vivants* that are presented at Offendene. She wishes to renew and extend the impact of her beauty upon local society. Similarly, for Lily "keenest of all was the exhilaration of displaying her own beauty under a new aspect: of showing that her loveliness was no mere fixed quality, but an element shaping all emotions to fresh forms of grace" (*HM*, 152). Gwendolen's concern—like Lily's—is that she should be the focal point of all attention, and she devotes considerable time to discovering a propitious role for herself. Finally, she selects the role of Hermione as the statue in *The Winter's Tale*—because she can wear the Greek dress which she believes is more flattering to her than any other. Certain changes are effected under Gwendolen's direction: "Leontes, instead of embracing her, was to keel and kiss the hem of her garment" (*DD*, 90) and the platform on which Gwendolen stands was to be "elevated by about six inches, which she counted on as a means of showing her pretty foot and instep" (*DD*, 91).

There are ironies attached to Gwendolen's choice of the part of Hermione. The first of these is that she chooses to be a statue, and so underscores the object status which is implicit throughout. Secondly, she refuses the part of the captive Briseis, a slave girl, for the role of the triumphant and long-suffering Hermione—with the intended emphasis upon triumphant. But as Hermione was a slave to Leontes' jealousy, so Gwendolen will find herself captive to Grandcourt.

Despite its successful framing of her beauty, the *tableau vivant* itself is anything but a success. Through a strange working of fate, Gwendolen as Hermione does not return to life on cue. Instead, a panel in the wall of the music room springs open to reveal a macabre representation of death, and Gwendolen is reduced to a state of near-hysteria. It is a striking lesson against vanity that Gwendolen should behold a *mememto mori* on such an occasion, but the image does not stop at this. The dead face and fleeing figure behind the panel had first astonished Gwendolen following her brief imper-sonation of Saint Cecelia—a fact which emphasizes that Gwendolen is often engaged in a species of *tableau vivant.* And they continue to haunt her throughout the book as a prefiguring of the moment when Grandcourt's face will look up to her at the point of drowning. The suggestion is that Gwendolen (the fleeing figure) will be tempted to commit murder as a means of escape from the slavery for which she prepares herself in the self-marketing procedure of the *tableau.* Later in the novel, in what George Eliot explicitly recalls to us as the same room in which Gwendolen had "pleased herself with acting Saint Cecelia" and "achieved the wearing of her Greek dress as Hermione" (*DD*, 294), Gwendolen will seek professional advice from a brilliant musician (Herr Klesmer) who had witnessed and seemingly been impressed by her performance in the *tableau vivant.* There she will discover that such abilities as she has demonstrated would serve her in a career on the stage only as a kind of veil for the role of courtesan. In preference to this, Gwendolen chooses marriage—whereupon another veil descends.

As for the *tableau vivant* in which Lily Bart figures, we are told:

> The impulse to show herself in a splendid setting—she had thought for a moment of representing Tiepolo's Cleopatra—had yielded to the truer instinct of trusting to her unassisted beauty, and she had purposely chosen a picture without distracting accessories of dress or surroundings. (*HM*, 156)

Whereas Gwendolen sought magnificence, limiting suitability to her dress and ignoring such matters as the discrepancy between Hermione's age and her own, Lily (with a more developed sense of her own worth) resists the appeal of a borrowed grandeur and chooses instead "a type so like her own that she could embody the person represented without ceasing to be herself"

(*HM*, 156). She selects Reynolds' portrait of "Mrs. Lloyd Carving Her Husband's Initials in a Tree," as if to remind us that Lily herself is in need of a husband. Like Gwendolen, she chooses the part of an emphatically married woman: symbolically, she capitulates to obtain praise. Lily knows the fate that is required for her ascendancy: in the *tableau* all eyes are satisfactorily focused upon Lily, but at the Van Osburgh wedding she had been obliged to regret that she was not the "mystically veiled figure occupying the center of attention" (*HM*, 102). As Mrs. Lloyd, she wears pseudo-Classical draperies which (although amply accounted for by the conventions of nineteenth century portraiture) may descend in part from Gwendolen's Greek dress.

Both women strive to distinguish themselves from other participants in the *tableaux*. Gwendolen's appearance in "the *tableau* of Hermione was doubly striking from its dissimilarity with what had gone before" (*DD*, 91). The "thrill of contrast" experienced by Lily's audience, however, is specified: while in all the earlier *tableaux* "the personality of the actors had been subdued to the scenes they figured in, "Lily's *tableau* is "simply and undisguisedly the portrait of Miss Bart" (*HM*, 156). The audience is as much shocked by this as by Miss Bart's decidedly inefficient drapery. She disguises nothing of her body, just as she disguises nothing of her ambition or her insistent personality. In something of the same way that George Eliot had manipulated the *tableau* to reveal Gwendolen's fettered strength of personality, so Edith Wharton suggests that Lily desires most passionately to be herself.

Taken together, the responses issuing from various male observers suggest the complex truth of Lily's position in the *tableau vivant*. One such observer is Paul Morpeth, a distinguished portrait painter who is prevailed upon to organize the *tableaux*. In his "abhorrence of the world in which he had seen her" and because he is "immensely struck by Lily's plastic possibilities," (*HM*, 175) Morpeth recalls another unprostituted artist, Herr Klesmer— who had twice described Gwendolen's finale as a magnificent " 'bit of *plastik*' " (*DD*, 92–93). The musician kindly pretends that Gwendolen's loss of control is intentional "plastik"; the painter decides that Lily, for all her "vivid plastic sense" (*HM*, 152) and the grace of her body, has a face " 'too self-controlled for expression" (*HM*, 275). As Gwendolen and Lily feel to their perpetual chagrin, the "plastic possibilities" of woman are sorely limited. Yet both women believe in the necessity of that self-control which chains them to society's mold; they fear a loss of control which hints at their desired freedom.

Lawrence Selden believes that in the *tableau* he has seen "the real Lily Bart, divested of the trivialities of her little world, and catching for a moment a note of that eternal harmony of which her beauty was a part" (*HM*, 157). This response is like Rex Gascoigne's to Gwendolen, each man being half-deluded in the faith "that the fundamental identity of the good, the true and the beautiful . . . is manifest in the object of his love" (*DD*, 99). Both authors (because they are in love with beauty) are attracted to this idea, and they allow themselves to credit some vague, residual truth that it contains. But clearly for Eliot and Wharton there is no necessary connection between beauty and moral worth. Although "some of the goodness which Rex believed in was there," the youthful lover is absurd in his inability to "conceive a more perfect girl" (*DD*, 99). And Selden's sentiments are undercut by Lily's bestowal of the same melting look upon Ned Van Alstyne and George Dorset as upon Selden himself; under the spell of male admiration "she lost something of her natural fastidiousness, and cared less for the quality of admiration received than for its quantity" (*HM*, 158).

Both women attempt to convert object status to dominion by the assertion of personality, and in so far as they reach for themselves as well as for power over others the response of an observer like Selden is justified. However deeply enmeshed they are at the moment by the "trivialities" of their society, "the real Lily Bart" and the real Gwendolen Harleth (both what is captive and what is free in them) are fully represented in the still point of the *tableaux*. Only the worst of it is contained in Jack Stepney's brutally accurate observation that Lily is "a girl standing there as if she were up at auction" (*HM*, 183). Thus, both women—Gwendolen in *Daniel Deronda* and Lily in *The House of Mirth*—are caught forever between a world in which they may appear to rule but are in fact up at auction, and a world not yet realized in which they can own and be themselves.

Notes

1. Richard Poirer, "Edith Wharton: *The House of Mirth,*" *The American Novel from James Fenimore Cooper to William Faulkner* (N.Y.: Basic Books, 1965), p. 126.

2. Ibid., p. 128.

3. Ibid., p. 129.

4. Edith Wharton, *The House of Mirth* (New York: Holt, Rinehart and Winston, 1962), p. 371. All subsequent references are to this edition and are indicated parenthetically in the text.

5. George Eliot, *Daniel Deronda* (Middlesex: Penguin Books, 1973), p. 50. All subsequent references are to this edition and are indicated parenthetically in the text.

6. Edith Wharton, Review of *George Eliot* by Leslie Stephen, in *Bookman,* XV (May 1902), 247–251.

Rebellions of Good Women

PATRICIA MEYER SPACKS

When Kate Millett, in 1970, declared Charlotte Brontë's novel *Villette* "an expression of revolutionary sensibility," she inaugurated a new view of the Brontë sisters.[1] Virginia Woolf, half a century earlier, had noted the "anger" of Charlotte Brontë's fiction as a female emotion marring the writer's achievement.[2] In the context of a new wave of feminism, that anger seemed, rather, a valuable source of literary energy. Both Charlotte and Emily Brontë wrote of women who defied convention, declaring the individual's right to freedom; behind the disguise of romantic fiction both authors can be seen to articulate fundamental feminist principles and the psychic forces that underlie them.

Although this view represents a valuable new perspective, it requires modification. The emotional power of the Brontës' fiction derives not from their anger alone but also from a complex perception of the needs and desires of women in relation to their realizable possibilities. The women the Brontës imagine want to be free, certainly. But they also want intensely to be *good*. To examine the moral issue of Brontë novels as the characters themselves perceive them suggests that the heroines depicted suffer less from the class between personal impulse and conventional restriction than from a profound inner conflict of opposed needs. Victorian convention, as it happens, supports one set of needs and not the other; but both remain real. Charlotte and Emily Brontë both fantasize powerful male beings who surmount or avoid the fundamental conflict and who express without penalty their aggressive wishes, but both novelists prove unable to imagine such fully successful reconciliation for females. Women's moral condition, the Brontë novels make us feel, almost inevitably involves serious psychic conflict. Partly for social, partly for personal reasons, women experience with special intensity the opposing claims of self and others, valuing the fulfillments of selflessness as well as the gritifications of self-indulgence.

The nature of female moral experience has always caused perplexity, for both sexes. Consider the first *O.E.D.* definition of the word *moral*: "pertaining to the distinction between right and wrong, or good and evil, in relation to the actions, volition, or character of responsible beings." The very terms of the definition raise problems. Are women "responsible beings" in precisely the same sense as men? Presumably so, in relation to God; certainly not—so it has at various times been thought—in relation to society. Are "right and wrong" perceived in the same ways by women and men? Both sexes might agree in the abstract about the wrongness of killing, say, but disagree about the particular circumstances that would allow homicide to be condoned. Are the possibilities for female volition equivalent to those for male exercise of will?

Such questions remain cogent even in the era of the Equal Rights Amendment; a hundred years ago they were yet more pressing. The Brontë novels I plan to discuss—Emily Brontë's *Wuthering Heights,* Charlotte Brontë's *Villette*—provoked moral indignation in early audiences. The *Quarterly Review,* alluding to the "repulsive vulgarity" of the vice depicted in *Wuthering Heights,* concluded that no woman could have written the novel except one who had "long forfeited the society of her own sex."[3] A reviewer in the *Christian Remembrancer* ferociously attacked *Villette,* remarking that Brontë's female characters overturn traditional morality—"their own un-aided reason, their individual opinion of right and wrong, discreet or im-prudent, sole guides of conduct and rules of manners,—the whole hedge of immemorial scruple and habit broken down and trampled upon." We may sympathize with the novel's heroine for her orphaned state and her poverty, the female critic grants, but we cannot ever feel affection for her, given "her unscrupulous and self-dependent intellect."[4] As fictional characters and as writers of fiction, contemporary criticism of the Brontë's implies, women are subject to particularly rigorous moral standards.

The male Victorian view of female moral possibility is predictably epito-mized by John Ruskin, who in the 1871 preface to *Sesame and Lilies* set forth a series of imperatives for feminine conduct. His specificity may be partly accounted for by his view that imagination is "a far rarer and weaker faculty in women than in men," but he also believes "that no man ever lived a right life who had not been chastened by a woman's love, strengthened by her courage, and guided by her discretion." Ruskin admits that he has actually *seen* "the utmost evil that is in women," while he has been forced merely to *believe* in "the utmost good." Good women are hard to find, he explains; they sometimes "seem almost helpless except in their homes," and "they are recognized chiefly in the happiness of their husbands and the nobleness of their children."[5] His lengthy account of female power and potentiality in the essay "Of Queens' Gardens" elaborates the implications of these obser-vations, clearly delineating the view that woman's morality must focus on service, her justification deriving from those she helps, her natural impulses of gentleness and love compensating for male aggressiveness, but her pro-pensities toward sloth if not vice requiring constant discipline.

In a world dominated by such a view—although, of course, living quite outside normal social contexts—the Brontë sisters wrote. Motherless, having spent years in acquiescent subservience to an irascible father and dissipated brother, they had demonstrated their possession of conventional female virtue. Yet questions about the dimensions of moral possibility in a woman's experience appear to have occurred, at some level of consciousness, to both Emily and Charlotte. Their novels may be understood as detailed investigation of moral life, systematically opposing the situations of women to those of men and using the juxtaposition to clarify the dimensions of the female dilemma. The moral schemes of these books reflect a special woman's viewpoint and suggest structural principles vital to the Brontë's novelistic craft.

To look at *Wuthering Heights* from the point of view of its moral implications may seem wildly inappropriate—may seem, in fact, positively *Victorian*. But of course this is, after all, a Victorian novel, with a surprisingly emphatic stress on moral questions. Nor does the conventional resolution of the Cathy-Hareton plot represent merely a retreat from the implications of the more romantic sequence involving the elder Catherine and Heathcliff. Even the story of the impossible passion between two extraordinary narcissists suggests that women require more than passion for their fulfillment.

The "more" required by Catherine remains slightly indistinct. Certainly she demands admiration as well as love from everyone she encounters; at times, despite her apparent amorality, she specifically wishes to be admired for her "goodness." After her marriage, she boasts to Nelly Dean of her lack of envy for Isabella's beauty, grace, and charm, arguing that she acts toward Isaballa like an indulgent mother—maternal love being, of course, the ultimate standard of female virtue—and that she gratifies every desire expressed by her husband and his sister. Nelly disputes these claims; but the important point is that Catherine feels impelled to make them. Earlier, in a similar vein, she has explained that she plans to marry Edward Linton in order to benefit Heathcliff. "Did it never strike you," she inquires of Nelly, "that if Heathcliff and I married, we should be beggars? whereas, if I marry Linton, I can aid Heathcliff to rise, and place him out of my brother's power."[6] This logic, she insists, provides her best motive for marriage.

The reader presumably agrees with Nelly that such self-descriptions merely rationalize Catherine's self-willed conduct, embodying her efforts to assimilate her behavior to the Ruskinian model of good womanhood based on the ideal of female service and subordination and reminding the reader of the standard she flouts. The events of Catherine's life in fact follow a stereotypical moral pattern. A little girl, deprived of a mother's care, grows up predictably self-indulgent and subject to uncontrolled passions. For a time she believes it possible to gratify all her desires, possessing the love of two men representing opposed human types, but nemesis descends: like so many other Victorian heroines, Catherine suffers and succumbs to mysterious "brain fever," ambiguously an expression of her passive resistance to and resentment of conventional expectation as well as a punishment for her failure to meet it. She dies in giving birth, conveying both her unfitness for active motherhood and her fulfillment of female destiny despite all efforts to avoid it. Of course this is not the whole story—not even the whole of Catherine's story. But as far as it goes, it supports nineteenth-century expectations of womanhood by recording the punishment of deviation from those expectations.

Nelly Dean, that model of convenitonality, embodies as well as articulates a more acceptable standard of female behavior: Charlotte Brontë, for example, defending her sister's novel against charges of immorality in an 1850 preface to it, praises Nelly's "true benevolence and homely fidelity."[7] Vicariously participating in the moral and emotional struggles around her, Nelly enforces her views of proper behavior. In talking with the elder and the younger Catherine, with Heathcliff, with Edgar Linton, as well as in telling the story to Lockwood, she constantly and explicitly judges conduct, always certain how other people should behave. Relatively powerless in social terms, she actually exercises considerable force by decisions to withhold or to reveal information. Her sense of virtue rests in her dedication to the interests of others—her benevolence and fidelity, to repeat Charlotte Brontë's terms. Twentieth-century readers may see her as a busy-body; Edgar Linton accuses her of causing trouble; but Nelly sees herself as doing what a woman should do: taking care, serving.

Indeed, the virtues painfully developed by the younger Cathy are more aristocratic versions of Nelly's. Cathy, instinctively motivated toward helplessness, wishes only to make a pet of her sickly cousin Linton, as unaware of the moral ambiguities of such a desire as Nelly is of the evil consequences of meddling. Her compulsion to help traps her into an empty and brief marriage, in which serving a man becomes her only possible enterprise, a matter of life and death. After Linton dies, after a period of mourning followed by depression and anger, Cathy finds her need to love and to help once more overpowering. Remorseful over her earlier cruelty to Hareton, she showers kisses and flowers on him; he digs a garden for her, she teaches him to read; at the novel's end, educated by love, she looks forward to a marriage based on mutuality, deriving from her discovery of the utter necessity of a human interchange of love and service. Isabella, whose interest in Heathcliff rests on sexual attraction alone, comes to a bad end. Cathy, more "womanly," shows no overt sexuality. Her kisses and flowers and games, her attitude toward Hareton, resemble a child's—and of course one finds striking similarities between nineteenth-century notions of good woman and good child. Cathy's is the solution endorsed by Nelly and by Lockwood.

But not, of course, by Heathcliff, whose towering presence expresses fantasies opposed to those implicit in the women's careers. His Byronic aspect as a figure of dark, brooding power has been more often noted than the novel's stress on his curious moral nature. Manifestly sadistic and vindictive, he defines his morality in terms of such character traits. Thrusting his wife from the room, he returns muttering, "I have no pity! I have no pity! The more the worms writhe, the more I yearn to crush out their entrails! It's a moral teething; and I grind with greater energy, in proportion to the increase of pain" (p. 189). The infliction of pain, he believes, exercises and develops his moral powers (so the metaphor of teething implies), morality demanding, in his perverse opinion, the utter dehumanization of others. He equates his moral position with his obsession.

This vision of romantic grandeur associated with the reversal of normal ethical assumptions belongs to a woman's fantasy about something imaginable in men, but not in women. Cathy defines Heathcliff's isolation as misery—"You are miserable, are you not? Lonely, like the devil, and envious like him? *Nobody* loves you—*nobody* will cry for you when you die! I wouldn't be you!" (p. 319). This is the orthodox female point of view about Heathcliff's condition. He, on the other hand, perceives his isolation as strength. His passionate devotion to a ghost pre-dates Catherine's death: the woman he loves is always a phantom even while a living person bears the phantom's name. His proclamations of love are largely competitive self-assertions, declaring his superiority to Edgar Linton. Nor is he "punished" for his vindictiveness, destructiveness, or perversity. Unlike Catherine's, his death has no stated moral overtones. He welcomes it as a reunion with the object of his obsession.

Other male characters in the novel, although strikingly different from Heathcliff, reiterate the implication that the masculine nature involves moral possibilities inconceivable for even the most passionate of women. Edgar Linton makes the point negatively. Displaying the "feminine" trait of compassionate concern for others, he has little effectual force, judged "unmanly" by his own wife and even by right-thinking Nelly Dean. Like a woman, he pines away. The other men endure, impervious to life's vicissitudes. Joseph espouses a strict morality of externally-imposed rules, with no apparent capacity for entering into the feelings of others. Lockwood, a professional onlooker at life, implies a morality of disengagement. Men—*manly* men—it seems, have sources of strength unavailable to women, whose need to love and be loved forms their moral nature, as Ruskin suggests, but also makes them vulnerable. If, like Catherine, they indulge in self-love (and her passion for Heathcliff, by her own confession, is directed toward a projection of herself), they cannot survive. The man dedicated to comparable narcissism, Heathcliff, triumphs; Joseph ahd Lockwood, also narcissistic after their fashions, lead lives which they appear to find satisfactory; the man whose morality approaches a woman's loses wife and sister, yields his daughter to his enemy's maneuvers, gains no one's respect. We do not know, of course, what will happen to Hareton, who appears to be developing some "female" virtues.

Occasionally the novel hints women's moral arrogance in relation to men, as when Catherine boasts her magnanimity or Cathy announces that she knows Linton has a bad nature and she's glad she has a better one, to forgive it. But the imaginative energy of *Wuthering Heights,* as most readers immediately feel, focuses in the fantasy-figure of Heathcliff, allowing a powerful morality of sadism—not only full self-indulgence, but a language to justify it—and allowed this quite specifically because he is a man. Many critics have recognized the ambiguous implications of *Wuthering Heights,* its plot declaring that one must learn, like Cathy, to be a good child-woman in order to find happiness, in emotional energy revealing the high value of that grand passion which makes happiness irrelevant. But one may note also how consistently the novel reiterates that men can create their own morality, or rest happily in pre-existent systems of rule, while women, doomed to the morality of nurturant service, inevitably destroy themselves if they yield to passions which almost literally tear them apart, as Catherine is torn. The many-layered perspectives, the narrative intricacies through which we perceive the action may obscure the fact that despite the irony directed at the narrow convenitonalities of Lockwood and Nelly Dean, despite the compelling figure of Heathcliff, Emily Brontë has implied a view of good womanhood which Ruskin himself might endorse—although also some resentment at the necessity of holding it. Perhaps she does not dare allow Catherine to go unpunished; perhaps, on the other hand, she literally cannot imagine such a woman's survival. Catherine's meaning inheres in her death. Her incapacity to compromise dooms her; she sounds shrill and petulant, not splendid at all, as her death approaches. Splendor is reserved for uncompromising Heathcliff, increasingly powerful even as he starves, consciously rejecting all the world can offer him. Cathy, who makes her peace with actuality, belongs to the realm of domestic tranquillity—the most a woman can hope for in life. The novelist's rebellious impulse expresses itself successfully only through a male figure.

Villette, Charlotte Brontë's last novel, offers a remarkably advanced delineation of the psychology of female self-suppression, telling a story of deprivation which appears to issue from a sensibility altogether opposed to that governing *Wuthering Heights.* Lucy Snowe, orphaned and dependent on her own efforts for economic survival, makes her way in the world first as paid companion to Miss Marchmont, a servile position made tolerable by affection, then as nursery-governess and later schoolmistress in a girls' school in a foreign city, a thinly-disguised version of the Brussels where Charlotte Brontë had actually taught. Infatuated with the handsome Dr. John, whom she had known in her girlhood, she endures his kindly but patronizing treatment of her as an object of pity and concern, watches his abortive affair with a frivolous, heartless student, sees him fall in love with and marry tiny, beautiful, feminine Polly. Lucy comes to love tyrannical M. Paul, who finally proposes to her, but events deprive her of him too. Gradually she learns to live with virtually no emotional sustenance from without.

Lucy thinks less consciously or persistently than Jane Eyre, her fictional predecessor, about the problem of being and doing good. But she describes more explicitly than Jane the feminine equation between love and service and the degree to which the opportunity for loving service may focus a woman's most passionate aspiration. The deprivation of this opportunity constitutes her heavy burden. Toward the end of the novel, as she formulates her vision of running her own school, she reflects that this object in life "is too selfish, too limited, and lacks interest." Perhaps, she reflects, her effort to win independence for herself will entitle her to "look higher." She yearns for something "dearer to me than myself," someone "at whose feet I can willingly lay down the whole burden of human egotism, and gloriously take up the nobler charge of labouring and living for others." Concluding that she is unlikely to achieve such fulfillment, she consoles herself with the thought that "a great many men, and more women, hold their span of life on conditions of denial and privation."[8] Why should she be more blessed than they?

To consider lack of opportunity to labor and live for others as "denial and privation" reveals the speaker's emotional commitment, which has been substantiated in various ways throughout the novel. Yet more revealing is her anxiety about the "burden of human egotism"—a problem of much concern to nineteenth-century thinkers, egotism being defined as "the vice of thinking too much of oneself." Lucy believes service an alternative to egotism; other characters, however, demonstrate their creator's awareness that a woman's serving may both express and conceal egotism. Little Polly Home, for instance, whom Q. D. Leavis rightly perceives as a kind of alter ego for Lucy, possessing the same sensitivities but blessed with fuller freedom to manifest them[9]—Polly, wheedling cakes for Graham Bretton, is described as one who "must necessarily live, move, and have her being in another: now that her father was taken from her, she nestled to Graham, and seemed to feel by his feelings: to exist in his existence" (p. 20). Her sense of self depends on discovering a strong male in whose experience she can hide. Dying Miss Marchmont, whose emotionally-deprived career suggests a parable for Lucy's, directly equates love and goodness in her memory. She explains that she has rarely loved because she is not "particularly good" (p. 34). Her one grand passion, however, lives splendidly for her still because it ennobled her. The elevating force of human attachment, for Polly and for Miss Marchmont, involves losing or merging the self in another, perceived as superior, thus paradoxically asserting the self's significance.

Lucy struggles with many forms of egotism. Her social position denies her manifest indulgence in self-importance, but her astringent commentary on those she encounters declares her preservation not merely of self-respect but of covert intense feelings of superiority. Although she repeatedly, almost constantly, points out that the world forbids her what it allows others— freedom, pleasure, love—it cannot forbid her her vigorous inner life, her imaginative explorations of experience. Systematically limiting herself, she declares herself "a mere looker-on at life" (p. 135). But such a self-description cannot contain Lucy: her "looking on" is no passive role. She finds private ways toward self-realization. Invoking imagination as "our divine Hope," she declares her "secret and sworn allegiance" to this "good angel" (p. 223). Reason, she explains, denies her opportunity to express her feelings; imagination supplies it, if only in dreams—waking as well as sleeping dreams. Reality, however, limiting, provides relatively few checks on her imaginative life, that hidden expression of ego. Her private drama of correspondence with Dr. John, for example, flourishes on the basis of very few letters, and many fantasies. Quite deliberately she treasures her imaginative formulations even when she knows them to contradict actuality. Dr. John, she now knows, was in fact "not nearly so perfect" as she believed him. None the less, she will "hold him to be" heroic, for the pleasure of the fantasy (p. 240). Her starved experience creates the need for rich inner life; imagination abundantly supplies it.

The planned marriage between Lucy and M. Paul seems to belong to this realm of imagination. As Mrs. Leavis points out, it is a dream of reconciled opposites, of Catholic and Protestant sensibilities, with all the antipathies concealed in those terms, functioning in harmony. It is in detail unimaginable—for Lucy and apparently for Charlotte Brontë, who insisted despite all suggestions to the contrary that her novel could not have a conventional happy ending. The marriage is quite impossible. The *imagining* of the marriage, on the other hand, provides a sustaining force which makes the period of her lover's absence avowedly Lucy's happiest years. Working for the sake of another, growing plants because he will value them, nourished by his letters and by her dreams, she lives fruitfully. Such happiness, however, in its nature cannot last: imagination finally collides with actuality in the hinted shipwreck which deprives Lucy of the object of her dreams. But the novel literally ends with an explicit invitation to readers to exercise Lucy's, imaginations" if such they have. In their imaginations as in Lucy's, happiness and goodness can be simultaneously sustained; in actuality, probably not.

Lucy and Brontë recognize the precariousness of imgination as a guiding principle of life. Excessive indulgence in the fantasies of solitude leads to Lucy's collapse after the strange episode in which her isolation and the fears and fantasies it engenders drive her to confess to a Catholic priest. Charlotte Brontë had done the same thing, under the strain of her Brussels solitude; she wrote her sister Emily at the time, "I felt as if I did not care what I did, provided it was not absolutely wrong, and that it served to vary my life and yield a moment's interest."[10] The sense of desperate blankness in her own experience belongs to Lucy as well. Brontë acknowledged to her publisher that she believes her heroine "both morbid and weak at times; . . . anybody living her life would necessarily become morbid." She specifically refers to the confessional episode as issuing from "no impetus of healthy feeling."[11] *Villette,* extensively and profoundly autobiographical, refers to Charlotte Brontë's bitter experience of unrequited love for the Belgian schoolmaster M. Heger and probably also for her publisher, George Smith, and reflects her frightful isolation after the death of all her sisters. For her as for Lucy, imagination provides the sole resources. But it is, Lucy makes clear, a source of torment as well as of solace, encouraging her to believe in the reality of ghosts, torturing her with visions of other people's happiness, causing her to exaggerate her own inadequacies and to create false explanations of the feelings others have toward her. The life of imagination, this novel insists, is a life of egotism—we would say narcissism. Yet the imagination—supported, of course, by a firm structure of social assumption—also generates Lucy's dream of release, the woman's release through a Ruskinian exaltation of loving service.

She sees how readily men seem to resolve the opposed demands of self and others. Dr. John, in his professional function, achieves, "amongst a very wretched population, a world of active good," beloved by his patients, admired by Lucy, "oblivious," she says, "of self." At home, on the other hand, he seeks "nutriment to his masculine self-love: his delight was to feed that ravenous sentiment, without thought of the price of provender" (p. 190). Women, of course, pay that price for him; his "provender" comes from his mother, from Polly, even from Lucy herself. M. Paul, the other significant male figure in the narrative, tyrannizes over throngs of devoted females in the very act of "doing good": as teacher, he is also free to be dictator. Lucy, on the other hand, feels no comparable freedom in her profession, forced to ingenuities of tact in her dealings with students, fellow-teachers, and head-mistress. Men both find greater opportunities for meaningful service and greater license for the indulgence of the narcissism. Women live to indulge them; and unattractive, proud Lucy, adept at teasing and challenging a man, is happy to gratify M. Paul in every way she can find.

Men, then, the novel says, can have it both ways: can demand that others gratify them, can gratify the needs of others. For Lucy, such fulfillment comes only in imagination. This fact is at the heart of *Villette*'s moral scheme. Harriet Martineau, who had been the novelist's friend, came to feel that Charlotte Brontë's books were immoral. She objected to her "dominant . . . idea, . . . the need of being loved" as unrealistic.[12] Without concurring in Martineau's judgment, one may admire her critical penetration: this idea indeed dominates the Brontë novels. But it is also central to the rigorous morality the books convey. Only by being loved, Lucy Snowe insists, can she be effectively good. The yearning to be good, to help and serve the object of devotion, has the same passionate intensity as the desire to be loved.

The "rebellious women" created by Emily and Charlotte Brontë, in short, however powerful their opposition to conventional standards and assumptions, enable their imaginers to express also a deep desire for conformity to the most powerful Victorian view of women's function; or perhaps an awareness of the psychic necessity of such conformity, given existent social possibility. As energetically as they assert the female drive toward psychic independence and the freedom of passion, they assert also the need for relationship as an opportunity for service. *Wuthering Heights* and *Villette* also share a deep pessimism about the possibility of achieving the double fulfillment declared to be women's need. These books present men as stronger and freer partly because they are simpler in their needs: Catherine, more racked by conflict and less successful than Heathcliff, is also less grand. Women never quite win. Emily Brontë isolates passion from fulfilling relationship: Catherine, full of passion, can relate only to versions of herself; she must die. Her daughter Cathy achieves attachment by subduing her powerful hostility; she seems to sacrifice intensity for harmony. Lucy Snowe manages simultaneous passion and service only in imagination. Yet the intense and complicated feminine dream conveyed through the heroines' strivings shapes both novels. The convoluted narrative scheme of *Wuthering Heights* allows different moralities to comment on one another and asserts (without emotionally accepting) the sad necessity of female compromise. The melancholy movement of *Villette,* a pattern of repeated frustration for the heroine, sustained happiness achievable only for half-fantasized others, seems designed to declare more unmistakably than its predecessors the impossibilities of women's hope of integrating service and passion.

Notes

1. Kate Millett, *Sexual Politics* (Garden City, N.Y.: Doubleday, 1970), p. 147.

2. Virginia Woolf, *A Room of One's Own* (New York: Harcourt, Brace & World, 1957), p. 73.

3. *Quarterly Review,* 84 (Dec. 1848), 175.

4. Quoted in Margot Peters, *Unquiet Soul* (Garden City, N.Y.: Doubleday, 1975), p. 371.

5. John Ruskin, *Sesame and Lilies* (New York: Lupton, n.d.), pp. 17, 27, 28.

6. Emily Brontë, *Wuthering Heights,* ed. David Daiches (Baltimore: Penguin Books, 1965), p. 122. Subsequent references to this edition included in text.

7. Printed in *Wuthering Heights,* p. 39.

8. Charlotte Brontë, *Villette* (New York: Harper and Row, 1972), p. 350. Subsequent references to this edition incorporated in text.

9. Introduction to *Villette,* p. xxix.

10. 29 May 1843; quoted in Peters, p. 133.

11. To William Smith Williams, 6 Nov. 1852; quoted in Peters, p. 354.

12. Quoted by Helene Moglen, *Charlotte Brontë: The Self Conceived* (New York: Norton, 1976), p. 225.

The Modern Period

Virginia Woolf's Miss Latrobe: The Artist's Last Struggle Against Masculine Values

DIANE FILBY GILLESPIE

In Woolf's fiction the outcome of the artist's struggle is never wholly positive. Miss La Trobe's situation and achievement in *Between the Acts,* however, is one of the more ambiguous. Partly for this reason, the overall tone of the novel has caused confusion.[1] *Between the Acts,* like *Orlando,* deals with English literary and social history. Unlike *Orlando,* Woolf's last novel portrays the world on the verge of another major war. In this ominous context the unifying effect of Miss LaTrobe's pageant may be tentatively affirmative; but far more definitive is her struggle to direct the play.[2] Miss LaTrobe's anguish represents Woolf's final and most complex attempt to deal with an idea that has preoccupied her since her first novel.

' 'What a miracle the masculine conception of life is—judges, civil servants, army, navy, Houses of Parliament, lord mayors—what a world we've made of it,' " remarks Terence Hewet, the novelist in *The Voyage Out* (VO 253).[3] Hewet is the first artist in Woolf's fiction whose work is hampered by the dominant value system of his society. *A Room of One's Own* and *Three Guineas* make clear that a country in which men compete for symbols to designate their ranks in a rigid hierarchical system and demand flattery from the women they bar from competition is not civilized; it is essentially barbaric. The results are acquisitive and possessive men and nations as well as violent responses to anything that threatens mastery.[4] Within such an environment artists compete for recognition by following aesthetic traditions and fashions. The extent to which they doubt such values and progress towards a more inclusive perspective, however, determines their true artistic success. Orlando is not the only artist in Woolf's fiction to change, aesthetically if not physically, from male to female.

Of all Woolf's artist characters, Terence Hewet has the shortest distance to go to reach androgyny. As an artist he is more likely than most men to criticize traditional values and their artistic correlatives if only because his society disapproves of his career choice.[5] Hewet's mother thinks her son's early interest in music is effeminate and prefers that he " 'kill rats and birds' " (VO 266). Older, he moves among men like Richard Dalloway, who insists that, while politicians at least try to define and solve social problems, artists behave irresponsibly (VO 45). Rachel Vinrace, who like Hewet is an artist, objects: politicians may improve the material well-being of certain groups of people, but they ignore their minds and feelings (VO 71–2).

Rachel's charge against politicians parallels Hewett's increasing dissatisfaction with novelists who value only external facts and public activities and with readers who are more interested in gossip about the author and his friends than in metaphysics (VO 262). Attempting to achieve greater reality, Hewet has already defied " 'absurd conventions' " like the happy ending and the tendency to present people of the past as a different species (VO 264). Now, in a novel on " 'Silence' . . . 'the things people don't say' " (VO 262), he will shift his focus from external facts to unspoken thoughts and feelings. Hewet recognizes, too, that because most novels present a masculine view of the world, the characterizations of women are inadequate (VO 258). His efforts to discover from Rachel what women think and feel suggest that they will be prominent among his future characters.

Hewet's inclusive perspective is evident when one contrasts him with the male egoists in Woolf's fiction who, subservient to aesthetic traditions developed by men, skillfully execute lifeless works of art. The most benighted of these is William Rodney in Woolf's second novel, *Night and Day*. Although his characters speak in a variety of meters, Rodney's poetic dramas are soporific. His technical skills, Katharine Hilbery decides, "are almost exclusively masculine; women neither practice them nor know how to value them" (ND 143). Yet Rodney, who is disturbed because Katharine's passion "never took the normal channel of glorification of him and his doings" (ND 253), expects her homage.

In *The Waves* Woolf's characterization of two male artists with similar problems is more complex. Nevil, another poet with a command of form and technique, executes works of art which, like Rodney's, remain lifeless. They remain so because he distrusts emotion. But even emotion is insufficient if the traditional forms do not provide a vehicle for its expression. Bernard, in spite of his "double capacity to feel, to reason" (W 82), is still unsuccessful. He waits for the fragments he writes to form the definitive story, but he waits in vain. He realizes that the meanings he intuits only at moments cannot be expressed in the neat sequences demanded by the traditional story line or the neat phrases demanded by conventional notions of style. What he needs, he decides too late, is " 'some little language such as lovers use, broken words, inarticulate words, like the shuffling of feet on the pavement' " as well as " 'some design more in accordance with those moments of humiliation and triumph that come now and then undeniably' " (W 261).

Woolf's female artist characters are more successful in finding the new language and design that Bernard wants. The difficulties resulting from their existence in a society dominated by the masculine conception of life are multiplied because they are women. As Woolf points out in *A Room of One's Own* and in a number of other essays, society may consider the abilities of male artists misdirected, but it does not doubt those abilities; female artists must struggle, in addition, against inferiority feelings resulting from definitions of "woman" and "artist" that are mutually exclusive. Because of the eighteenth-century emphasis on the controlling power of the male intellect and the exaggerated sex segregation of the nineteenth century, both the female Orlando in *Orlando* and Lily Briscoe in *To the Lighthouse* must cope with varying degrees of self-doubt. Nevertheless, the obscurity in which they, like most women, live is the cause as well as the predicted effect of both their choices to seek artistic forms appropriate to their similar visions of continuity underlying change.[6]

In her last novel, Woolf is no longer concerned with the specific problems the female artist confronts because she is a woman. Like Lily Briscoe and Orlando, Miss LaTrobe ultimately is more interested in the integrity of her work of art than in public acclaim, but this idea is subordinate in the novel to another—the necessity of modifying, in art as in society, the role of "Man the Master" (BA 215) who responds with violence to what he cannot control. Like Lily Briscoe in *To the Lighthouse,* Woolf moves from a preoccupation with injustices done to women to a recognition of the general plight of humankind of which those injustices are symptomatic: its failure to establish what Peggy in *The Years* calls "a world in which people were whole, in which people were free" (Y 421).

Miss LaTrobe is, in many respects, a cariacture of the masculine conception of life. The characters in the novel and the narrative voice usually think of and refer to her as "Miss." Her rumored sexual preferences for women, her stocky body, cigarettes, whip, strong language, and authoritative manner, however, are not conventionally feminine. As a decisive and peremptory leader, she is disliked by individuals but appealed to by groups who need someone to assume responsibility for decisions and, more important, blame for failures. A relatively successful leader, Miss LaTrobe knows how to exploit the vanity of her amateur actors and actresses to gain her ends.

More than anything else, however, Miss LaTrobe wants to possess her audience. By arousing its emotions, by making it perceive (as she does) English history and the literature that reflects it, she wants to unite its disparate members and imbue them with a sense of common purpose. Miss LaTrobe's ends may be admirable, but her means are doubtful. If, as has been suggested, her preoccupation with her audience is a love relationship paralleling others in the novel, then it is one in which she plays the most reprehensible of traditionally masculine roles.[7] Like Mr. Ramsay berating his wife for her lack of attention to facts, like old Bart Oliver scoffing at his sister's religious beliefs, she is the superior, aggressive party, needing what she often scorns and wishes she could do without. Because of its flightiness, its short attention span, its ignorance, its biases, the audience again and again slips her "noose" (BA 145). With it, Miss LaTrobe not only would surround and gather together, metaphorically, the members of her audience but also capture and coerce them. She is like one of the troopers in the ludicrous newspaper account Isa reads who lures a girl to see a horse with a green tail and then attacks her.

Although several images in the book assume the importance of symbols, the most powerful image of violence resulting from a frustrated attempt to wield power is Giles' killing of the snake:[8]

> Dead? No, choked with a toad in its mouth. The snake was unable to swallow; the toad was unable to die. A spasm made the ribs contract; blood oozed. It was birth the wrong way round—a monstrous inversion. So, raising his foot, he stamped on them. The mass crushed and slithered. The white canvas on his tennis shoes was bloodstained and sticky. But it was action. Action relieved him. He strode to the Barn, with blood on his shoes (BA 119).

In this passage, all traditionally positive associations of snakes with eternity, androgyny, wisdom, healing, and various life forces are thwarted. Instead the snake, unable to live, choking on the toad, unable to die, suggests the indeterminate condition of many people in the novel and of England and Europe as well.[9] William Dodge's reference to himself as " 'a flickering, mind-divided little snake in the grass' " (BA 90) has the conventional associations of treachery and danger. Indeed, to Giles, William Dodge exemplifies "perversion" (BA 118), a threat to traditional notions of sexuality and sex roles. Miss LaTrobe, in this respect, is liked with Dodge. Moreover, it is her pageant that forces Giles into the passive role of audience member when he wants to be active. His killing of the snake partly relieves the frustration that results from the contempt he feels for some of the people around him and from the inactive role he must play in a world confronting war. He gets further relief from the kind of woman Woolf criticizes in *A Room of One's Own* and *Three Guineas,* one who makes him feel important and in control rather than peripheral. Unlike Isa, who sees Giles as a " 'Silly little boy, with blood on his boots' " (BA 133), Mrs. Manressa notices the blood and is pleased: "Vaguely some sense that he had proved his valour for her admiration flattered her." He plays the "sulky hero" to her "Queen" (BA 128).

Miss LaTrobe embodies both Giles's violence and the snake's indeterminate position. She has some of his intolerance and contempt, although it is directed at the behavior of her actors and her audience rather than at individuals. She has a similar desire to act, to assert herself, to control a situation, and a similar dislike of details beyond her control. Like Giles, too, she relieves herself of her frustration by resorting to possessiveness, jealousy, and violence. Again and again, she curses the members of her audience from behind a tree. Tormented by their inattention, she gnashes her teeth, clenches her fists, grates her fingers in the bark of the tree, stubs her toe on a root, and grinds a hole in the grass with her heels. Like the world surrounding her pageant, Miss LaTrobe is at war; she must overwhelm or be overwhelmed. So intense is her desire to master and possess, so fearful and jealous is she of interruptions and distractions, that creation becomes destruction; birth becomes death: "Panic seized her. Blood seemed to pour from her shoes. This is death, death, death, she noted in the margin of her mind; when illusion fails" (BA 210). The blood in this passage is as much related to the blood oozing from the choking snake as it is to the blood on Giles's shoes. Like the snake, and like the continent on the verge of war, she has overextended herself. Ominously, she is not relieved by her violence. The failure of her illusion, death without the relief of dying, is, like the situation of the choking snake and undying toad, a "birth the wrong way round—a monstrous inversion." Mis LaTrobe chokes on a vision she can neither rid herself of nor communicate.

Her dilemma is that, as a writer, she both parodies and reflects the values of male dominated society and art. Parody, however critical in its implications, is not an aesthetic alternative. At intervals during the pageant, for example, she plays a recording of a "pompous popular" march tune:

> Armed against fate
> The valiant Rhoderick
> Armed and valiant
> Bold and blatant
> Firm elatant
> See the warriors—here they come (BA 96).

William Dodge associates the tune with Giles, pursued by Mrs. Manressa (BA 132). Later it introduces Budge, the publican, wielding his truncheon and representing patriarchal authority over all aspects of public and private life in the age of Victoria. In that age, as Miss LaTrobe represents it, the men sing "Rule Britannia" and the women, " 'I'd be a Butterfly' " (BA 188–89); the king counts money in his counting house while the queen eats bread and honey in her parlor (BA 211–12). Mocking a society which separates the sexes so drastically, Miss LaTrobe still tries to impose her views upon her audience as if she were the valiant Rhoderick or the indomitable Budge herself.

Miss LaTrobe's name further underscores this irony. "With that name," thinks a member of the audience, "she wasn't presumably pure English." She has Russian blood in her, perhaps, or French (BA 72). Some of Woolf's first English readers may have remembered an actual family of LaTrobes, one relatively old and prominent in nineteenth-century England, but not originally English. Thought to have descended from the Huguenots and to have come initially to Ireland with William of Orange, the five LaTrobes mentioned in the three brief biographies included in the *Dictionary of National Biography* were all men who composed and wrote about music as well as played musical instruments. Four of the five were clergymen. Although associated with a traditionally male-dominated institution, the church, the LaTrobes were Moravians, an evangelical Protestant sect that challenged older religious traditions and that remained strongest, not in England, but on the continent.

The emergence of their name in connection with a figure often so ludicrous as "Bossy" LaTrobe is mock-heroic; nevertheless, like the LaTrobes, Miss LaTrobe is artistic, evangelical in her efforts to communicate, and, while in England, not necessarily of it. As Woolf says in *Three Guineas*, women have no countries (TG 197). As *Between the Acts* indicates, national distinctions are questionable for men as well. Miss LaTrobe is one of several reminders in the book that England is not isolated from the continent and the imminent violence there. Nor is that link merely geographical. "Consider the gun slayers, bomb droppers here or there," indicts the voice from Miss LaTrobe's megaphone. "They do openly what we do slyly" (BA 218).

Miss LaTrobe includes herself in this indictment. She goes even further: *"Do I escape my own reprobation, simulating indignation, in the bush, among the leaves? There's s rhyme, to suggest, in spite of protestation and the desire for immolation, I too have had some, what's called, educa- tion . . ."* (BA 219). The word *"simulating"* is important. Miss LaTrobe's cursing, clenching, gnashing, gashing, grinding, grating, and metaphorical noose-throwing belong to a role in a larger play she did not write. It is a melodrama in which she plays the villain; her audience is the victim. At the same time, she is "a slave to her audience" (BA 113), victimized by her own tyranny. In war, as the saying goes, no one wins. Isa Oliver, wishing love and hate would stop tearing her apart, also perceives that it is "time someone invented a new plot, or that the author came out from the bushes" (BA 252). Like Pirandello's six characters, Woolf's are in search of an author. The play in which they perform their hackneyed roles is *The Masculine Conception of Life*, a melodrama which looks increasingly like tragedy.

Although caught in her role, Miss LaTrobe is at least partially conscious of her entrapment. If national boundaries are fundamentally artificial, so, she discovers, is the traditional way of defining man's relationship with the natural world. One of the major rivals for her audience's attention is nature. At least twice she wishes she could shut out the view. Moreover, the wind consistently blows away the words that the villagers sing and competes by rustling the leaves. Miss LaTrobe does plan to utilize the natural world in her production, but only on her terms. She is the product of a society that has left its mark, from Roman roads to cesspools, upon the landscape. Although her "ten mins. of present time" (BA 209) does not have the predicted effect, on two important and much cited occasions bellowing cows and rain help her to maintain the illusion she has created. In other lesser ways too, the natural world aids in the creation of illusion. Finally, when actors and actresses hold up to the members of the audience mirrors reflecting themselves, the noise and activity arouses the natural world and the cows and dogs join in: "the barriers which should divide Man the Master from the Brute were dissolved" (BA 215).[10] On these occasions Miss LaTrobe relinquishes her traditionally ordained power. In this way, not through violence, she is relieved of her frustration.

If the pageant defies neat summations, it does so in spite of Miss LaTrobe's desire to control every aspect of it. That she at moments loses control, relaxes out of the mood of frustration and fury resulting from her violent exercise of will is to her credit rather than to her discredit as an artist. When she is artist enough to accept gratefully the unanticipated intercessions of the natural world and to intuit that a work of art evolves to some extent according to its inner laws, she begins to produce an alternative to works of art dominated by masculine values. Miss LaTrobe, like Hewet, loses interest in producing or parodying art forms of the past. At the end of *Between the Acts* she conceives a new play. She envisions midnight and "two figures, half concealed by a rock" (BA 210) who, several pages later, are identified with Giles and Isa Oliver. These figures are actors in the drama of modern life ongoing between the acts of Miss LaTrobe's previous play. Stripped of shelter and transported into prehistory, Giles and Isa are parts of the entire drama of the human and prehuman past Lusy Swithin reads about in her *Outline of History*. In a way even more inclusive than Orlando's or Lily Briscoe's, Miss LaTrobe tries to present the permanent as well as the transient.

The artist's struggle against masculine values is one of Woolf's consistent preoccupations. Against the artist characters enslaved by aesthetic traditions which do not present reality in a sufficiently complex way, Woolf sets other artists. These men and women do not question the idea that art is an ordering, unifying force; they do question and even reject particular ordering mechanisms inappropriate for the expression of a reality as much internal as external, as much enduring as transitory. *Between the Acts* makes clear that the struggle is not confined to artists. It has implications for both human interaction and international relations within the realm of nature. Conflict resulting from the dominance of one person, group, nation, or realm by another is resolved by a perspective that contains disparities within some larger unity. Woolf's novels reveal the extreme difficulty of attaining and the even greater difficulty of maintaining this inclusive perspective in a society structured upon its denial. Miss LaTrobe and several of Woolf's other artist characters vacillate between confinement to separate parts of the human experience and perceptions of the whole. These glimpses, however brief, are the only bulwark they have against chaos. That bulwark, although very real, may not suffice. Woolf's last novel leaves us as Miss LaTrobe leaves her audience: "The gramophone gurled *Unity—Dispersity*. It gurgled *Un . . . dis . . .* And ceased" (BA 235).

Notes

1. Among those who see the book as pessimistic are Bernard Blackstone, *Virginia Woolf: A Commentary* (New York: Harcourt, Brace, 1949), pp. 237–238; and Jean Guiguet, *Virginia Woolf and Her Works*, trans. Jean Stewart (London: Hogarth, 1965), pp. 326–327. Among those who see it as optimistic are Warren Beck, "For Virginia Woolf," *Forms of Modern Fiction,* ed. William Van O'Connor (Minneapolis; Univ. of Minnesota Press, 1948), p. 253; Marilyn Zorn, "The Pageant in *Between the Acts,*" *MFS*, 2 (February 1956), 32–35; and Ann Y. Wilkinson, "A Principle of Unity in *Between the Acts,*" *Virginia Woolf: A Collection of Critical Essays*, ed. Claire Sprague (Englewood Cliffs, N.J.: Prentice-Hall, 1961), pp. 145–154. Several writers find the book affirmative, though bleak. See, for example, Don Summerhayes, "Society, Morality, Analogy: Virginia Woolf's World Between the Acts," *MFS*, 9 (1963), 332; and Stuart Hampshire, "Virginia Woolf," *Modern Writers and Other Essays* (London: Chatto and Windus, 1970), pp. 40, 45–46.

2. A number of critics make this point. See for example, James Naremore, *The World Without a Self: Virginia Woolf and the Novel* (New Haven and London: Yale Univ. Press, 1973), p. 229; and Nancy Topping Bazin, *Virginia Woolf and the Androgynous Vision* (New Brunswick, N.J.: Rutgers Univ. Press, 1973), p. 201.

3. The following Hogarth Press editions of Woolf's works are abbreviated and documented parenthetically in the text: BA *Between the Acts* (1947); ND *Night and Day* (1919); TG *Three Guineas* (1938); VO *The Voyage Out* (1929); W *The Waves* (1931); Y *The Years* (1951).

4. Mary Steussy Shanahan, in "*Between the Acts:* Virginia Woolf's Final Endeavor in Art," *Texas Studies in Literature and Language*, 14, 1 (Spring 1972), 123–138, discusses Woolf's views on civilization in the context of impending war. Her approach is Freudian, however, and she does not discuss the impact of masculine values on the creative struggle of the artist in *Between the Acts* or elsewhere in Woolf's work. Neither does Werner J. Deiman in "History, Pattern, and Continuity in Virginia Woolf," *Contemp. Lit.*, 15, 1 (Winter 1974), 49–66.

5. As Virginia Stephen, Woolf wrote on this problem in "Street Music," *National and English Review*, 45 (1905), 144–148.

6. For a more complete discussion of Lily Briscoe and Orlando as well as female artist characters in the works of other writers, see my "Virginia Woolf and the 'Reign of Error,' " *Research Studies*, 43 (1975), 222–234.

7. See Jean Alexander, *The Venture of Form in the Novels of Virginia Woolf* (Port Washington, New York, and London: Kennikat Press, 1974), p. 215.

8. See, for example, Stephen D. Fox, "The Fish Pond as Symbolic Center in *Between the Acts,'* *MFS*, 18, 3 (Autumn 1972), 467–473.

9. Among a number of critics who comment on the snake in similar ways, see Renee Watkins, "Survival in Discontinuity—Virginia Woolf's *Between the Acts,*" *The Massachusetts Review*, 10, 2 (Spring 1969), 368, 375.

10. Avrom Fleishman, in *Virginia Woolf: A Critical Reading* (Baltimore and London: The Johns Hopkins Univ. Press, 1975), p. 207, says that Miss LaTrobe "recognizes her mistake in trying to appropriate the materials of nature whole, without modifying them by esthetic design." Such a comment applies to her use of ten minutes from the present, but it does not define her relationship to nature in general.

A Passage to India
as "Marriage Fiction":
Forster's Sexual Politics

ELAINE SHOWALTER

> Marriage is too absurd in any case. It begins and
> continues for such very slight reasons. The social
> business props it up on one side, and the theolog-
> ical business on the other, but neither of them are
> marriage, are they? I've friends who can't remem-
> ber why they married, no more can their wives. I
> suspect that it mostly happens haphazard, although
> afterwards various noble reasons are invented.
> About marriage I am cynical.[1]

Admirers of *A Passage to India* will readily identify in this quotation the
voice of Cyril Fielding. It is a voice which is detached, skeptical, and
urbane—a voice, in fact, like Forster's own. When he speaks like this,
Fielding is very British, very Bloomsbury. In this speech, too, we can
recognize the characteristic distrust of the marriage-code, "the family in its
economic aspect," which forms an important theme in Forster's earlier
novels, such as *The Longest Journey* and *Howards End.* Like John Stuart
Mill, Forster saw the family as the primary socializing force; and like Mill, he
suspected that the nuclear patriarchal family was the source of all other
human power relations. "All the selfish propensities," Mill declared, "the
self-worship, the unjust self-preference, which exist among mankind, have
their source and root in, and derive their principal nourishment from, the
present constitution of the relation of men and women."[2] Forster concurred.
At the heart of marriage he saw the desire for ownership. Moreover, his
homosexuality made him an outsider despite himself, and forced him to
consider alternative lifestyles, even if he never dared to realize them. As
Forster's biographer, P. N. Furbank, tells us, he "quite seriously and on fully
thought out grounds, distrusted marriage as an institution, and fretted at
having to write "marriage-fiction." He suspected marriage might do more
harm than good; he was sure, at least, that there were finer possibilities
outside it."[3]

It is all the more surprising, therefore, to discover at the end of *Passage to India*, that Fielding has married. Are we to see this match as "haphazard," and, as critics, to invent *postfacto* noble reasons for it? Warned by Forster, we are inclined to be cynical. Biographical evidence, particularly in the wake of the long-suppressed homosexual fiction (*Maurice* and the short stories in *The Life to Come*) tempts us to conclude that Fielding's marriage is yet another reluctant artistic surrender to bourgeois and heterosexual morality. On the other hand, we might agree with George Steiner that *Passage* represents a sublimation and reworking of the plot of *Maurice*, with "the encounters between white and native, between emancipated rulers and 'advanced' Indians . . . a brilliant projection of the confrontation between society and the homosexual."[4] In either case, we would have to see the marriage of Fielding and Stella as hypocrisy, Forster's concession to the conventions of "marriage-fiction." For if Fielding is a homosexual hero it is Aziz to whom he owes a commitment.

Yet I think such a critical conclusion underestimates the complexity of Forster's dilemma. All of his novels and stories show that he was far from militant in his homosexuality and far from dogmatic in his personal values. An an artist, the other side of his frustration, his "weariness of the only subject that I both can and may treat—the love of men for women and vice versa," was the search for a marriage of true minds, a bond which could satisfy all of his needs for unity, fellowship, love, and continuance, without possessiveness or dominance.[5] Beyond his cynicism, Forster dreamed of the potential of a permanent union. In *A Passage to India*, he analyzed the failures of institutions to live up to his ideal. But the book is more than an exploration of an aesthetic and personal impasse. In the development of Fielding as a character, and in his surprising conversion to husbandhood, Forster resolved some of his feelings about human relationships in a manner neither cynical nor cowardly. Yet the Anglo-Indian setting, the structure which so liberated Forster's imagination, also reveals some shadows, some unilluminated corners where the author stands in ambiguous relation to the values of his novel. In this essay I wish to show how Forster's ambivalence toward women and marriage is a central quality of his book.

Passage to India, which has as its central incident an alleged sexual assault, assumes in its narrative a correspondence between sexual and political relations. This aspect of the novel, which we would now call sexual politics, has not received much notice; Oliver Stallybrass is probably representative in regarding sex as a minor theme in *Passage*. Perhaps the oversight is due to the scale of the political and religious dramas in the book, which seem to dwarf its personal and sexual elements. Yet Forster sees connections between the British family and imperialism, between purdah and Indian nationalism, Forster asks not only whether an Indian can be friends with an Englishman, but more profoundly, whether the institutions of marriage and the state are shaped to protect us from the threat of equality. The quality of "asking" should be emphasized. Just as the ambiguous nature of the incident in the caves is central to his novel, ambiguous views on sexual relationships are at its peripheries.

An essential part of this demonstration is Forster's portrayal of his female characters. With the exception of Mrs. Moore, the Englishwoman in the novel have been harshly treated by the critics. Forster, it is true, is hard on them; but not as hard as are critics, who notice the women only to condemn them. Wilfred Stone, for example, comments that "Anglo-Indian women are even more obnoxious than their men."[6] Lionel Trilling observes that:

> Of all the English it is the women who insist most strongly on their superiority, who are the rawest and crudest in their manner. The men have a certain rough liking for the men of the subject race; for instance, Turton, Collector of the District, has a "contemptuous affection for the pawns he moved about for so many years; they must be worth his pains." But the women, unchecked by any professional necessity or pride, think wholly in terms of the most elementary social prestige and Turton's wife lives for nothing else.[7]

Trilling writes as if the Englishwomen were morally inferior to their men; it is closer to the truth to say that the enforced togetherness of marriage and cultural isolation has stunted their development.

As Trilling inadvertently suggests, social prestige becomes central to their lives because they have nothing else to live for. There is no function for them as individuals in India; their husbands wish them to remain aloof from the natives. Their main responsibility is to their children, whom they must accompany in the hot season. Like the other appurtenances of Anglo-India, the women are exports, the "food of exile," reminders of home. Placed in a situation where they have no real identity, the recognition of others becomes their only guarantee of existence. Fielding is therefore a threat to them, because he ignores them. (In "feminist England," Forster points out, his notice would be unessential.)

Their relationship to the Indian natives is even more threatening, because the women do not wish to confront the fact of their own subjection; to see themselves mirrored in this "subject race," and to realize that they too are the objects of a "contemptuous affection." Maintaining status over the Indians gives them some reassurance. Yet Forster underlines the similarities between their positions and the natives. Like the Indians, the women are presented as intuitive, emotional, sensitive, inconsistent, and vain, living a precarious existence, dependent on the approval of the master race, and dimly aware that they always stand in danger of losing it. Like the "uncertain, cowering, recovering, giggling" (42) purdah women, to whom they feel a complacent superiority, the Englishwomen are infantilized. Narcissistic, weak, and helpless, they exert a childish tyranny over the men, for absolute powerlessness corrupts as well as absolute power. Collector Turton states, "It's our women who make everything more difficult out here," and he is not the only man in the novel who resents them. Perhaps as Forster notes, "There is a grain of resentment in all chivalry."

Nonetheless, men and women together have managed to collaborate in the pretense that marriage brings them mutual contentment and fulfillment. Together, in the annual ritual of the Club play, they celebrate the marriage-ethic of England, tinned for belated export to the colonies like the peas and the salmon. Forster points up the irony of the occasion with particular care. First of all, in their isolation in the hot dark clubhouse, where the windows have been barred "lest the servants should see their mem-sahibs acting" (24), the Anglo-Indian women are in a kind of purdah themselves. Second, the play they have chosen, *Cousin Kate*, is a mildly anti-feminist comedy, a hit of the London season of 1903 by H. H. Davies, in which the eponymous heroine, a successful novelist, yearns only for marriage. "A woman's life is so meaningless by itself," Kate insists. "I have a profession, I'm successful, I'm invited and welcomed everywhere—but I'm lonely . . . I'd give it all up for a real home with a husband and children."[8] As a final touch to this scene, the part of Kate is played by the adventurous Miss Derek, who, we later learn, is having an adulterous affair with Colonial McBride. No irony, however, is perceived by the Englishwomen, who have persuaded themselves that marriage and motherhood should be the central realities of their lives.

The narrowness and specialization of the lives makes them especially susceptible to moral atrophy, the occupational disease of the Anglo-Indian. Aziz points out at the beginning of the novel that while the British men, on the average, last about two years before surrendering their integrity, the women disintegrate in six months.

Forster's portrayal of the Englishwomen could be taken as an expansion of his friend G. L. Dickinson's hostile description in a letter:

> It's the women more than the men that are at fault. There they are, without their children, with no duties, with empty minds and hearts, trying to fill them by playing tennis and despising the natives.[9]

How much sympathy, then, does he feel for the women? I think we must accept the fact that Forster often saw women as part of the enemy camp. While not precisely antagonistic to them, he believed them to be allied with the forces and institutions of repression. As Quentin Bell puts it, Forster was "happier with his own sex."[10] And he was not very enthusiastic about feminism even as Virginia Woolf articulated it. Thus his attitude in this novel may simply be contemptuous, in the tradition of most male British travellers in India.

On the other hand, Forster tells us enough about the circumstances in which the women find themselves to make it clear that they are the victims and not the villains of their culture. They too are exports from England, symbols of the distance between the rulers and the natives. It is not their fault that their presence is necessary to keep the men from sexual contact with the natives—male and female—as the food and tobacco shipments keep them from curry and *pan*. Forster resents the restraints—first external, and then absorbed—which keep the British from experiencing the mixture of the sensual and the holy which characterized India to him. In this sense, he sympathizes to a considerable degree with at least one Englishwoman, Adela

Quested. In fact, there is much of Forster himself in Adela's struggle not to be pinned down by the codes of the compound.

A significant subplot in *A Passage to India* is the struggle of Adela Quested to avoid this fate. A pilgrim, as her name suggests, Adela is in double jeopardy in India. Both British and female, she confronts forces in Chandrapore which work to make her smaller, duller, and weaker. In her painful quest, she succumbs temporarily to the marriage-ethic of Anglo-India, and to its corrupting and deadening influence; but ultimately she is able to cast it off, and to escape destruction, at the price of renouncing love.

Critics have usually extended to Adela the contempt they express for the other Englishwomen. Wilfred Stone, for example, has compared her to Hermione Roddice in Lawrence's *Women in Love*: "Both women are catastrophes of modern civilization—repressed, class-bound, over-intellectualized" (382). Yet Adela is one of the least class-bound characters in the book, except in the sense that she is limited by her sex; and rather than being repressed and intellectualized, she is extremely sensitive. In an early draft, Forster wrote of Adela that "it seemed to her that she was a bird, an unimportant one, shut up in a cage with two perches labelled 'marriage' and 'not marriage' and that she hopped from perch to perch in order not to notice the cage."[11] In her rejection of the marriage-convention, she is yet unable to escape the cage of sex-roles.

Forster is chiefly interested in the claustrophobic codes of western marriage, demanding "eternal union and external ownership." But he also touches on marriage-customs of India, which are much more sinister. While critics have acknowledged that Indian society is not the ideal antithesis of British imperialism, no one has pointed out the radical immorality of India's male supremacist culture, or even commented on the effects of purdah on Indian character.

The institution of purdah, under which nearly 40 million women, mostly Moselm, were living as late as 1930, was a form of slavery responsible for widespread ignorance and disease. Among the poor, purdah was not strictly enforced, since the demands of survival often left no room for convention; and among the rich, adequate provision could be mde to render a life of sequestration comfortable, healthy, and even luxurious. But among the middle classes (to which Azia would belong) doctors found that women were coerced by "conventional respectability [to adopt purdah] in its most rigid form without having the means to render the seclusion healthy or even tolerable."[12] The women's apartments were deliberately kept dark and airless; thus *purdahnashi* women were particularly prone to tuberculosis, and to many other diseases as well; in Calcutta in 1912, the death rate for women was 1.6 times that of men. Vitamin D deficiency produced disastrous effects; according to Dr. K. Vaughn, "the present working of the purdah system, by depriving the girls and women of sunlight, is directly responsible for the production of osteomalacia [a condition, especially frequent in pregnancy, characterized by softening of the bones, with subsequent deformity, weakness, and pain], gross pelvic deformity, and the deaths of thousands of mothers and children in childbirth annually."[13] Aziz's wife, we should recall, is a purdah woman who dies in childbirth.

Reforms sought by the All-India Women's Educational and Social Conference in 1917 included abolition of purdah and child marriage, prevention of polygamy and enforced widowhood, and an end to commercial and religious prostitution. In a 1921 census, Calcutta (where Aziz plans to visit a brothel) was discovered to have 10,000 prostitutes, 2,000 under the age of thirteen; the practice of kidnapping lower-caste girls was widespread, as was their sale by parents. Marriage, moreover, resembled a legalized rape. Fully half of the female population was married by the age of fifteen; their consent was not an issue, much less mutual love.[14]

Forster's emphasis on the novel is not on the appalling conditions under which Indian women lived, but rather on the corruption of the marital relationship when it is enforced on all; and on the effects of purdah on the moral and spiritual character of Indian men. In the character of Aziz particularly can be traced the egoism and limited vision which is the darker side of heroic and romantic nationalism.

As a doctor and as a humanist, Aziz ought from the beginning to reject purdah, but his ego is deeply involved in it. "I believe in the purdah," he tells Fielding; he makes exceptions for his friends to see his wife: "All men are brothers, and as soon as one behaves as such he may see my wife" (116). For Aziz, women are possessions, albeit prized ones; that woman is exhibited to her husband's friends is one more sign of her subjection; his convenience, and not her autonomy, is involved. Aziz's theory that the purdah can go when all men are brothers supposes that humanity resides in men only; he does not see that the need to enslave women must be overcome before brotherhood can be achieved.

In all his sexual relations, Aziz consults his needs alone and reduces the woman to the level of an object. "He begat his first child in mere animality' (55), with a wife chosen by his parents and physically unattractive to him. The patient suffering and eventual death of this woman won his love, and he grieves for her. The experience, however, teaches him nothing about love; his attitudes toward women continue to be superficial and egotistical. For Adela he can feel no sympathy because he finds her ugly. Her "angular body" and freckles are hideous to him (68); furthermore, "she has practically no breasts" (126). His reaction to the rape charge is largely one of outraged sexual pride. Although Aziz is painfully aware of the racist myth believed by the British, that the darker races lust after the pinko-greys, he has his own sexual mythology; he believes that only physical beauty makes a woman desirable, and that plain women really yearn to be raped. Only an acknowledgement of this from Adela will pacify his outrage; he wants her to write an apology reading "Dear Dr. Aziz, I wish you had come into the cave; I am an awful old hag and it is my last chance." Before the trip to the caves, he is planning an excursion to a Calcutta brothel, where he offers to find for Fielding a whore "with breasts like mangoes" (120). His lust is "hard and direct," in contrast to the English, whom he perceives as either frigid or indiscriminating, willing to satisfy their needs in the Chandrapore bazaar. Even in prostitutes, Aziz's standards are high.

Aziz's inability to perceive women as other than objects alienates Fielding, who understands Adela's complexity and appreciates the nobility of her self-immolation. Fielding is puzzled by the crudity of Aziz's response to the trial:

> The underlying notion was, "It disgraces me to have been mentioned in connection with such a hag." It enraged him that he had been accused by a woman who had no personal beauty; sexually, he was a snob. This had puzzled and worried Fielding. Sensuality, as long as it is straightforward, did not repel him, but this derived sensuality—the sort that classes a mistress among motor-cars if she is beautiful, and among eye-flies if she isn't—was alien to his own emotions, and he felt a barrier between himself and Aziz whenever it arose. It was, in a new form, the old, old trouble that eats the heart out of every civilization: snobbery, the desire for possessions, creditable appendages; and it is to escape this rather than the lusts of the flesh that saints retreat into the Himalayas. (214).

After the trial, Aziz, who has become "chief medicine man" to a Hindu court, takes up the cause of the emancipation of women, but it is not at all clear that his theories are more than frivolous. "His poems were all on one topic—Oriental womanhood. 'The purdah must go,' was their burden, 'other-wise we shall never be free!' " (293). Yet he has a vague notion of hiding the women away from "the foreigner"; women are still possessions, to be released or held as nationalist feeling dictates. And as Fielding reminds him, his private life with his mistress contradicts his espoused doctrine: "Free your own lady in the first place, and see who'll wash Ahmed, Karim and Jemila's faces. A nice situation" (321).

The central event of *A Passage to India* is a trial, and Forster uses it in the traditional literary way, as a spiritual test for all the characters in the book. The mysterious episode in the Marabar Cave is a screen upon which all the characters project their obsessions, personalities, and philosophies. It is important to see that the central male characters in the novel, Aziz and Fielding, undergo a trial as well as Adela; and that all three are guilty in some sense.

Freudian criticism has placed the blame for the incident in the Cave on Adela's projected sexual fantasies. Frederick Crews' analysis is a representa-tive one; "The echo that is metaphorically sounded in Adela's hallucination (if it is a hallucination) of sexual attack is that it is her unvoiced desire for physical love."[15]

Wilfred Stone has also written at some length on this point:

> In clinical terms, Adela no doubt suffered a form of sexual hysteria. She had been tense all that day and, just before entering the cave, had suddenly noticed that Aziz was a very handsome man. She had just as suddenly realized that she and Ronny did not love each other. Moreover, she was in a near panic about sex generally—virginal, frigid, afraid of being entered, afraid of that return down-ward and backward which is as illicitly tempting for women as for men. (335)

But the events in the Marabar Caves are too complicated, too closely connected to the moral experience of the main characters to be reduced to the hallucinations of a repressed spinster, even if there were evidence for such a view in the novel and in its early drafts. In fact, the evidence suggests the opposite—that Adela was not physically attracted to Aziz, and that she longed for emotion rather than sex. "She did not admire him with personal warmth" (153), according to the novel; in a manuscript Forster wrote emphatically that Aziz "did not attract her in any sense."[16] Instead, Adela is undergoing a spiritual crisis; the deadly apathy of Anglo-India has infected her, and for a fortnight she has "felt nothing acutely." Committed to a loveless marriage with Ronny, she confronts the evil meaning of the legalized rape such a marriage will entail.

That the Caves are connected in Adela's mind with intense anxiety over her forthcoming marriage has been frequently observed. Forster emphasizes the connection by carefully underlining the parallels between this incident and the scene of Adela's betrothal during the car accident in the Marabar Road in Chapter VIII. In many details, besides location, the accident is like the assault, only more neutral because externalized. The car hits a mysterious animal which only Adela sees, and in her excitement she destroys all the evidence of its appearance (89–90).[17] All the characters interpret the accident in terms of their personalities and cultural tradition; the Nawals and Mrs. Moore are sure the animal was a ghost; Ronny suspects a hyena, and uses the occasion to justify his views on the incapacities of Indians in an emergency; Adela is uncertain. Yet a fleeting sense of unity and sexual excitement brings Ronny and Adela together. On her way to the Caves, Adela recalls the accident twice, once on the train, once just before entering the Cave. Although she realizes that she and Ronny do not love each other, she determines to go through with the marriage: to break if off "would cause so much trouble to others; besides, she wasn't convinced that love is necessary to a successful union" (152). For this blackest of Forsterian heresies, she will have to suffer.

Aziz's complicity in the collective evil which culminates in the cave has not been recognized, but it is as appropriate that he undergo a trial as Adela.[18] Generally, readers of the novel have accepted his defense: that rape is a compliment to the woman, and that he does not admire Adela, but finds her repulsive. Even Adela, in dreadful self-abasement, asks Fielding if he thinks she has had the sort of hallucination "that makes some women think they've had an offer of marriage when none was made" (240). It is ironic that Forster here brackets marriage with sexual assault. He fails to make clear that rape is not a gesture of admiration but an expression of contempt or hatred. Aziz certainly does not love Adela, but he is contemptuous of her as he is of women generally.

Cultural blindness is apparent in the responses of all participants in the trial. Since both the British and the Indian cultures are permeated by notions of hierarchy, exclusion, and dominance, they are unified internally only in opposition to a common enemy; the trial provides a temporary illusion of unity for both sides. Forster notes ironically and at some length how sheer racism, and *machismo*—the imperialistic *duo* so neatly connected in the work of an earlier passenger to India, Rudyard Kipling—are the sources of "all that was fine" (179) in the British character. Suddenly, faced with Adela-as-Victim, the women feel like sisters, and resolve not to be snobs in the future. The men are dizzy with the sense of patriarchal outrage: "They had started speaking of 'women and children'—the phrase that exempts the male from sanity when it has been repeated a few times" (183). Britannia appears in the form of a Mrs. Blakeston—"a brainless but most beautiful girl," who with her "abundant figure" and "masses of corn-gold hair," symbolizes "all that is worth fighting and dying for." The intoxicating combination of sex and the possessive instinct stimulates aggressive feelings and behavior in the men whose irrational urges to conquer and avenge are re-awakened. In their metonymic system, the attack on Adela is construed as an attack on male honor and British authority; when Ronny enters the room, the men rise to their feet "in instinctive homage" (183); his property rights have been challenged as much as Adela's virtue.

For Fielding the trial poses a series of dilemmas, and challenges. A detached and dispassionate liberal, whose virtues have been "equilibrium" (118) and "travelling light" (121), he is forced to commit himself to Aziz's party. In the long run, the trial changes his life, for he meets Mrs. Moore's daughter Stella, and marries her. Fielding's independence and rootlessness protect him from the hysteria of the British colony; yet, as Aziz perceives, there is something cold and inhuman in his isolation. Working his way back into society presents Fielding with many problems. At first he is intimidated by the code of virile fellowship, even though he rejects the crude chauvinism of the British. Aziz makes him ashamed of his own predilections for privacy and sensual control, and he apologizes: "It is on my mind that you think me a prude about women. I had rather you thought anything else of me" (280).

Throughout the novel, Fielding is the most consistent critic of marriage; yet at the end he marries, and if we can trust Forster's hints (in Ronny's congratulations on his "son and heir" [307] and the comment that "their union had been blessed" [381]), will be a father. What has happened to the "holy" ideal of travelling light? In many ways, Fielding seems diminished by his marriage; in dwindling into a husband his values have changed, and he has become part of the community: "He had thrown in his lot with Anglo-India by marrying a countrywoman, and he was acquiring some of its limitations, and already felt surprise at his own past heroism" (319). His marriage separates him from Aziz, and it is a sexual, as well as a political betrayal, for the idea of interracial love as a solution to international conflict is the underlying significance of their relationship.

Yet Fielding's commitment suggests that Forster recognized the sterility in his own ideal. Independence and singleness have personal but short-term satisfactions to offer. The other characters pay for their mistakes by exile and renunciation: Adela no longer wants love; Aziz returns to superstition, separation and the comic and suitable punishment of writing long and unpublishable poems on female liberation; he will no longer try to befriend an Englishman. Their decisions, while wholly understandable in terms of circumstances and psychology, are regressive. Fielding's marriage, on the other hand, is a role which holds out the promise of a new generation.

The "elemental hunger for continuance" as F. R. Leavis puts it, is as insistent in *A Passage to India* as in any of Forster's works. Aziz is "placed"—although he lives in squalor, "He belonged to a tradition which found him, and he had brought children into the world, the society of the future" (121). Yet his society is tainted by dominance; no new union can spring from it, "not yet . . . not there." The hope of Fielding's marriage is that the negative aspects of the family—its possessiveness, its patterns of mastery and submission—will be cancelled by the mixture of the urbane and rational Fielding strain with the sympathetic and mystical Moore strain. the descendents of the Fieldings and the Moores may evolve spiritually beyond their parents.

While it comes as a kind of comic reversal in the novel, Fielding's marriage is also the resolution of themes which Forster has carefully set out. In the *Mosque* section, a conversation between Fielding and Aziz has revealed the differences between their feelings about self-perpetuation. Aziz cannot understand a man who is indifferent to the immortality of paternity; Fielding insists that he would "far rather leave a thought behind me than a child" (119). Fielding echoes Bacon's adage when he suggests that "any man can travel light until he has a wife or children" (121); and Aziz sees the meaning of this at once: Fielding has nothing to lose. In fact, Fielding has nothing; and in the aftermath of his encounter with Ronny at the Club—his finest moment of public heroism—he experiences with sorrow the fact of his emptiness: "he felt dubious and discontented suddenly, and wondered whether he was really and truly successful as a human being" (191).

The marriage to Stella Moore resolves the question of Fielding's success by linking him both to the promise of new life and continuity, and to the regenerative cycles of Hinduism. It is to witness the rebirth festival of Shri Krishna that the Fieldings come to Mau; Stella and her brother Ralph are wordlessly responsive to what Fielding calls "this Krishna business." There are hopeful signs that "the Marabar is wiped out," that the participants have ended that cycle of pain and misunderstanding, and are ready to begin anew.

Yet Forster's uneasiness about this compromise is revealed in numerous details and omissions. The marriage to Stella takes place off stage, and is revealed in the *Temple* section to the astonishment of Aziz (who thought Fielding had married Adela) and the reader (who barely recalled that Stella existed). Although she actually meets Aziz, and is involved in the baptism-accident at the festival, Stella is never directly described; she is more shadowy and incorporeal than any character in Forster's fiction. In fact, she exists for the reader chiefly through her relationships as daughter, sister, and wife. Her brother Ralph is far more realized as a character. It seems as if Forster does not want to imagine her very fully. Furthermore, Fielding's attitudes toward his marriage are anxious ones. "He was not quite happy about his marriage. He was passionate physically again—the final flare-up before the clinkers of middle age—and he knew that his wife did not love him as much as he loved her, and he was ashamed of pestering her" (318). Here Forster seems to be hinting that this is a December-May marriage, with Fielding driven by unreciprocated lust. A vaguer kind of sexual incompatibility is also suggested by this description; its disturbing implications for Fielding are reinforced by his statement that Stella's spiritual intensity makes him feel "half dead and half blind" (318). Despite all the symbolism of birth and rebirth in this section of the book, Fielding's marriage appears to have crippled and unmanned him.

Thus ultimately the view we have of Fielding's marriage is mixed, and undercut by Forster's own skepticism and mistrust. Even when it holds out the promise of the future, Fielding's marriage is a union of unequal partners: unequal in age, unequal in loving, and thus finally unequal in power. Although he worried much about continuance, Forster could not rejoice in the institutions which made it possible. Fielding's marriage is the most positive gesture towards spiritual evolution he can make; but at the same time, it is a surrender, and a microcosm of the failure of human relationships to solve human problems.

Notes

1. E. M. Forster, *A Passage to India* (New York: Harcourt, Brace and World, Inc., 1924), p. 262. All references to the novel will be given in the text; the edition I have used in the Harvest paperback.

2. "The Subjection of Women," in *Essays on Sex Equlity*, ed. Alice S. Rossi (Chicago: University of Chicago Press, 1970), p. 218.

3. "The Personality of E. M. Forster," *Encounter*, Vol. 35 (November 1970), p. 62.

4. "Under the Greenwood Tree," *New Yorker*, October 9, 1971, p. 166.

5. Quoted from Forster's diary for June 16, 1911, in Oliver Stallybrass' Introduction to *The Life to Come and Other Stories* (London: Edward Arnold, 1972), xiv.

6. *The Cave and the Mountain: A Study of E. M. Forster* (Stanford: Stanford University Press, 1966), p. 324.

7. From *E. M. Forster* (New York: New Directions, 1943); reprinted in *E. M. Forster: A Passage to India*, ed. Malcolm Bradbury (London: Macmillan, 1970), p. 83. In a feminist analysis of Forster, Bonnie Finkelstein reaches surprisingly similar conclusions: "Indian men oppress their women, while British women manipulate their men," *Forster's Women: Eternal Differences* (New York: Columbia Univrsity Press, 1975), p. 117.

8. *The Plays of Hubert Henry Davies* (London: Chatto and Windus, 1921), Vol. I, p. 100.

9.   Stone, p. 327.

10.   *Virginia Woolf,* Vol. II (London, 1972), p. 133.

11.   June Perry Levine, "An Analysis of the Manuscripts of 'A Passage to India,' " *PMLA*, Vol. 85 (March 1970), 290.

12.   E. Martelli, in *the Key of Progress: A Survey of the Status and Conditions of Women in India*, ed. A. R. Caton (London: Oxford University Press, 1930), p. 116.

13.   Caton, p. 120.

14.   Caton, pp. 83–107. Despite modernization and reforms, the status of Indian Moslem women remains shockingly low. In the aftermath of the India-Pakistani War about 200,000 Pakistani wives who had been raped by Bengali soldiers were "ostracized by the Moselm communities and had virtually no place to turn to . . . By tradition, no Moslem husband will take back a wife touched by another man, even if she was subdued by force" (*New York Times*, January 18, 1972).

15.   Frederick C. Crews, *E. M. Forster: The Perils of Humanism* (Princeton: Princeton University Press, 1962), p. 139.

16.   Levine, p. 288.

17.   Bonnie Finkelstein makes the interesting suggestion that the "animal thing" that hits them is Adela's repressed sexuality. But her analysis emphasizes Adela's realization of her "major character defect . . . an undeveloped heart." This seems like an extreme case of blaming the victim. *Forster's Women*, pp. 130–34.

18.   Aziz's (and Fielding's) guilt may also have a source in the homosexual aspect of their relationship.

Violet Hunt's *Tales of the Uneasy:* Ghost Stories of a Worldly Woman

MARIE AND ROBERT SECOR

Today Violet Hunt is remembered only as a woman who had her circle, a circle which encompassed most of the notable literary figures in late Victorian and Edwardian England. With some of these she became, or claimed to have become, romantically involved. Oscar Wilde is said to have proposed to her; Oswald Crawfurd, editor of *Black and White,* gave her syphilis; H. G. Wells, Somerset Maugham, and Arnold Bennett were close friends; Ford Madox Ford lived with her for almost ten years. The annual parties she and Ford gave at South Lodge were important social and literary events, and Violet Hunt earned a reputation as "a beauty of the Edwardian era" with an assassin's wit, "disconcerting . . . for the way she pounced."[1] "A catfish in a decorous aquarium," Douglas Goldring called her.[2] Goldring gives us a good sense of what her name evoked in the early part of the century, when he was an Oxford undergraduate:

> By 1906, if Violet Hunt's name cropped up in the conversation of literary aspirants, it immediately caused a stir. "Do you really know Miss Hunt? Do tell us what she's like. Is she as fascinating as people say?" . . . Several of my friends enjoyed a reflected prestige from the fact that they had met Violet in London and had actually danced with her. In our youthful . . . eyes, she ranked, by hearsay, as one of the most exciting figures in the Edwardian capital . . . "Fast," fashionable, brilliant, daring; leading spirit, as we imagined, in a circle of metropolitan celebrities of both sexes, from our undergraduate standpoint, she was glamour personified.[3]

David Garnett remembers her less kindly as "a thin viperish-looking beauty with a pointed chin and deep-set, burning brown eyes under hooded lids. There was a driving force within her, which I afterwards recognised as insatiable ambition."[4] Hunt's ambition was literary as well as social, for she was a writer of fiction of considerable merit. D. H. Lawrence appreciated her fully, both as a friend ("She was charming and I loved her") and as a writer. Kyle S. Chrichton remembers Lawrence once launching "into a long defense of Violet Hunt as a novelist, saying that she wasn't at all appreciated."[5]

Another admirer was Henry James, of whom Hunt was "an older and more intimate friend . . . than Ford ever claimed to be."[6] Hunt understood the subtleties in the relationships of James's characters, of which he was so fully aware, and the sexual impulses behind them, of which Hunt felt James was less conscious. She was especially intrigued by the sexual undercurrents of her favorite ghost tale, James's "The Turn of the Screw."[7]

Perhaps inspired by James's story, Hunt produced in 1911 her own volume of ghost stories, *Tales of the Uneasy,* which was reviewed widely and well. "Her style is excellent, her grasp of her subjects sure, and her insight exceptionally clear and sane" (*The Athenaeum,* Apr. 15, 1911, p. 418). "The hard, pungent, scintillating cleverness that marked Hunt's earlier method . . . taken into conjunction with the high seriousness and insistent pathos that found so fine an expression in *White Rose of Weary Leaf,* lifts the cleverness at times into something not unlike genius" (*The Outlook,* Apr. 1, 1911, p. 419). "Miss Violent Hunt is . . . one of the few nowadays who can write a really good short story" (*The English Review,* VIII, 1911, p. 176). "The collection can do nothing but add to an already considerable reputation" (*The Bookman,* May, 1911, p. 97). Today these remarkable stories remain both an important contribution to the genre of the ghost story and a record of the response of a sensitive but strong-willed woman to the weak and indecisive men who seemed to inhabit Edwardian England.

Violet Hunt was conscious of and articulate about her commitment as a writer to present experience from the woman's point of view. In a letter to the *New Statesman* (Dec. 9, 1922), she accused men writers of worrying the "little innocent preoccupations" of Leopold Bloom, "his business deals, his physical prowess," while relegating the thoughts of Molly Bloom to the back of the book. Hunt's interest in the weak and indecisive man was shared by the men writers of her age—he appears as Eliot's Prufrock, James's Winterbourne in *Daisy Miller,* Conrad's Heyst in *Victory*—but her main interest was in the psychology of women affected by such men. Hunt had her own experiences to go by—from her early affair with the painter George Boughton to her life with Ford at the time she was publishing *Tales of the Uneasy.* Hunt considered Ford "a cold, patient man, without fire, lazy of habit: his heart, dull-beating"[8] and was exasperated by his dependency:

> He would bear quite meekly, like the "exceedingly patient donkey" to which his father had compared him in boyhood, the weals of fate . . . But I am different. I won't bear things unless I have to. I have to live always in the boiling middle of things. . . . It seems to be my fate always to be up against people who prefer solvency to sentiment and pawkiness to passion. . . . I was always one that, refusing to notice when the signals were against me, made haste to the rendezvous that is to bring down misfortune on my head.[9]

The first three stories in *Tales of the Uneasy,* "The Telegram," "The Operation," and "The Memoir," treat from the woman's point of view the weak-willed man whose passivity makes him subject to the superior will of a woman. In her affairs with married men (Boughton, Crawfurd, Ford), Hunt recognized the superior power of the wife over the mistress along with the passivity of men who drift under the control of stronger wills. At the same time Hunt was horrified at the vision of the powerful, unchecked will of a woman, a will fed by the passivity of an unmanly man. In these ghost stories Violet Hunt often seem most frightened of herself.

In "The Telegram," the first of the volume's nine stories, Alice Damer, like Violet Hunt herself, is an attractive flirtatious woman impatient with the passivity of men. Alice rejects marriage for the two reasons which make others marry, love and money: she is incapable of the former and has plenty of the latter. Her victim is Everard Jenkyns who wants to marry her, but she rejects him and uses him as a social convenience until (too late) she changes her mind. Alice is a drawingroom vampire, a modern "belle dame sans merci." She attracts Everard, enthralls him, teases him with one kiss, feeds him dinner but starves his heart, and ultimately sucks the life from him. Everard becomes, figuratively and then literally, one of the walking dead, inspiring only revulsion by the time Alice decides to put him out of his misery and marry him for her convenience.

The story's basic situation resembles that of James's novel, *The Sacred Fount* (1901), in which the vitality of one person grows in proportion to its depletion in another. In "The Telegram" Alice thrives on Everard's devotion. Although she is nearing forty, her mirror shows her "very few lines, no look of fatigue, even in a bad glass! And as much color in her hair, that poor Everard admired so, as ever there was" (p. 15). Everard, meanwhile, declines into "the ruin of a man, a pale, thin, hectic mask, sitting opposite her, pretending to eat" (p. 19). Jamesian too is the sense of lost opportunity, of life wasted by those who refuse to live and recognize too late what they have missed.

The contest between Alice and Everard is unequal from the start, for hers is the superior will, while he passively lets her dictate the terms of their relationship. He comes when Alice calls, accepts being used, and so doing earns her contempt: "other and more full-blooded men would not have been content with so merely spiritual a sustenance" (p. 8). Eventually, however, without any encouragement from Alice, Everard loses all interest in life and virtually starves himself to death. He declines Alice's summons to dine only when he dies; ironically, that act of self-determination is enough to pique her into deciding to marry him.

"The Operation," which *The Outlook* (April 1, 1911) called "one of the weirdest and most powerful short stories we ever remember to have read," appeared first in *The Fortnightly Review* (Nov. 2, 1908) under the title "A Physical Lien." The earlier title defines more precisely the story's theme: it is about the sway one personality can exercise over another. Like "The Telegram" it concerns the relationship between a strong woman and a weak man. This time the man is fought over by two women, his first wife Julia (whose love for him is so strong she is able to give him up to another woman) and his second wife Florence (whose strength is in her will: "A man all to oneself or nothing" [p. 43]).

Joe Mardell, the object of the struggle, is an actor, "susceptible, weak, hustled and busy" (p. 42), a man who lives by assuming the identity of more powerful personalities. Julia, an actress, is wholly committed to him and their marriage. She takes unsuitable roles to be with him and eventually, out of love and self-abnegation, relinquishes him when he wants a divorce. Florence is pretty and wilful, "of an acquisitive, pugnacious, predatory habit of mind" (p. 41). She wins the battle of wills over Joe and values her prize not for what he is, "but for what he means to me—light and kisses and frocks and champagne" (p. 62). Julia loves deeply and abnegates her will; Florence wills intensely and reduces love to flirtation. Joe, a little man, is the pawn in the battle between love and will.

The story questions the nature of emotional commitment. Julia's power extends over Joe even after the divorce. It extends even to Florence, who must share Julia's death pains in acknowledgement of her love's power. Florence, on the other hand, refuses to make the emotional commitment necessary to sustain a relationship. She carefully maintains her social power and emotional independence in marriage. She dines when and with whom she pleases, refuses to wait up for Joe; he in turn "never attempted to control her social movements, . . . took what she gave him and was always as ready to flirt with her as if he were not married to her! She had managed Joe well!" (p. 51).

Hunt takes Julia's side in the struggle because she appreciates the value and respects the power of fidelity. She considered "Conrad's deification of the sense of responsibility in emotional affairs" to be "the high-water mark of civilisation."[10] The opposite of this emotional responsibility is the emotional selfishness (like Florence's) which may preserve the polite social forms, but undermines the relationship between men and women and the substance of civilization. Hunt herself knew what emotional responsibility ought to be. Boughton, Crawfurd, and Ford all disappointed her by their failure to make any permanent emotional commitment to her.

"The Memoir" is also a story of a weak man fought over by two women. Again the question of possession is raised, and again the plain wife, the "little brown bird" (p. 90), triumphs over the brilliant mistress. Sir Hilary Greenwell is weak and pliable, "a male bone of contention" (p. 74) between the two women who love him. He is a romantic figure (a traveller, writer, and social lion), "and women simply 'clawed him' for their parties, and adored him for their boudoirs" (p. 75). His wife Mabel is eight years older than he, plain in spite of her expensive clothes. She lives vicariously in Sir Hilary's social triumphs. "She herself never triumphed" (p. 73), we are told—at least not until she becomes a widow and gains the upper hand over her husband's ex-mistress, the brilliant, "over-powering," and "astonishingly indiscreet" (p. 91) Cynthia Chenies.

The women in "The Memoir" are left by their weak man to work out for themselves the question of disputed possession. Sir Hilary is careful merely to preserve appearances for both his wife and his mistress; he makes no hard choices. "He loved Cynthia with every fibre of his being—all save the domestic ones" (p. 80). Cynthia, on the other hand, risks indiscretion for her love, while the less attractive Mabel must use her wits and her position as Sir Hilary's widow in order to settle the score between them. "She was neither young nor beautiful: it behoved her to be clever" (p. 83). The women control the game, and the man, for all his apparent worldly success, is but a pawn.

"The Prayer" and "The Blue Bonnet," show possession to be the ultimate motive of women determined to rescue their men. The irresistible impulse to save another's soul, as well as the folly of attempting to build a relationship on such a basis, intrigued Hunt around 1909 at the beginning of her affair with Ford Madox Ford. She got to know Ford at a time he was particularly vulnerable, separated from his wife, financially troubled and professional unappreciated. With the wisdom of hindsight she writes in her memoirs of her attempt at salvation: "I was ready to commit the eternal error. I was full, not of love, but of Loving kindness, and obsessed by the permanent illusion of all women that they can save." She comes upon Ford as he is about to take morphia and confiscates the bottle (perhaps the attempted suicide was just a melodramatic gesture, but Hunt took it seriously). Later after their affair ends she writes bitterly, "as for salvage, it is well known that the shipwrecked mariner turns against his rescuer: and sailors, wise and primitive men, will let a man drown lest he live to do him an injury."[11]

"The Prayer" is a macabre tale about the refusal of a young wife, Alice Arne, to let her husband die. Dead, he returns to life in answer to her desperate prayer, and she then must live with the consequences of this unnatural act. Alice's is a death- and God-defying possessiveness: "My God, my God, he's mine," she cries, "he's my husband, he's my lover—give him back to me!" (p. 99). To save Edward is to possess and control him. He can will neither to die nor to live; he has no say in his own salvation. Like Everard in "The Telegram," Edward Arne tries to exercise his will by dying, but Alice refuses to accept this assertion of independence.

"The Prayer" also assumes an imbalance of power between the sexes. Excess of will results in emotional and physical vampirism. Alice's un- natural will deprives Edward of his, so that although returned to life he is really death-in-life, a vampire reversed, struggling to return below the earth where he belongs: "The crust of the earth seems a barrier between me and my own place" (p. 127), he complains. In his unnatural revived state he is not a ghost, a spirit without a body, but "a body—senseless—lonely—stranded on this earth—without a spirit" (p. 117).

If Edward is death-in-life, Alice's life with him becomes another kind of living death. As vampire, Edward now drains her of vitality: "Where she was pale he was well-coloured; the network of little filmy wrinkles that, on close inspection, covered her face, had no parallel on his smooth skin" (p. 104). Alice's punishment for her unnatural act is the destruction of their relation- ship and her own life. To redress the balance she is driven at the end to take back the "gift" that was not hers to give.

We see a similar destructive possessiveness at work in Christina Daunet, the heroine of "The Blue Bonnet." She is the woman left behind, the faithful fiancée, while her lover partakes of a man's life of adventure. Charles Daunet is a soldier committed to the Stuart cause, "more of a fighter than a lover" (p. 164). His blue bonnet, visible when he "fought like the devil at Preston" (p. 157), is the symbol of his prowess in battle. While he fights for the losing cause, Christina remains at home, "loyal—as women are loyal" (p. 163), to care for her house and her dying mother. Their wedding is postponed and Christina's happiness must depend on the outcome of a political struggle which concerns her little but deprives her of her lover and protector when she needs him most.

When Charles returns to beg protection, his once blue bonnet "faded by sun and wind and rain" (p. 169), Christina takes him in even though she believes he has been faithless to her. She gets her revenge by rescuing her man from the Hanoverian soldiers. Again Hunt demonstrates the impossibility of a woman's building a relationship with a man by becoming his savior and distinguishes carefully between "Love" and "Loving-kindness." As she writes in *The Flurried Years,* the relationship between man and woman "is bound to be Love, or nothing, with a dash of hate."[12] In "The Blue Bonnet" we see the hatred and resentment which motivate the rescuer, inspired by the passivity of the man who gives himself over to her: "She was revengeful—then she would give him up? She meant perhaps to save him? Well, his life belonged to her" (p. 170).

Christina demonstrates her power over her frightened lover both by agreeing to save him and by deliberately humiliating him in doing so. For once she is in total control of the situation: she invites the enemy soldier into the house where Charles is hiding, pointedly welcomes the sight of a "real" man, initiates the flirtation with Captain Butler, leads him to the servant's corner where Charles hides, and completes Charles's degradation by identifying him as her idiot bastard half-brother and forcing him to witness her seductive behavior.

The story's attitude towards Christina is ambiguous, her actions both courageous and vindictive. But instead of being grateful for his rescue, Charles sees Christiana only as a slut. While she awaits his return with the "Loving-kindness" that kills—"she would dress his wound, and shelter him and be a mother, not a mistress, to him a while" (p. 179)—Charles can escape degradation only in death. He commits suicide as his only act of independence; Christina then falls on her knife, her only act of fidelity.

Hunt's theme of relationships gone wrong is also treated in four Gothic stories: "The Coach," "The Witness," "The Barometer," and "The Tiger Skin." All four are set in the Northcountry where Hunt was born (Her mother's family, the Raines, were long inhabitants of Durham, and Hunt saw in herself a strong streak of her mother's "northern, Valkyrie-like hardness and grimness.")[13] In these stories Hunt uses Northcountry settings and superstitions to achieve her Gothic effects. Her emphasis is on the individual as victim of the perverse relationship he cannot control.

"The Coach," which Hunt considered "the best story I ever wrote,"[14] is based on the country superstition of a Coach of Death, a phantom carriage with a headless coachman, which can be seen on St. John's Eve with its cargo of departed souls. Hunt's coach carries along the Great Northern Road five characters: a fashionable lady, a philanthropic millionaire, a baby farmer who takes in unwanted babies and lets them die, a mental degenerate who has sliced up his sweetheart, and a working man who has killed the millionaire.

"The Coach" investigates the premise on which perverse relationships rest. In the other stories the men are all enthralled by women who destroy them, while they destroy their women by helping them become the monsters they are. As a vampire needs its victim, the victim may seek his vampire. So in "The Coach" the fashionable woman and the millionare are guilty of both their vacuous lives and their own violent deaths. The less the fashionable woman's life was worth, the more she flashed her jewels, until she met the death she had invited. Similarly, the millionaire, having found his wealth a burden and his life empty, created the circumstances of his own murder, walking home alone from the station at night despite his fears. The worker is thus a victim of his victim; his crime, like that of the baby farmer, an inevitable product of social injustice. While he lived in poverty he found unbearable the rich man who complained about his burden of wealth and then eased his guilt with gifts of money to libraries and charities but never to people in need. The worker's family complained (" 'Lord bless them, they never thought as they were 'citing their man to murder' ") and the papers carried stories about the millionaire's fear of robbers. All circumstances seem to conspire to drive the worker, half drunk, towards his fatal act.

"The Witness," a strange and powerful tale of murder, madness, and guilt told by an obsessed narrator, takes us into the Gothic world of Edgar Allan Poe, as Hunt continues to explore the psychology of the murderer as victim of self and circumstance. "Hard Sally James" (p. 186) is another of Hunt's passionate but calculating self-sufficient women of superior will. When "poor mad Mary" (p. 188), the narrator's wife, tracks him down in her bedroom, Sally with serene and amoral singlemindedness strikes her down and with the narrator's help buries her in a deep pit shaft. The narrator is another of Hunt's weakwilled men. He passively watches Sally kill for him, then follows her orders for burying the body, but refuses to acknowledge his complicity in the murder: "Sally was sure to know what to do. It was her murder" (p. 189).

At the time she wrote the story, Hunt was feeling the frustration of a reversal of roles in her own affair with Ford, "the exceedingly patient donkey." Like Ford, who eventually solves his problems with Hunt by joining the Welsh Regiment, the narrator is capable only of running from responsibility, first from Mary when she degenerates into madness and prostitution, then from Sally. He runs all the way to America, taking with him his dog Roger, the only witness to their crime. There he remains in self-imposed isolation, obsessed with one idea: "I must see her again" (p. 194).

On his return, the narrator at first thinks Sally mad, raving as she does about how dogs can be made under torture to betray the secrets of their masters. Eventually, however, the narrator seems to believe Sally and her story. Perhaps we are meant to as well, but there is good reason to suspect Sally. She had dominated the narrator by her will on the night of the murder; perhaps now her insane will distorts his weak, uneasy mind into the image of her own.

Even more than the narrator, Sally has been left to brood over her crime—made pointless by his desertion—in the prison cell of her mind and room, "a cell ten feet square" (p. 187). Sally recoils from Roger both as the only companion to whom the narrator has remained faithful and as a reminder of things past, but the narrator can no longer be dissociated from his dog and their deed. " 'You and me'll never be parted,' " he tells Roger. " 'She must take us both for better or worse, eh?' " (p. 196). At the story's close we learn that the narrator has been telling his tale from Durham jail, where he is soon to be hanged for killing the woman who had killed for him as she was about o strike a blow against the witness to their crime. It really does not matter how deep the pit shaft goes.

"The Barometer" is another Gothic tale, the shortest and starkest in the collection. It evokes the oppressive atmosphere of a country vicarage in Yorkshire during a period of drought. The story is simple: two boys are terrorized by their own foreboding, their fears ignored by their stern parents, until they meet their doom. The starkness of the moors, the grimness of the vicarage, and most of all the fright of the children are realized with an economy and power that impressed May Sinclair: "When I read these tales I find myself wondering what wild turn Violent Hunt's talent might have taken if she had never lived in London, never seen Fleet Street, but had been brought up, like Emile Brontë, in the Yorkshire country of her people and had never left the moors."[15]

The dry heat which in "The Barometer" has soured the milk and parched the earth only intensifies and symbolizes the arid lives of these country people, "sad human beings, sighing and complaining, full of vague physical uneasiness and sense of stress of longing" (p. 215). The dominant force in the house is Mrs. Cooper, who withholds human warmth from her children with the "helpless shyness of a hard woman" (p. 222). Her husband, the Rev. Matthew Cooper, is "a hard, cold, God-fearing, painstaking, undeveloped man, conscious of having a wife who managed him" (p. 220), but of little else. This time it is the children who are victims of the wilful woman and the passive man who accepts her management.

While the uncanny foreboding of the children (the true barometers) and their death in bed by lightning suggest the supernatural, the children are natural victims of the dried out emotional springs of their mother, who refuses them her bed despite their fears and pleas. As the maid says: "If they were mine, shouldn't I like them to nestle aside o' me! This room is fair lonesome. Naebody could hear them if they were to strike out" (p. 227). The children, however, have learned not to "strike out," to stifle their own impulses of joy and pain. "Crying was never allowed" (p. 223). The heavens but mirror their condition.

If "The Barometer" depicts the death of children whose fears are ignored by a cold, hard mother, "The Tiger Skin," the longest, most grotesque and Gothic of the tales, reveals in the figure of a woman so proud and so devoid of maternal instincts that she virtually murders her own deformed child because she believes that only the fittest should survive.

Adelaide Favarger is brought up motherless by her cynical and heartless father. Dr. Favarger seems to care more for his theories than for his daughter, whom he abuses to her face as "the only microbe in the establishment" (p. 235). Hunt may have gotten the situation from James's *Washington Square,* but unlike Catherine Sloper, Adelaide turns out to be all too much like her father, having spent his life drinking in the poison of his cynicism and his inhumane ideas. Her father's sterile laboratory will become her Gothic northern sanctuary at High Walls, where she will deliberately cut herself off from the judgment and values of the human community. "Adelaide had succeeded in creating a human vacuum all around her, an area sterilized of all gossip" (p. 271). Adelaide will carry out the doctor's theoretical beliefs about eugenics on Mary, her deformed child; the room he keeps locked for unnamed experiments will become the attic hovel where Mary meets her horrible death.

By twenty-five, Adelaide is a "meagre Circe, who gathered the ready made beasts about her" (p. 235). Wald Ensor may not seem a ready made beast, but there is no doubt that under Adelaide's spell he so fails in his human responsibility that by the end of the story he is transformed into a figure repellent to the townspeople. Ensor is the man of humane instincts without the will to act on them. He disapproves silently of the doctor's conversation in the early scenes of the story, then ignores or rationalizes away the horrors of High Walls in the later ones. He loves children and is so concerned for their morals that he wants to ban immoral books from the library, but can do no more for Mary than make ineffectual gestures of kindness—like carrying her wash pail or bringing her candy. Without vision or will, pity and compassion are useless and hypocritical.

Mary is the visible product of the relationship between Adelaide and Ensor, a monstrous birth which signifies their unhealthy union. She and not Phyllis, the cook's beautiful daughter whom Adelaide passes off as her own, is the proper mirror of Adelaide's increasingly depraved soul, the portrait of Dorian Gray made flesh. At the same time, she reflects her father, for Ensor is just as craven and deformed under Adelaide's influence. Ensor willingly unmans himself in his relationships with women: "He likes women to show grit, and did not on the whole object to be managed by any person exhibiting a marked competency" (p. 256).

Once again Hunt seems to be working out frustrations from her own life, particularly her relationship with Ford. She had had enough of men who threw themselves on her competency; she had no patience left with the blindness of ineffectual good nature, like Ford who could be "so knowledgeable," yet "a blind as those that can't see."[16] If Ensor is drawn from what Hunt saw as the worst in Ford, then the story's predatory tiger-woman, Adelaide, is a grotesque version of herself. Douglas Goldring, one who knew Violet best, said that "there was always a certain feline quality about her charm."[17]

"I was too old to be a New Woman,"[18] Hunt said, looking back at the Ford years, and she yearned for marriage and a conventional domestic life. But the men she knew never seemed quite equal to her, and she could not retreat from the sexual awareness and self-sufficiency by which she lived and with which she informed the women in her stories. They should be called, Henry James joked, "Ghost Stories of a Worldly Woman."[19] And so they are.

Notes

1.   Iris Barry, "The Ezra Pound Era," *The Bookman* (Oct. 1931), p. 165.

2.   "Violet Hunt" entry in *Twentieth Century Authors* (London: 1955).

3.   Douglas Goldring, *Life Interests* (London: 1948), p. 171.

4.   Edward Garnett, *The Golden Echo* (London: 1953), p. 183.

5.   The first statement Lawrence makes in a letter to Edward Garnett (Harry T. Moore, ed., *Collected Letters* [London: 1962], I, 98). Chrichton's recollection can be found in Edward Nehls, ed., *D.H. Lawrence: A Composite Biography* (Wisconsin: 1958), II, 412. Hunt in turn was one of the first to recognize Lawrence's talents. She was influential in getting his poems published in *The English Review* and recommended his first novel, *The White Peacock,* to her publisher, William Heinemann. After Heinemann published the book, she reviewed it favorably for the *Daily Chronicle* (Feb. 10, 1911).

6.   Douglas Goldring, *The Last Pre-Raphaelite* (London: 1948), p. 98.

7.   Hunt's comments on James's story in the Preface to her subsequent volume, *More Tales of the Uneasy* (London: 1925) reveal both literary and personal insight: "I, myself, think it is just a freak story which rose full-armed from the subliminal consciousness of—as the surface mind goes—a sexually unsophisticated man.... Perhaps as he sat down to write it, some sneaking abnormality crawled up from the underworld of the consciousness and, having perpetrated the Tale, he was almost childishly unaware of the Character of the fruit of his intelligence. He had the simplicity of genius which scorns, or at least is not careful to guard itself from, misunderstanding."

8.   Violet Hunt, *The Flurried Years* (London: 1926), p. 152.

9.   *The Flurried Years,* pp. 126–27.

10.   *The Flurried Years,* p. 6.

11.   *The Flurried Years,* p. 74.

12.   Ibid.

13.   *The Flurried Years,* p. 118.

14.   *The Flurried Years,* p. 14. "The Coach" was first published in March 1909, in *The English Review*. After appearing in *Tales* in 1911, it was anthologized in *Georgian Stories* of 1922 and then again by Somerset Maugham in *Tellers of Tales* in 1939.

15.   May Sinclair, "The Novels of Violet Hunt," *The English Review* (Feb. 1922), p. 118.

16.   *The Flurried Years,* p. 153.

17.   *Life Interests,* p. 180.

18.   *The Flurried Years,* p. 123.

19.   Preface to *More Tales of the Uneasy*.

The Contemporary Period

Women and Madness in the Fiction of Joyce Carol Oates

CHARLOTTE GOODMAN

The Gothic world which Joyce Carol Oates has projected in her novels and short stories[1] is one that is shaped by irrationality, extreme emotions, and violence. Oates's female characters, in particular, are born into a hostile world that fails to nurture them. Rejecting the lives of their unhappy mothers, they long to forge a more meaningful existence for themselves. However, few life options seem available to Oates's women. Most seek fulfillment through sexual relationships, or marriage and motherhood; but sexual relationships in Oates's fiction usually end disastrously, and wives and mothers fail to be affirmed by the traditional female roles they have chosen. Like the women whose lives Phyllis Chesler has documented in *Women and Madness,* Oates's female characters often experience acute psychological malaise because of their powerlessness, and many ultimately become suicidal or psychotic. Although Oates has received little attention to date from feminist critics, her fiction merits such consideration, for it dramatizes forcefully some of the factors that contribute to the despair and psychological disintegration of contemporary women.

In this article I shall focus on Oates's female characters who become psychologically disturbed, and shall consider the life choices of these women, the ways in which such choices prove to be destructive to their sense of self, and the nature of their psychological response.

I

The life choices made by Oates's female protagonists reflect both a desire on their part to live a more satisfying life than that of their mothers, and an inability to create alternate, more meaningful roles for themselves. Oates's prototypical young female protagonist sets forth from her family home in quest of a new life. Like Natasha in *Expensive People,* she runs away from her home, seeking a "rebirth and rebaptizing" (301). Observing the hardships and shortcomings of her mother's life, the young girl desperately wants to avoid the unhappy fate that has been her mother's lot. The determination to have a more fulfilling life is expressed as follows in "The Census Taker" by an adolescent girl whose mother was deserted by her father:

> I ain't goin' through the old ways—not comin' from a child to a woman, havin' children to keep on with the old ways, suffrin' them, suffrin' all agony to squeeze them out in no walled-in world. An' sick all your life, an' poor, an' got to get up in the mornin' to ice on the window (*By the North Gate,* 21).

It is this same determination to find a way out of the "walled-in world" of her mother that leads Clara in *A Garden of Earthly Delights* to run away from the migrant camp where her family lives. Having witnessed the death of her mother in childibrth, and the rapid transformation of her father's new wife from a vigorous young woman to a worn-out, bitter hag, Clara insists, "I want more things than just babies like my Ma and Nancy and everybody else!" (195). Similarly, Maureen Wendall in *Them* is desperately anxious to flee from her family's squalid, overcrowded apartment in a Detroit slum to a more harmonious world like the one she sees pictured in the glossy pages of women's magazines. An avid reader who often hides away in the public library, Maureen longs for the measured world of a Jane Austen novel, where men treat women with tenderness and courtesy, instead of the brutality with which her father treats her mother.

Poverty is one of the factors that contributes to the unhappiness of the women in the works that I have mentioned thus far. However, a similar determination to avoid the fate of their mothers is expressed by Oates's more affluent female protagonists: Nadine, a major character in *Them,* is as eager to escape from her family's richly carpeted Grosse Pointe mansion as is Maureen Wendall from her shabby apartment in the slums of Detroit, and in *Wonderland,* Shelley Vogel, daughter of a famous neurosurgeon, runs away repeatedly from her elegant home. Also in short stories like "Boy and Girl," "How I Contemplated The World From The Detroit House of Correction and Started My Life Over Again," "A Girl At the Edge of the Ocean," and "Pastoral Blood," young women flee from a suburban world that leaves them spiritually and emotionally impoverished. Grace, in "Pastoral Blood," epitomizes this type of Oates protagonist. Product of affluent suburbia, she looks with distaste at her mother, "pretty in a trim, girdled, impersonal way; her gray hair highlighted and streaked by the beautician . . ." (*By the North Gate,* 76); and she thinks that the sunshine in their well-equipped kitchen, with its blue counters, and milkglass china, and tiled floors, looks "oppressive" (77). Mirroring her own vapid life, for Grace, is the girl typically shown on the TV screen who

> has long hair and is a cheerleader, and there's a scene to show her and her boyfriend dancing some dance. The sponsor is shampoo or cereal (83).

About Grace, Oates writes, "She wondered if her death would be anything unusual or whether it would be another, final cliché" (87).

The means of escape usually chosen by Oates's young female protagonist is that of a sexual liaison. "A woman does not matter to another woman," says one of Oates's characters ("Inventions," *Marriage and Infidelities,* 382). What does "matter" to Oates's women are the attentions of men who will, they hope, validate their existence. Thus Clara, in *A Garden of Earthly Delights,* uses her beauty as a means of acquiring a lover who will offer her love and protection. Abandoned by her first lover when she becomes pregnant, Clara once again uses her sexual availability to arouse the interest of a man. This time she calculatingly chooses the older, more affluent Revere, a man who can provide her and her unborn child with the material comforts that Clara craves, and after her marriage she feels "safe and protected by Revere and his world" (291). Similarly, Maureen Wendall in *Them* sells her body in order to acquire the money that she needs to escape from her home. Jealous of her brother's ability to get jobs after school, while she herself is forced by her mother to stay at home and help with the housework and the new baby, Maureen seeks a quick way to get money. Though she has often heard her mother's unhappy sobbing, and feels as a result that she herself "did not want to live with a man, sleep with a man" (171), she begins to pick up men who offer her money in exchange for sex.

While the motives of characters like Clara and Maureen for seeking sexual relationships are in part economic ones, even Oates's affluent young women seek relationships with men as a means of adding excitement or fulfillment to their lives. Often these women seem to be searching for a father-substitute, a man who will provide them with the attention and security that they were denied by their own fathers. Grace, in "Pastoral Blood," for example, leaves home on the anniversary of her father's death; as the older man, whom she picks up in a bar, embraces her, she remembers her father and thinks, "Father, look around to me, take me into your heart!" (*By the North Gate,* 86). Another character who seeks her father in her lover is Shelley in *Wonderland.* Recalling that her father, a busy neurosurgeon, was never at home during the years when she was growing up, she thinks, "Father, I want to fall asleep in your arms" (431). Besides having in common the fact that they look on their lovers as father-substitutes, both Grace and Shelley are disdainful of their mothers, whose conservative values and domesticity they abhor. Grace's emotional distance from her proper, middle-class mother is revealed as she observes her mother approaching and thinks of her not as "Mother" or "her mother," but as "the Mother" (91). Shelley's disdain for her mother is similarly apparent: at the same time that she is thinking longingly of her father, she recalls her mother's nagging her about her posture and her dirty fingernails, and she whispers, "I don't love her" (383). It is ironic that the fathers who have abandoned them arouse the love and admiration of their daughters, while the mothers who have also been abandoned only arouse their daughter's contempt.

Though the mothers in Oates's fiction have suffered as a result of their own sexual and marital relationships, it is they who encourage their daughters, above all else, to seek the attentions of a man. Phyllis Chesler's explanation for such behavior is pertinent here: mothers, she says, "must be harsh in training their daughters to be 'feminine' in order that they learn how to serve in order to survive.[2] To train their daughters how to be "feminine" in Oates's world is to teach them how to exploit their sexual attractiveness. Loretta, the mother of Maureen Wendall in *Them,* for example, when presenting her daughter with a sweater that she herself had outgrown, comments, "If you'd stand up straight, you'd be all right. You'll have a nice shape . . ." (154); and she gives her daughter lipstick and restyles her hair in order to make her more attractive to men. However, Loretta also, perhaps unwittingly, reveals to Maureen the dangers of sexual attractiveness. Along with her beauty tips, she communicates to Maureen fears about dark places, public toilets, and pregnancy. "You . . . you better watch out for them boys, huh? Boys ever fool around with you?" Loretta asks her adolescent daughter (153). Another mother who encourages her daughter to seek the attentions of a man is the mother in "Matter and Energy" who has been hospitalized for depression. Despite the fact that her own marriage has been a tragically unhappy one, she says to her daughter, "I want you to be married. I want you to be happy" (*The Wheel of Love,* 34).

II

The search of Oates's female characters to better their status or find happiness and fulfillment through relationships with men, marriage, and motherhood usually ends in failure. Sexual relationships in Oates's fiction do not provide women with the sense of completion that they long for and often trigger off violence either directly or indirectly. Losing autonomy as they obsessively follow their lovers, the women who fall in love frequently become psychologically unbalanced. Marriage is destructive to Oates's women, who are frequently treated brutally, or ignored, betrayed, or abandoned by their husbands. The children who are the products of these unhappy marriages also fail to bring happiness to the mothers in Oates's fiction, and in several of her stories, in fact, mothers have death wishes for their offspring.

The reason that sexual relationships prove to be so destructive to Oates's female characters is that such relationships have an obsessive quality to them and that they ultimately fail to confirm the woman's sense of self. Oates, who called one of her short stories "What Is The Connection Between Men and Women?" and entitled a volume of poems *Love and Its Derangements,* seems to view the love/sex "connection" between men and women as a bewildering kind of disease, a fever in the blood which often succeeds in unbalancing both partners. Her comments about Sylvia Plath's attitude towards sexual relationships would seem to apply to herself as well. Plath, she writes,

> understood well the hellish state of being Swift's true counterpart, the woman who agrees that the physical side of life is a horror, an ungainly synthesis of flesh and spirit—the disappointment of all romantic poems and the nightmare of the monkish soul.[3]

Despite the fact that the women in Oates's fiction actively seek sexual partners, they are usually reluctant participants in sexual relations, and are often depicted as frigid or as passive recipients, rather than equal partners in the lovemaking process. Pejorative terms and words which suggest acts of a pathological nature are often used by Oates to describe sexual intercourse. In one passage, for example, the following words appear: "terrible," "spasm," "brutal," "scream," "wildly," "viciously," "agony," "crazy," "murderous," and "mad" (*Do With Me What You Will*, 370).

It is not surprising that Oates, who has such a negative and even idio- syncratic view of sexual relations, shows those characters who seek com- pletion through the sexual act as doomed to failure. Oates's women are driven to find sexual partners—and are in despair once the relationship has been consummated. A character like Ilena, a college professor in "The Dead," feels that she is being driven crazy because two men share her body—her husband and her lover. The "madness of loving two men" makes Ilena look enviously at the nuns who teach at her school because "their lives were unassailed and honest and open to any possibility, while hers had become fouled, complicated, criminal, snagged, somehow completed without her consent" (*Marriage and Infidelities*, 388). Ilena sees her own good looks as a liability, something which "conferred no blessing on the beautiful woman" (403) because beauty only makes a woman more sexually appealing to men, and relationships with men cause so much pain. In *With Shuddering Fall* an obsessive sexual attraction to a stranger leads the young protagonist to leave her devout Catholic home and follow her lover, a racing-car driver. When he dies in a crash, a crash in part precipitated by his negative feelings about their relationship, she goes mad. In the psychiatric ward where she is a patient, she "would cry aloud at the memory of his body, his muscles and sweating back, his clenched teeth, his strong thighs" (310). Nadine in *Them* also is hospitalized in a mental hospital after she is forcefully separated from her lover. Meeting her again years later, he feels "as if the two of them were fated for some final convulsion . . ." (342). As they make love, Oates calls them "enemies" (36), and though Nadine tells him over and over again how much she loves him, she becomes so desperate when he fails to satisfy her sexually that she shoots him. The protagonist of Oates's *Do With Me What You Will* is yet another woman who ends up in a psychiatric hospital because a love relationship has failed. Since in Oates's fiction, sadomasochism is such a major component of sexual relations, it is not surprising that she portrays physical relationships as certainly disappointing and even destructive.

Oates's fiction suggests that one of the major problems that women face in sexual relationships is that men place unreal expectations on them and fail to see them as they really are—not as lowly sex objects or lofty fertility god- desses, but as human beings with virtues and shortcomings like their own. "A body isn't very important; it doesn't last, it isn't like God, and yet men expect something like God," says a woman in the short story ". . . and Answers" (*The Goddess and Other Women*, 164). This woman requests to be treated by a female psychiatrist who will not be disappointed, as a male would, if another woman says there is "nothing mysterious" about women (165). A woman in "Unmailed, Unwritten Letters" expresses her view of the way men tend to see women through distorting lenses as follows:

> The actors in this play all seem to be wearing masks . . . Women who are loved are in perpetual motion, dancing. We dance and men follow us to the brink of madness and death, but what of us, the dancers?—when the dancing ends we stand back upon our heels, dazed and hurt. Beneath the golden cloth on our thighs is flesh, and flesh hurts. Men are not interested in the body, which feels pain, but in the rhythm of the body as it goes about its dance, the body of a woman who cannot stop dancing (*The Wheel of Love*, 54).

In this passage, woman is described as a ceremonial dancer, a faceless goddess in "golden cloth" whose individuality and human pain men would rather ignore.

Another reason given by Oates for the disappointment women experience in sexual relationships is that rather than trying to establish a mutually affirming bond with their partners, men seek instead from their lovers a narcissistic confirmation of their own powers. As the female protagonist in "Matter and Energy" observes about her lover:

> He does not love me, but he loves his own reflection in me, as if I were a screen in which he can view himself endlessly, admire himself, his word, his language, the magic of his manliness, his immortality (*The Wheel of Love*, 312).

The woman in such a relationship cannot help but feel diminished or negated.

In Oates's fiction, marriage and motherhood are also shown to be damaging to the female ego. Her lower class women are often physically assaulted by their husbands or abandoned by them, and the wives of successful men are frequently treated as menials. The work by Oates which perhaps best illustrates the way women can be damaged psychologically by marital relationships is *Wonderland*, a novel whose two main female characters are the wives of successful physicians. Women like these, with their big houses and expensive clothes, would be the envy of a poor girl like Maureen Wendall in *Them*; yet both Mrs. Pedersen and Helene Vogel are shown to be desperately unhappy. Mrs. Pedersen is an alcoholic, and Helene Vogel, the wife of Mrs. Pedersen's stepson, becomes so depressed that she is barely able to function. The complaints of the women about their busy husbands are similar: Mrs. Pedersen cries out angrily, "Men don't understand, they don't see that I am a human being of my own . . ." (165); and Helene Vogel expresses the feeling that she is being "annihilated" by her husband, who does not have "the time to imagine her existence" (412)

Unable to drive, lacking the confidence even to check into a hotel on her own, Mrs. Pedersen feels completely dependent on her sadistic husband, a man who insists that she get his approval before she buys anything, who locks her in her room, who enjoys making her cry, who forces her to shave off all her body hair, and if it isn't shaved off well enough to suit him, takes the razor and goes over her body himself (170). "I'm afraid I might go crazy, I might die if I don't leave him . . . I will have to take my own life," she tells her stepson (165).

Helene Vogel, who is the daughter of a famous physician and who once was a brilliant chemistry student herself, also feels that her role as wife and mother does not fulfill her. In the following passage, which seems significant enough to quote at length, Oates summarizes the ways in which Helene's married life has been a disappointment to her:

> She had thought that marriage would be the beginning of her life; she had had a long life as a famous man's daughter, and she had been eager to begin her life. She would be a woman, womanly and fulfilled. A wife. But this had not come about . . . And then, puzzled, she had believed that the birth of her first child would fulfill her. So much apprehension and pain and joy . . . But the birth had left her exhausted and at a distance from herself, from her own body. Her baby had overwhelmed her. She was ashamed to herself and it occurred to her that she must have another baby to make her normal, a real woman. But after the second baby nothing was different. She felt a final, terrible certainty about her strangeness: she would never become a real woman (412).

Helene has obviously been misled by some of the patriarchal myths about the supreme joys of marriage and motherhood. Neither having an intimate relationship with a man nor bearing his children enhances her sense of self, and her elusive quest for fulfillment ends in failure.

Helene Vogel is typical of many of Oates's women who are devastated when motherhood fails to be as positive an experience as it is touted to be. Despite her sense of disappointment, Helene tries to be a good mother; several mothers in Oates's fiction, however, actually turn against their children. In two stories mothers have subconscious death wishes for their children, and they experience breakdowns when the children accidentally die. "Jackie died because I wanted his father dead," the unhappy wife of a brutal man in "Puzzles" admits to herself months after her 3-year-old has accidentally drowned in a drainage ditch. Unable to bear the notion that her son might grow up to be a brutal man like his father, she prefers her son to die. About her husband she thinks:

> Now I will tell this man the things I must tell him. It is time. It is time for me to tell him of my hatred for him, and my love, and the terrible anger that has wanted to scream its way out of me for years, screaming into his face, into his body (*Marriage and Infidelities,* 511).

A mother in ". . . and Answers" also seems to have willed subconsciously her child's death—or so her psychiatrist believes. The evidence in the story, which is presented through the answers that the woman gives the psychiatrist, seems to corroborate her psychiatrist's point of view. Although the woman vehemently denies that she deliberately wrecked the car she was driving and in which her daughter was a passenger, she also reveals that she could not bear the look of fear that she had begun to observe in her daughter's eyes, a look that reminded her of the fear that she herself used to feel for her father.

"I looked at my daughter and it was like looking at myself in a mirror . . . ,"
she says (*The Goddess and Other Stories,* 165). The mother in"Matter and
Energy" actually tries to kill her daughter. Abandoned by her husband and
suicidally depressed, she throws a crockery jar filled with flour at her
daughter. The daughter, who later visits the psychiatric hospital in which
her mother has been a patient for years, remembers that long ago, at home,
her mother would hide in the basement and cry. "She didn't want to be my
mother!" the daughter thinks bitterly, and she speculates that the "shape-
less, sleeping and smiling" women who are sitting in the hospital lounge are
"probably all mothers" (*The Wheel of Love,* 299).

III

The psychological disturbances that can be seen in Oates's female characters include anxiety, depression, and psychosis, and among her characters
are alcoholics, drug addicts, catatonics, and those who are suicidal. What a
good many of her characters commonly experience are feelings of depersonalization and disembodiment. In *The Divided Self,* R. D. Laing speaks of
these feelings as being characteristic of individuals who fear that their own
identity is in constant danger of being obliterated. Such individuals tend to
see themselves and others as objects rather than people. Laing uses the term
"petrification" to describe the process of depersonalization: "To turn oneself
into stone becomes a way of not being turned into a stone by someone else,"
Laing writes, and then he goes on to say that turning others into objects
serves to rob them of their power.[4] Many of Oates's characters see themselves and/or others as objects: Grace in "Pastoral Blood" thinks of herself
as the twin of the "mechanical girl" mannequin in the store window (*By the
North Gate,* 70); Maureen Wendall in *Them* likens the men with whom she
has sexual intercourse to "a machine, one of the machines at the laundromat
where she dragged the laundry" (194), and she believes a mirror will reveal
her own body to have "no reflection, no face" (292); Ilena in "The Dead"
conceives of both herself and her lovers as "protoplasm that had the sticky
formlessness of semen" (*Marriage and Infidelities,* 409).

Perhaps the best example in Oates's fiction of a "petrified" character is
Elena in *Do With Me What You Will.* As the title of the novel suggests,
Elena is a person completely lacking a will of her own, a mechanical doll who
can be manipulated by others. At the beginning of the novel we see how she is
traumatized in early childhood when her father, who is estranged from her
mother, abducts her from the school playground, transports her to the West
Coast, and keeps her confined and almost starving in his shabby apartment.
In response to this experience Elena develops an impassivity which insulates
her from others. Oates shows the adolescent Elena thinking of herself as a
statue: "I looked down upon my body and saw that it had gone to stone, and
the folds of my dress had become the creased folds of a gown. Such a body
does not need a head" (106), Elena says. Later in the novel a married Elena,
returning from a boring society charity luncheon, stands immobile, frozen as

it were before a statue in downtown Detroit. Oates uses Sylvia Plath's expression to describe Elena: "An invisible bell jar protected her" (299). Recalling that episode, Elena says, "I went into stone like the statue in front of me: I had gone into peace" (304). Awakened from her trance by a stranger who subsequently becomes her lover, Elena again moves through life in her detached way. However, she breaks down completely when her lover threatens to abandon her. "I know how holy you are, how dead and empty you are, you thing, you dead empty thing—you *thing,* you *thing,*" he shouts at her (447). Her behavior perfectly illustrates what Laing means by "petrification."

Phyllis Chesler has observed that depression, rather than aggression, is the characteristic female response to disappointment or loss.[5] Depression is commonly found in many of Oates's female characters. Though a rare female character commits a violent or aggressive act,[6] it is usually Oates's male characters who react violently, and her female characters who are the victims of their violence. Clara, in *A Garden of Earthly Delights,* for example, becomes psychotically withdrawn after her son, who blames her for dooming him to be forever branded a "bastard," attempts to shoot her, and then commits suicide. "But what did I do wrong? All my life was for you!" Clara shouts at him when he turns on her (382). The final scene of the novel shows Clara in the nursing home where she is a patient, sitting before the television set and watching men commit acts of violence. Another character who becomes psychotic when she is attacked by a male is Maureen Wendall in *Them.* Maureen's breakdown is precipitated after her stepfather beats her because he discovers that she is earning money by sleeping with men. Perhaps his own anger is exacerbated by both guilt and lust, for he himself had been acting seductively towards Maureen. During the 13 months following the beating, she lies in bed; having regressed to an infantile oral stage, she bestirs herself only to eat the voluminous quantities of food that her concerned mother prepares for her. "Even when I was awake I was asleep," Maureen says of that period in her life (316). Violence is always ready to break out in Oates's fictional world, and therefore the most important goal of a vulnerable female character like Maureen is: "She does not want to be hurt" (295).

"What does it mean to be a woman?" the catatonic Maureen Wendall thinks in *Them* (301). This question is explored in work after work by Joyce Carol Oates as she examines the roles of women and their relationships. Oates's view of women's lives is certainly a bleak one, and she does not give easy answers to the question of how women should live their lives so as to avoid the anxiety and despair that often leads to madness. Her fiction, however, does provide valuable insights about the powerlessness of women and the causes of their desperation. Unable to gain autonomy over their lives, and threatened by a brutal world where violence against them may break out at any moment, Oates's female characters often become anxious or depressed, and sometimes retreat into madness, which confers upon them the blessings of safety and peace.

Notes

1.   Quotations from Oates's fiction will be made from the following volumes: *A Garden of Earthly Delights* (Connecticut: Fawcett Publications, 1971); *By the North Gate* (Connecticut: Fawcett Publications, 1971); *Do With Me What You Will* (Connecticut: Fawcett Publications, 1974); *Expensive People* (New York: Vanguard Press, 1968); *Marriage and Infidelities* (Connecticut: Fawcett Publications, 1973); *The Goddess and Other Women* (New York: Vanguard Press, 1974); *The Wheel of Love* (Connecticut: Fawcett Publications, 1973); *Them* (Connecticut: Fawcett Pulications, 1970); *With Shuddering Fall* (Connecticut: Fawcett Publications, 1971); *Wonderland* (Connecticut: Fawcett Publications, 1973).

2.   Phyllis Chesler, *Women and Madness* (New York: Avon Books, 1973), p. 42.

3.   "The Death of Romanticism: The Poetry of Sylvia Plath," *New Heaven, New Earth: The Visionary Experience in Literature* (New York: Vanguard Press, 1974), p. 136.

4.   R. D. Laing, *The Divided Self* (New York: Basic Books, 1971), p. 54.

5.   *Women and Madness*, p. 64.

6.   Two exceptions to this are Nadine in *Them*, who shoots her lover, and the mother in "Matter and Energy" who attacks her daughter.

A Conversation With May Sarton

Dolores Shelley

I'd only recently discovered May Sarton myself, but when I began to read her a year or two ago, a single question came to mind again and again. Why has she received so little critical attention? And why has it come so late in her career? Although her works have always been reviewed (William Rose Benet, John Holmes and others favorably reviewed her first volume of poetry, *Encounter in April,* in 1937, while *The Single Hound,* her first novel, published a year later in 1938, was highly praised) and she has had an impressive audience of readers, scholars and literary critics have ignored her. That is, until the past five years when women in the "Academy" began to discuss her work. In 1973, 1974 and 1975, the Modern Language Association convention included seminars on "The Art of May Sarton"; nearly all of the papers presented were written by women.

Her first response to the question, during a phone conversation prior to our meeting, was that it was "partly ill luck." She said then, "I've had a good many favorable reviews, my books are read by many people, but I've not been a member of an establishment, or *the* establishment. I've never had any kind of power behind me."

Today we explore the reasons. "Well," she says, "I was not an innovator, certainly, and I think that's one thing that gets attention. Secondly, there was a very interesting paper written by a woman this year discussing me in relation to French culture and poetry, saying that my emphasis on clarity was very unfashionable and made the work look more simple than it is. I appeared on the scene just after the women lyric poets: Millay, Wylie, Louise Bogan. They were the generation just preceding mine. The fashion was Eliot when I was young, not lyric poetry, so I've always been unfashionable."

"I never went to college, which I have no regrets about, except that I notice that people who did are usually helped by their former professors. Richard Wilbur had Matthieson (F.O. Matthieson of Harvard), for instance. The people who went to Columbia had Trilling. I've never been a part of any group, and groups help each other. I've been reading the new biography of Amy Lowell. One learns there how the Imagists backed each other, got each other published, wrote reviews for each other. The Bloomsbury group—another example. Virginia Woolf knew when a novel came out that E. M. Forster would reiew it; Strachey would review it. Imagine that!"

"The only group I've ever been a part of was a distinguished group of poets. This was when we were all young; John Ciardi, Richard Eberhardt, Richard Wilbur, John Holmes, who's dead now, and I. We met about four times a year, drank a lot and read each other our poems. We all criticized each other, but I had the feeling the men were not very interested in my poetry. Not because it wasn't good, but that somehow . . . when I got home, I just felt terribly lonely. That's what I'm really saying. And the proof of this lack of interest is that years later John Ciardi talked about our meetings in the preface to one of his books and failed to mention that I was there!"

I asked her about the support writers sometimes receive from each other at writers' colonies and her associations at Harvard and Wellesley, where she taught.

"I spent three weeks at Yaddo and was very unhappy there. I never went to MacDowell because about the time I might have gone, I lived fifteen miles away. At Harvard, there were people who were very kind to me. Archibald MacLeish and the Kenneth Murdocks couldn't have been kinder. They used to invite me to dinner parties, though I was never going to be great in the English department. I was only a lecturer, of course. I taught to make enough money so I could buy time to write. I never stayed anywhere more than three years."

"But to try to answer your quesiton," she continues, "I don't think the kind of writing I did presented an exciting tool for intellectual analysis by young professors who might want to make a name for themselves. And I have absolutely no doubt that it's harder for a woman. And then, I'm bi-sexual and, of course, men don't particularly like this. Of course, I didn't 'come out' for a long time. I'd written a great deal that I hoped would have broad, universal appeal. I want to be known as a universal, human writer. I dread being labeled, you see. I've never aligned myself with a lesbian group of writers, because I don't write only about that. That's a very small part of my work. I think it should be."

In May Sarton's fiction, self-fulfillment is strongly emphasized and women often reject the passive acceptance of traditional roles. Hilary Stevens, in *Mrs. Stevens Hears the Mermaids Singing,* is an outstanding example of this sort of woman. The most profound satisfaction she experiences in life does not come through marriage but her own artistic interests, her own writing. The same could be said of the painter Joanna in *Joanna and Ulysses*; Lucy Winter, the teacher and protagonist of *The Small Room*; and Caroline Spencer, the main character in *As We Are Now.* The traditional roles of marriage and motherhood are present in much of Sarton's fiction, but there are also new models for women who do not wait for their lives to be defined only by men.

"I'm very interested in the subject of marriage, though," she says. "I mean, anybody is; half the world is concerned with it. I've written about the marriage of young lovers in my third novel, *Shadow Of a Man* (which is not my best), of middle-aged marriage in *The Birth of a Grandfather* (which I think *is* an interesting novel), and, of course, in *Kinds of Love,* an old marriage, people in their old age. *Faithful are the Wounds* has quite a bit about marriage, though it also talks about a singular person who does live alone, the suicide, who was Matthieson."

She speaks again of the price she paid for admitting she was a lesbian.

"When *Mrs. Stevens* was first published, I lost two jobs right away. That was in 1965. You have no idea of the change since women's lib. Women's lib has made all the difference. I can now go on a television program and talk about this. People are much more liberal now, much more accepting. This in itself is good."

She was silent for a moment and then came back to the question of recognition. "There is a third reason why perhaps I have not had a break from the critics. I have worked seriously in two mediums, and in the last years, three, if one includes the memoirs and *Journal of a Solitude.* That meant that the poetry critics tended to think of me as primarily a novelist and the critics of the novel as a poet. Then, because I was not born in America, I did not have the advantage of being 'placed' in a regional sense."

"In my father's house . . ." are the first words of *I Knew a Phoenix,* the autobiography of May Sarton's early years. The opening pages are a daughter's loving tribute to George Sarton, author of *Introduction to the History of Science,* acknowledged even today, so many years after its publication, as one of the seminal works in its field. She writes of her birth at Ghent, Belgium, the birthplace of her father, her grandfather's house. And of her father leaving Belgium as a refugee of World War I, eventually to become the first American professor of the History of Science. She writes of England and Wales, her mother's countries and of conversations the two women have many years later of going back to Wales to find the valleys, farms, and orchards of her mother's childhood. She writes of her parents meeting in Ghent, when her mother, Mabel Elwes, was a professional portrait painter and her father a student at the university.

By the time May Sarton was five, in 1916, her parents, ardent socialists both, were in America, where George Sarton taught a half course at Harvard in exchange for a room at Widener Library. Her parents lived in Cambridge, then, from that time until their deaths many years later.

"Was it through your father that you knew people or had introductions to people such as Virginia Woolf?"

"Yes, through my father I met Charlie Singer, the great historian of science in England. I was looking for a place to live in London. You could get a room with breakfast for a pound a week those days—horrible, with brown walls, but I didn't care, I was so excited to be there. The Singers helped me find a room in a cooperative house in Bloomsbury. There I made friends with John Summerson; he took me to Elizabeth Bowen and Bowen introduced me to Virginia Woolf. And the Huxleys were at Charlie Singer's, Julian Huxley, that's right, and *they* introduced me to Koteliansky.

A young May Sarton, twenty-five in 1937, paid a visit to Virginia Woolf, after sending her a copy of her first book of poems and a small bunch of primroses. She saw her alone in her drawing room, talked about writing poetry, talking about writing novels. When Leonard Woolf arrived, she impetuously invited them both to dinner at Whipsnade, thirty miles outside of London. Here tigers stalked the flowering hawthornes, but by the time they arrived, the tigers (caged, of course) had been put to bed and May Sarton had to hope that filet mignon and claret were enough.

From Virginia Woolf to Adrienne Rich, May Sarton has known many of the important writers of this century. When asked if she had ever met Carson McCullers, she replies, "No, she didn't interest me, because I think she was totally corrupted by the time she was thirty. It was fatal that she left the South. Here's an example of a person who was pushed by a group, if you will, and whom it ruined. That first house where she lived in Brooklyn with Auden and Gypsy Rose Lee, whom she was in love with, was disastrous for her. Carson was a sucker of people's marrow. She didn't give; she ate people up; she used them. I have a very terrible impression of an angel stuck in a monkey. She was certainly enormously talented, but I find somebody as neurotic as that not interesting. She was destructive to herself and to everybody who ever loved her. Destructive to her husband."

"But I think it's very hard for a woman to be married and have children and be a first rate artist. If you try to think of the first rate artists who are women, practically none of them have married and have had children except Kay Boyle who had three or four husbands and eight children, which is sort of like having none. She never has had a settled life. Katherine Anne Porter, you see, take her; take George Eliot, Jane Austen, Elizabeth Bowen, who was married but had no children. Look at the great women writers: Christina Rossetti, Emily Dickinson, Millay—she did finally marry, but Boissevain was a kind of nurse. Adrienne Rich married, of course, had children, but divorced. And Plath committed suicide trying to do it all. Now we are coming to understand that men can give more than they've ever been asked to give in a marriage, that a woman is not going to be expected to be everything; that is, to be all the time mother, all the time cook and also to be an artist."

"Do you think the woman artist is subverting her desires for a family, children, through art?" I ask.

"Not subverting, exactly, but perhaps it uses the same kind of creative energy. It's really a matter of energy. You can't do first rate work and not give it your first rate energy, I think. I write a fantastic amount according to other people. I never feel this myself, because I actually write very few hours a day. And I fight for the time, because of the letters, keeping a house going. I do everything: garden, make cookies, all these things. I don't have a secretary. I've been reading Edith Wharton's life and I'm just mad with envy. She wrote in bed, threw the sheets on the floor and her secretary picked them up and typed them! Meanwhile, the cook came in and was told what to have for dinner and the chauffeur took her out. I don't have any of those things, nor do I really want them, frankly."

"For a while you had a column in—"

"*Family Circle,*" she says. "Oh, that was heaven! I loved it. It was like being Colette. *Why* did they ever have me? I mean, *FAMILY Circle?* All the pieces were about living alone. They pushed the column to the back of the book and surrounded it with advertisements of bread so nobody could find it. But I enjoyed it. I thought the pieces were quite good; they were casual essays about life as I was living it in Nelson, New Hampshire. There are certain things I'm gathering for my senility; I'll bring those twelve pieces together and add a little, yes." "I'm very leery," she says, "of too strong a theoretical structure before the novel is written. Forster talks about this. My theory is that you have a theme and you put the characters down into a strong enough situation so that they're going to work out whatever it is you want to know about them. I write to a question, not an answer. I think it's terribly dangerous to have too definite an idea of what you're going to say before you say it, because your characters teach you so much."

"With regard to the universal appeal of my work, I think it has to do with the themes of family life and the woman. All the problems of being a woman, which are dealt with in various ways in the books. It's a generally humanistic view. This is another reason I haven't had criticial attention. Had I been a political writer, I might have. Had I been more psychoanalytically oriented, I might have. But I love the medium voice. I love Turgenev. I love Chekhov. Chekhov, Turgenev, Trollope, of course Virginia Woolf, Jane Austen. This is what I call the middle voice. It's not the screamer. It's not the extremely original, except for possibly Woolf. By original, I mean the person who, really, like Joyce, breaks through a whole new thing. These people have not particularly moved me. I was influenced by Mauriac. As a novelist, I think he's one of the greatest technicians there's ever been. Incredible economy. Technically, I've learned more from the French, there's no doubt, than I ever have from the English or Americans. But French is half my language; I was born in Belgium."

"One of the problems of novelists is that any human life of *any* depth and passion is far more complex and more happens in it in even what *looks* like a fairly tranquil married life than one can readily accept. There are episodes. There are things that happen. Life *is* stranger than fiction and nobody would believe, really if . . . nobody would believe, for example, the number of love affairs I've had. And I don't believe it myself."

"Why not?"

"I don't know. I mean, it just seems to be unlike me. But I think you have to live a lot before you can write. You learn from the person you love. You're so concentrated, really, that you almost become that person. And if you multiply this by thirty, or whatever it may be, then you have all these people you're made up of. It's great riches."

"I'm talking about women, mostly. That's the whole thing for me. Women have been the muse and it's the most aggressive side of me which falls in love with women. I feel more able to write and more myself than I ever do at any other time. This is not going to happen anymore, and I don't even want it to, but when I was young, it was always people older. It was always people who had much to teach me with whom I fell in love."

"You wrote of a love affair in *Journal of a Solitude* when you were fifty-eight?"

"Yes, at least," she replied. "I brought out *A Durable Fire* then, the poems of that love affair, which ended badly as the book notes. I wanted to say to Americans, don't think people are dead when they're sixty, because they're not. The more we learn about gerontology, the more it becomes clear that people go on having a capacity for passion, love, really, into their eighties. This shocks Americans to death, you know. They think that at a certain age, when you retire, you retire from everything. For me now, the stars, the horoscope, everything says more love affairs, but I say no."

"Do you think you have a particularly strong Freudian influence in your work?" I ask.

"No, I would not say so. Much more Jung. But I only came to Jung when I was fifty. I think Jung is for people who are fifty. Freud is for the young because he helps them to understand. Nobody's pure Freud anymore, not even Freudian analysts. They're all mixtures; they're all eclectic. There are certain ways in which I think Freud is helpful, but it's all being questioned now."

"I would be anti-Freudian in that I never believed that a homosexual was a cripple. I've always believed that there are neurotic homosexuals just as there are neurotic heterosexuals. But the fact that you're in love with your own sex does not make you sick. At the same time, I think that it may be that you do not develop fully in that life, the homosexual life, because you do not take in the stranger in the same way. And there's no doubt that men are different from women. There's no point in pretending they're the same. So that it's much easier, I think, to love your own sex. It doesn't ask such a great giving and taking in of the stranger and therefore you don't grow as much. Often, homosexual relationships don't last for this reason. It's all happened, you know, and then it gets thrown away because there's not enough room for growth in it. It's too narcissistic."

"I started falling in love with women when I was nine or ten years old and it's gone right through my life. I was in love with men. I had a long affair with a rather famous man, but I always felt I was a nurse. I always felt I was taking care of him. I was *exhausted* at the end of the week by trying to do what he wanted. He was older than I. I was trying to be a good wife, but I felt depleted and unable to work. Or rather, since I'd given everything, there was nothing left. With a woman, on the contrary, I felt very excited, wrote poems, you see. And that's the only way I can judge."

"As you're speaking about this," I ask, "I'm wondering what your feelings are in regard to the women's liberation movement, the feminist movement.

Many women in the movement must ally themselves with you whether they're homosexual or not."

"Yes. It's also because I live alone. I have proved that you can do it and have a wonderful life, except that the day isn't long enough. That's the only problem. I'm always in a state of guilt about the letters that don't get written. That's the insoluble part of my life. Because I love to get them, when they're intelligent, and I'd miss them very much. But if you think of something that is never finished—see, a book is finished—oh, and that's a marvelous feeling— but if I take two days off and don't write letters, it means there are thirty there. Every single day I have to write letters. Otherwise, they accumulate. Do what can be done every day and don't let it get to you. Easier said than done, you know."

"I get letters from all over the world, all over the country, and this is what's exciting. People write who have read the works and so often they feel they've been made alive by them again. People of all ages and of every walk of life. Farmer's wives, old women out in Wichita, Kansas and young people. The young are writing because of *Journal of a Solitude* and *As We are Now.* Children write, of course, about the children's book and old people write a great deal. I got very interesting letters about *As We are Now* and also about other books, *Kinds of Love,* for example, because many women are dealing with failing husbands and vice versa."

"Do people send you their own writing?"

"Oh, yes. I just received a story by a young woman who said she can't afford failure at this point. This is what I have to talk to her about. You *have* to be able to afford failure if you're going to be an artist. You've got to fail most of the time. It's inevitable. Nobody's going to produce a masterpiece every day. You *can't* say I can't afford to fail."

"Sometimes I get angry because I think people just don't realize at all how good you have to be to get there. What it takes in self-criticism and per- sistence . . . especially in self-criticism, being able to break down your own work and remake it because you see what's wrong. It takes guts."

"When you're writing, can you also rewrite at the same time?"

"In poetry, yes, because it's when I'm most excited that I'm able to criticize. I'm at a white heat critically as well as emotionally. I can put a poem through a hundred drafts and still keep working on it. With a novel, I don't revise that much. I usually put it through the typewriter twice, but then I revise a lot at the end for style and little things. Then you're helped with that by copy editors who really do a wonderful job because they pick you up with repetitions of a word, things like that, that you might not notice in a paragraph."

We turn once again to the question of the critics. "Of course," she says, I used to feel as if I were underground. That's the image I think I used somewhere in *Plant Dreaming Deep.* As if I were underground and trying to push up a gravestone and say, 'I'm here, I'm here.' It's started, though, and I'm not worried now. Now it's all very different."

"All I want now, which is very arrogant of me and vain, is a really big money success. I'd like to make a lot of money to give away and to not worry anymore. Now I have to write a book a year to live. And that's a lot, because it means you can never rest on your laurels. It's a precarious business at best."

"It sounds as if you're running a race."

"Well," she says, "that's it."

Quebec Women Writers

CHRISTIANE MAKWARD

A young militant writer from Montreal, Nicole Brossard, raised several pertinent questions at the international writers' convention devoted to "Woman and writing" held in Montreal in 1975:

> How is it that women have played such an important part in our literature: Gabrielle Roy, Germaine Guèvremont, Marie-Claire Blais, Anne Hébert.... How come, in particular, that their works knew how to get through to a wide section of the Quebecan public? With what collective schizophrenia did their own phantasms connect? On what oppression did they throw light?[1]

Statistics show that women hold more space in reference books on Quebec literature than on French literature. They represent 13 percent of the writers listed in the *Dictionnaire pratique des auteurs québécois* by Hamel, Hare and Wyczynsski (Montreal: FIDES, 1976) as compared to 3.7 percent in the *Histoire des littératures III* (Paris: Gallimard/Pléiade, 1958) and 4.9 percent in Bersani & al. *La Littérature en France depuis 1945* (Paris: Bordas, 1970).

The standard literary history manual in Quebec by G. Bessette & al., *La Littérature canadienne-française* (s.l.: CEC, 1968), opens with a presentation of the founding mother of the Quebec Ursulines Order, French-born Marie de l'Incarnation (1599–1672), who lived in Quebec for 33 years and wrote some 13,000 letters. The same source quotes Laure Conan as the founder of the French-Canadian novel in 1884. Another critic mentions that the first Quebec-born writer was another nun, Sister Marie Morin, who left chronicles of her order as well as descriptions of the pioneers' wives fighting "the Indians" (commonly referred to as "the savages") side by side with their men in the 1660s.[2]

It is important to bear in mind certain historical data in order to appreciate the specificity of Quebec literature and, within it, the myth of the French-Canadian mother. This is the only female archetype in Quebec literature according to Jean Le Moyne.[3] In a recent novel, Monique Bosco deals with the "dangerous mother" or Medea archetype as being "the most sensitive in the collective subconscious" of today's Quebec.[4]

In the late seventeenth century the then few thousand residents of Quebec (New France at the time) were under moral and legal obligation to comply with the Lord's order to multiply and people the earth! Shipments of volunteer "King's daughters" were sent to Quebec to marry within two weeks of their landing. Fishing and hunting permits were withheld from bachelors and child-bearing was rewarded by monetary recompense. In the middle of the eighteenth century, Madame Bëgon's diary comments on the "crisis of absolution" when confession was refused to persons who would not pledge to refrain from dancing, an activity associated by the clergy with promiscuity and venereal diseases. From 1763 to 1867, the French-Canadian population grew from 60,000 to one million—an enduring wonder to demographers. In the late nineteenth century young women were pressured into weaning their babies so they could fast like everyone else (and conceive again). By the middle of the twentieth century, women could still be denied absolution if they were not pregnant or nursing.

The iron clasp of the Catholic Church on the people and the women of Quebec has only begun to be forced open since 1960. These facts are not evoked as entertaining details, but are cited in order to throw light on the special ambiguity of the myth of the mother in Quebec literature. Until recent years, French-Canadians found the basis of their identity as a group in their religion. Catholic faith and religious life were the primary forms of political resistance: the collapse of the old educational system—entirely in the hands of the Church until then—coincides with a new liberal government (subsequently displaced by a socialist-separatist government). It also coincides with a renewal of the literature and culture of Quebec, one symptom of which is the use of the adjective "Quebecan" instead of "French-Canadian" to describe them. This phenomenon has the same implications as the lexical pairs lady/woman or Negro/Black.

The second specific character of Quebec literature (seen in works by women and men alike) is defined as a pervasive, oppressive pessimism. It is as obvious and as dominant as the mother archetype and has the same roots: the political and religious questions. Only mystical writings (and mystical poetry such as Rina Lasnier's) can escape this "uninterrupted vocation for distress" that thrives on fear—fear of the body, of sex, of the city, of the present, of chance, of dream, of imagination.[5] Mystical writings escape this pessimism because the experience of the mystic is holistic in essence and poverty, repression of the senses, physical hardships are the normal prerequisites of ecstasy and spiritual endurance. As for people in general, those ordinary subjects and objects of fiction, they function under the ordinary tensions and dilemmas of spiritual and earthly drives, physiological laws and upheavals of society. The repression of sensual enjoyment and the systematic negative representation of the couple are salient traits of French-Canadian literature. As a well-known poet put it: "When did we eat up our joy?" (Saint-Denis Garneau, 1912–1943). It seems that the exclusive identification of womanhood and motherhood, and the political "castration" of the French-Canadians, have kept hope and joy out of the literature until recently.

Again, it is through women writers that "the body electric" (to use Whitman's phrase) entered Quebec literature in the 1920s—however discreetly. The poet Medjé Vezina wrote: "For the mouth retains an indelible trace/ The shape of pleasure emerges like an island."[6] Today, new women's writings (in Quebec as well as in France) explore and celebrate the body. They "write their bodies" and, to use a more esoteric phrase, they "copulate with their mother-tongue." This is the central preoccupation of feminist writers like Monique Wittig, Hélène Cixous, Annie Leclerc as well as Madeleine Gagnon and Nicole Brossard in Quebec. To quote the latter again: "The entire history of poetry, the novel and fiction generally is essentially linked to the quest of the body . . . what is stifled and fantasizes beneath the law, order and herarchy . . . must be allowed to speak through all possible distortions: violence, irony, pornography, idealism, madness. . . ."[7]

The body is rarely glorious in French-Canadian fiction. A significant case in point is to be found in Laure Conan, the acknowledged pioneer of the novel. She was a single and very withdrawn woman who wrote historical and psychological novels in the late nineteenth century. Her two best known feminine characters are "embodiments" (or "disembodiments" rather) of sacrificial femininity. Both renounce their fiancés for "higher truths," one in the name of patriotism ("his" honor), the other under the spell of an extraordinary "Electra complex." *Angéline de Montbrun* (1884) is not haphazardly named. In a case Freud would have loved to unravel, she mourns for her father by developing an ugly growth on her face, which forces her to break her engagement. She can then retire from society altogether and consume herself in her father's memory. Laure Conan's novels were widely read and praised, abiding as they did by the classical heroic ideal and the Church's teaching. A woman reduced to angelic martyrdom dies of love but cannot live for it.

In the 1940s two distinguished novelists produced complementary works. Germaine Guèvremont analyzes problems and passions (greed, alcoholism, jealousy, insecurity, love, thirst for power) in rural settings. She does create richly convincing "good mothers" but she also conceives tormented characters driven to criminal negligence and madness. Guèvremont piles up catastrophes with great skill and conforms to the novelistic tradition (and most likely to sociological reality) of the wandering male and the domineering female figures. She diversifies impressively the theme of female relationships which range from rivalry (leading to murder) to friendship, empathy, and mother-daughter couples.

Gabrielle Roy (born 1909) is definitely the best-known of the Quebec writers, female or male. She has been celebrated as the first full-fledged novelist of Quebec. In the late 1940s her novel *Bonheur d'occasion*, the chronicle of a poor family of Montreal during the second World War, put an end to the century-old tradition in fiction that emphasized the "devirilization of the French-Canadian man, the virilization of his woman and on the other hand, the recourse to compensatory myths."[8] Still considered her masterpiece, although it has been follow by two other novels and five collections of shor stories, *Bonheur d'occasion* renews the archetypes of the endlessly fertile good mother (Rose-Anna produces a sixteenth baby by the end of the novel) and the irresponsible, self-centered father. It also deals very powerfully with the frustrations of the poor and their active desire to emerge by any means. Florentine, the eldest daughter, both empathizes with her mother and rebels against the values her mother upholds. The war, by enabling the men to provide better income for their families, constitutes a way out of despair and starvation. While the mother bemoans the fact, Florentine rejoices in it; her new husband, her brother and finally her father enlist and leave.

There is no doubt in critics' minds that Roy's novel contributed extensively to the rise of the new Quebec consciousness by dealing (for some five hundred pages) with the economic, linguistic, political, sexual and religious alienations of the people described. Denouncing reality as unbearable, Roy departs from the idealistic tragic and mystical tradition in Quebec fiction. She creates in Florentine a character who succeeds, out of unfailing determination, in pulling out of misery. At the painful cost of emotional repression, Florentine saves herself, rejects all her mother's values except solidarity with the family.

Another three prominent Quebec women writers are quite well-established, if publication in France is any measure of recognition. One is a "pure" poet: Rina Lasnier (born 1915); the other two have written poetry as well as plays and fiction: Anne Hébert (born 1916) and Marie-Claire Blais (born 1939). Lasnier is a mystic poet, mysticism being a not uncommon way of resolving existential anxiety. She has experienced fully the collective alienation of her people and expresses in accomplished modern verse her quest for God which mostly takes the form of universalist effusion.[9] Her contemporary, Anne Hébert, is the poet of fascination with death, of human exile and enclosure, of fear of the flesh, and the destructive or liberating power of sexuality. Her prose works are dominated by stifling mother figures, the most extraordinary one being Claudine in "Le torrent," and by revengeful servants or socially inferior women.[10] Like Gabrielle Roy, but in symbolic modes which question ancient values on different levels from those of realistic fiction, Hébert powerfully describes the alienation of her countrywomen.

After 1960 a new trend emerged in women's writings: humor, irony, ferocious satire, brilliant word-play were all introduced and *laughter* was powerfully present. The trend can be traced back to Claire Martin's memoirs of the mid-sixties. Martin (born 1914) has been suspected of darkening the picture to laugh louder! Unforgettable scenes such as "Jeanne's leg" (or how to put a saint on the calendar) and "Friday dinner at the nun's school" (or the multiplication of green peas) in *Dans un gant de fer* place Claire Martin among the truly striking satirists in contemporary francophone literature. Her follower in realist fiction and satire seems to be Michèle Mailhot (born 1932) who has published six novels to date (*Le Fou de la reine, La mort de L'Araignée, Veuillez agréer*, among others).

There is irony in feminist writing of today (it works best for feminist readers of course). "Witches laugh," to quote Xavière Gauthier's introduction to the first issue of the journal *Sorcières*. They laugh in Montreal as well, even though light-heartedness is certainly not the dominant mood in any women's group. Irony may be the most efficient way of denouncing the wrongs of society. In *La Barre du Jour 50*, devoted to women and language, there is a picture of a doll-like little girl on a tricycle, who, in a caption, tells the reader: "mon pre est roffe, ma mère est toffe . . . pis moé chus roffe and toffe"! Recently, on the cover page of the *Quinzaine Littéraire* (May 1977, issue #255) a "Québec dossier" was announced. One of the cover items was the photo of a bilingual sign on a Montreal street. It read: No Trespassing/ Pas trépasser. Do not trespass/Do not die. (Trépasser" in French means to die!) Those are the stakes indeed for the two communities in Montreal. If Quebec literature has reached the healthy stage of laughter here and there, it is largely because of the vitality and the creativity of its women writers.

Another recent landmark achievement is *La Nef des Sorcières*, a collective dramatic production that was very well received in 1976.[11] The *Nef des Sorcières* (The nave of the Witches or the Witches' Boat) was a collective composition and production, first conceived by Luce Guilbeault and Nicole Brossard. Several writers were assigned a particular monologue to voice separately the actress, the worker, the menopausal woman, the lesbian, the prostitute, and the writer. All of the writers took part in the selection of the actresses and in the production of the play. Although this is the best-known example, there are many more signs of the liveliness of women playwrights in Quebec, not to mention the "established" ones such as Anne Hébert, Suzanne Loranger and Marie-Claire Blais, whose plays have entered anthologies and literary history books. As elsewhere, some of them write, perform and work anonymously. This is highly significant of the change in the writers' function in Quebec society: *collective* undertaking, new lifestyles and relationships, a sense of solidarity and strength are presented to the public's attention and are received favorably. There can be no sequel to *La Nef des Sorcières:* it demonstrated that once women can be heard and can collectively represent themselves as isolated, alienated and deprived, then their enclosure is definitely broken.

A noteworthy group to be mentioned here is the *Théâtre des cuisines* who take their works to schools and colleges, ignoring official theater houses, and consider their activity to be essentially a political "prise de parole" (conquest/seizing of speech). Some 20 productions have thus taken place in the past three years following the pattern of *La Nef des Sorcières*. Like post-1968 theater in France, it is basically an experimental, sometimes informal, ephemeral, but always political form of drama. Currently women are eagerly waiting for the production of Denise Boucher's *Les fées ont soif*. The author is a colorful, exuberant and very talented new figure on the literary scene whose conception of writing is clear: "I write in French and in the feminine because I know both languages."[12] Indeed, *Cyprine* pursues the search initiated in *Retailles* for a deeper and more reliable conception of femininity than can be captured in rational language: "to this woman of the end of the world, I shall tell: 'I am happy' . . . the primeval woman whose trace I am looking for, the one I shall find in myself, the one we would find in ourselves, the one we shall look for until we can say: 'this is what I am.' "

The most impressive text by Quebec women writers in the past few years is undoubtedly *L'Euguélionne*, a work of fiction by Louky Bersianik, a modest, unprepossessing woman in her forties.[13] The book has recently been published in France and is bound to inspire serious critical studies for years to come.[14] It has been viewed as a "transformation of the *Second Sex*" and can also be said to evoke simultaneously the poetic seduction of Wittig's *Les Guérillères*, and the narrative fascination of *Star Trek* or Ursula LeGuin's *Left Hand of Darkness*. Beyond these indeed, it has the seriousness and scope of Beauvoir's monument and yet is an entirely original work, involving Quebec culture and literature to a notable degree. Both sophisticated and easily readable, the science-fiction mode of the text is laced with effective satire and irresistible humor. It is the loose narrative of the human world as we know it, visited by an advanced female from outer-space. She investigates and judges everything from her "different" and very free point of view; she makes friends and is caught and condemned for the disruption she causes. She is sentenced to disappear, which she willingly does by disintegrating, having decided that earth was not her own "positive planet" nor the place where she could ever find "the male of her own species."

As a "character," l'Euguélionne is in fact a beautiful allegory of the new women's spirit of freedom, "the Statue of Libery, stepped down from her pedestal." She is said to be born from all women and to be down on earth to spread the good word—the end of a certain type of slavery. Ubiquitous and immortal, L'Euguélionne stands as a revised Christ figure, not to be crucified but to live in all women (she does delegate her knowledge to female friends); a spirit of change, disruption, and progress ("to transgress is to progress") to be transmitted to both sexes. In this alternating series of adventures and meditations, contemporary civilization, from Freud as "Saint Siegfried" to language and capitalism, is thoroughly scrutinized in unforgettable fashion.

In a sense, *L'Euguélionne* is a formidable sibling of Wittig's *Les Guérillères*. More remarkable still, it is both unpretentious and brilliantly, irresistibly funny: "If a woman has genius, they say she is made. If a man is mad, they say he is a genius. . . . The criterion of genius is its misogyny." The pun is more efficient in French because of the rhyme: "Si une femme a du génie, on dit qu'elle est folle. Si un homme est fou, on dit qu'il a du génie. . . . Le critère du génie est sa misogynie!"[15]

Among the general reading public in Quebec, the new women writers are not as uniformly popular as the previous generation (Anne Hébert, Rina Lasnier, Gabrielle Roy). The generation gap here is as obvious as it is in France where few older women writers have taken the time or made an effort to understand the new women's language and thereby deny any association between sex and creativity. The younger generation (Marie-Claire Blais could be said to straddle the gap) largely identifies as feminist and engages in *disruptive forms* of writing. No more do we see novels, short stories, or poems, but fragmented, sometimes collective, sometimes hermetic, texts that are unfailingly free, daring, and politically *for women* and only secondarily for the general public, with Quebecan separatism in the background. They do not constitute a coherent group; one looks in vain for "dominant" figures or leaders. They include academic women as well as free-lance writers and "plain" housewives. They are mostly women in their thirties, declared feminists, and remarkably creative. In the opinion of some of this group, the best in Quebec literature will be produced by women, and this will last for some time to come because male intellectuals are either absorbed in politics or perturbed by the success of the socialist left in Quebec. They no longer have a vital cause to stimulate them. Women, on the contrary, still have *their* struggle to carry on against the conservative majority; they are in motion throughout Quebec, even in the Church, and the young intellectuals have a vital part to play in changing their society for the better. They boldly believe that, as Nicole Brossard phrased it poetically: "la rupture est inaugurale" or "disruption is inception."

Notes

1.   Nicole Brossard, *Liberté* 106–107, 1976 (Actes de la rencontre québécoise internationale des écrivains: La femme et l'Ecriture), p. 13. Poet and novelist, Nicole Brossard is a founding member of the Feminist journal *Les Têtes de Pioche.*

2.   Jean Le Moyne: "Le femme dans la civilisation canadienne-française" (1953) in *Convergences,* essai (Montréal: HMH, 1969), p. 79.

3.   "La femme dans la civilisation canadienne-française," p. 79.

4.   Monique Bosco, *Liberté* 106–107, p. 78 and *New Medea* (Montreal: L'Actuelle, 1974).

5.   Laurent Mailhot: "La critique et le roman québécois" in *Le roman contemporain d'expression française* (Actes du colloque de Sherbrook, recueillis et présentés par Antoine Naaman et Louis Painchaud), CELEF, 1971.

6.   Quoted by Le Moyne, *op. cit.,* p. 93.

7.   *Liberté* 106–107, p. 11.

8.   Jean Ethier-Blais: "le Roman québécois" in *Le roman contemporain . . . op. cit.,* pp. 158–160.

9.   Cf. G. Bessette, *La Littérature canadienne-française,* p. 226 and the special issue of *Liberté* 108.

10.   Madeleine Hage: "Anne Hébert" in a forthcoming encyclopedia of women writers in French (Stock, 1979). See also bibliography in *Dictionnaire pratique . . . op. cit.* and Josette Féral: "Clôture du moi, clôture du texte dans l'oeuvre d'Anne Hébert" in *Littérature* 20, déc. 1975.

11.   Cf. La nef des sorcières ou les paramécides massacrées" by Denis Saint-Jacques: *Les Lettres Québécoises* 3, sept. 1976.

12.   Address made at the Ottawa Conference of Inter-American Writers, May 20–24, 1978. Denise Boucher is the author of *Retailles, complaintes politiques,* with Madeleine Gagnon (Montréal: Ed. de l'Etincelle, 1977) and of *Cyprine* (id., 1978).

13.   Louky Bersianik, *L'Euguélionne* (Montréal: La Presse, 1976).

14.   A reading of *L'Euguélionne* linking the dynamics of disintegration/integration to Kazimierz Dabrowski's theory as exposed in *Mental growth through positive disintegration* was presented at the Ottawa Conference of Inter-American Women Writers by Pierrette Marcotte (Saint-Jean, Terre-Neuve). Louky Bersianik declined to comment on the analysis which rests on the key concepts of "primitive" as opposed to "advanced"/educated/intellectual mentalities and traditional hierarchical order.

15.   *L'Euguélionne,* p. 252.